Communications in Computer and Information Science   1096

Commenced Publication in 2007
Founding and Former Series Editors:
Phoebe Chen, Alfredo Cuzzocrea, Xiaoyong Du, Orhun Kara, Ting Liu,
Krishna M. Sivalingam, Dominik Ślęzak, Takashi Washio, Xiaokang Yang,
and Junsong Yuan

Editorial Board Members

More information about this series at http://www.springer.com/series/7899

Alvaro David Orjuela-Cañón ·
Juan Carlos Figueroa-García ·
Julián David Arias-Londoño (Eds.)

Applications of Computational Intelligence

Second IEEE Colombian Conference, ColCACI 2019
Barranquilla, Colombia, June 5–7, 2019
Revised Selected Papers

Springer

Editors
Alvaro David Orjuela-Cañón 🆔
Universidad del Rosario
Bogotá, Colombia

Julián David Arias-Londoño 🆔
Universidad de Antioquia
Medellín, Colombia

Juan Carlos Figueroa-García 🆔
Universidad Distrital Francisco José
de Caldas
Bogotá, Colombia

ISSN 1865-0929   ISSN 1865-0937 (electronic)
Communications in Computer and Information Science
ISBN 978-3-030-36210-2   ISBN 978-3-030-36211-9 (eBook)
https://doi.org/10.1007/978-3-030-36211-9

This Springer imprint is published by the registered company Springer Nature Switzerland AG
The registered company address is: Gewerbestrasse 11, 6330 Cham, Switzerland

Preface

The Computational Intelligence (CI) area is increasingly employed in engineering problems of the Latin America (LA) region. LA scientists have focused their efforts on the CI field as a way to deal with problems of interest for the international community but also of great impact in the LA region. Many different areas including optimization of energy and transportation systems, computer-aided medical diagnoses, bioinformatics, mining of massive data sets, robotics, automatic surveillance systems, and more are commonly addressed problems from this part of the world, because of the great potential those applications could also have in developing countries.

In this way, the IEEE Colombian Conference on Computational Intelligence (IEEE ColCACI 2019) is being fortified to contribute to all scientists working on applications/theory of CI techniques. In this version of IEEE ColCACI, we received 59 papers by authors from 8 different countries. In this way, the conference is an international forum for CI researchers and practitioners to share their more recent advancements and results. The present proceedings include the 21 best papers presented as extended versions of works exhibited at the conference.

All participants enjoyed the conference, which was manifested through their positive comments. This motivates us to continue working on offering an excellent IEEE ColCACI in future editions. We would like to thank the IEEE Colombia Section, the IEEE Colombian Caribbean Section, the IEEE Computational Intelligence Colombian Chapter, the IEEE Computational Intelligence Society, the Universidad del Norte, the Universidad del Rosario, the Universidad Distrital Francisco Jose de Caldas, and the Universidad de Antioquia. Finally, special thanks to all volunteers, participants, and the whole crew that worked together to ensure a successful conference. See you at IEEE ColCACI 2020!

June 2019

Alvaro David Orjuela-Cañón
Julián David Arias-Londoño
Juan Carlos Figueroa-García

Preface

Organization

General Chair

Alvaro David Orjuela-Cañón   Universidad del Rosario, Colombia

Technical Co-chairs

Julián David Arias-Londoño   Universidad de Antioquia, Colombia
Juan Carlos Figueroa-García   Universidad Distrital Francisco José de Caldas, Colombia

Keynote and Tutorials Chair

Fabián Peña   Universidad de los Andes, Colombia

Publication Chairs

Diana Briceño   Universidad Distrital Francisco José de Caldas, Colombia
Alvaro David Orjuela-Cañón   Universidad del Rosario, Colombia

Financial Chair

José David Cely   Universidad Distrital Francisco José de Caldas, Colombia

Webmaster

Fabian Martinez   IEEE Colombia, Colombia

Program Committee

Alvaro David Orjuela Cañón   Universidad del Rosario, Colombia
Julián David Arias Londoño   Universidad de Antioquia, Colombia
Juan Carlos Figueroa García   Universidad Distrital Francisco José de Caldas, Colombia
Danton Ferreira   Universidade Federal de Lavras, Brazil
Efren Gorrostieta   Universidad Autónoma de Queretaro, Mexico
Cristian Rodríguez Rivero   UCDavis Center for Neuroscience, USA

Jose Alfredo Costa	Universidade Federal do Rio Grande do Norte, Brazil
Javier Mauricio Antelis	Instituto Tecnológico de Monterrey, Mexico
Leonardo Forero Mendoza	Universidade Estadual do Rio de Janeiro, Brazil
Carmelo Bastos Filho	Universidade de Pernambuco, Brazil
Edgar Sánchez	CINVESTAV, Unidad Guadalajara, Mexico
Guilherme Alencar Barreto	Universidade Federal do Ceará, Brazil
Gonzalo Acuña Leiva	Universidad de Santiago de Chile, Chile
Carlos Alberto Cobos Lozada	Universidad del Cauca, Colombia
Juan Bernardo Gómez Mendoza	Universidad Nacional de Colombia, Sede Manizales, Colombia
Diego Peluffo Ordóñez	Universidad Técnica del Norte, Ecuador
Gerardo Muñoz Quiñones	Universidad Distrital Francisco José de Caldas, Colombia
Alvaro David Orjuela Cañón	Universidad del Rosario, Colombia
Jorge Eliécer Camargo Mendoza	Universidad Antonio Nariño, Colombia
Claudia Victoria Isaza Narvaez	Universidad de Antioquia, Colombia
Sandra Esperanza Nope Rodríguez	Universidad del Valle, Colombia
Jesús Alfonso López Sotelo	Universidad Autónoma de Occidente, Colombia
Cesar Hernando Valencia Niño	Universidad Santo Tomás, Sede Bucaramanga, Colombia
Miguel Melgarejo Rey	Universidad Distrital Francisco José de Caldas, Colombia
Wilfredo Alfonso Morales	Universidad del Valle, Colombia
Alfonso Perez Gama	Fundación Educación Superior San Jose, Colombia
Diana Consuelo Rodríguez	Universidad del Rosario, Colombia
Oscar Julián Perdomo Charry	Universidad del Rosario, Colombia
Humberto Loaiza	Universidad del Valle, Colombia
Eduardo Francisco Caicedo Bravo	Universidad del Valle, Colombia
Juan Carlos Niebles	Universidad del Norte, Colombia
Carlos Andrés Quintero Peña	Universidad Santo Tomás, Sede Bogotá, Colombia
Alexander Molina Cabrera	Universidad Tecnológica de Pereira, Colombia
Luiz Pereira Caloba	Universidade Federal de Rio de Janeiro, Brazil
Leonardo Forero Mendoza	Universidade Estadual de Rio de Janeiro, Brazil
Alvaro Gustavo Talavera	Universidad del Pacífico, Peru
Efraín Mayhua-López	Universidad Católica San Pablo, Peru
Yván Tupac	Universidad Católica San Pablo, Peru
Ana Teresa Tapia	Escuela Superior Politécnica del Litoral, Ecuador
Miguel Núñez del Prado	Universidad del Pacífico, Peru
Heitor Silvério Lopes	Universidade Tecnológica Federal de Paraná, Brazil
Waldimar Amaya	ICFO-The Institute of Photonic Sciences, Spain
Leonardo Franco	Universidad de Málaga, Spain

Carlos Andrés Peña   University of Applied Sciences Western
                              Switzerland, Switzerland
Edwin Alexander Cerquera   University of Florida, USA
Nadia Nedjah   Universidade Estadual do Río de Janeiro, Brazil
María Daniela López de Luise CI2S Lab, Argentina
Gustavo Eduardo Juarez   Universidad Nacional de Tucuman, Argentina
Ernesto Cuadros   Universidad Católica San Pablo, Peru

Contents

Video Processing

SVM and SSD for Classification of Mobility Actors on the Edge

Andrés Heredia[1]([✉])[ID] and Gabriel Barros-Gavilanes[1,2][ID]

[1] LIDI, Universidad del Azuay, Av. 24 de Mayo 7-77, 010204 Cuenca, Ecuador
{andres.heredia,gbarrosg}@uazuay.edu.ec
[2] tivo.ec Research, Don Bosco 2-07, 010205 Cuenca, Ecuador
http://www.uazuay.edu.ec

Abstract. In the context of video processing, transmission to a remote server is not always possible nor suitable. Video processing on the edge could offer a solution. However, lower processing capacities constraint the number of techniques available for devices, in this work we report the performance of two techniques for classification from video on a mini-computer. The implementation of a real-time vehicle counting and classification system is evaluated through Support Vector Machine (SVM) and the Single Shot Detector Framework (SSD) in a minicomputer. We compare two SVM bases techniques, IPHOG and a MBF using Scale Invariant Features. The obtained results show that with a video resolution of 1280×720 pixels and using SVM, precision and recognition rates of 86% and 94% are obtained respectively, while with SSD 93% and 67% rates are reached with times of processing higher than SVM.

Keywords: Computer vision · Raspberry Pi · Support Vector Machine · Single Shot Detection · Performance evaluation · Convolutional Neural Network

1 Introduction

Smart-cities and Integrated Transport Systems (ITS) require to collect, process and integrate information about the state of public infrastructure through multiple sensors and methods, see guide presented in [17]. We focus our efforts on technology for automated counts in video to detect pedestrians, bicycles, autos, etc. This mainly because video capture seems less intrusive and requires minimal physical intervention to be installed in comparison to inductions loops or pneumatic tube counters. Then an important question arises: Are minicomputers able to execute vehicular classification algorithms? This is an alternative to

Thanks to the Ecuadorian Corporation for the Development of Research and Academia, CEDIA, for the financing provided to research, through the CEPRA projects, especially the CEPRA project - XII -2018; Clasificador-video para actores de la movilidad como alternativa a conteos volumetricos manuales.

A. D. Orjuela-Cañón et al. (Eds.): ColCACI 2019, CCIS 1096, pp. 3–15, 2019.
https://doi.org/10.1007/978-3-030-36211-9_1

streaming flows of video to servers on the cloud. Our approach allows to process the video "in situ", which is also called Edge processing. Edge computing address this kind of problem where bandwidth consumption is a big constraint.

Our contribution includes the performance evaluation on an embedded device of two techniques for Support Vector Machine (SVM), namely Inverse Pyramid Histogram of Gradients (IPHOG) and a Measure Based Features (MBF) method called "Scale invariant". Additionally, a Convolutional Neural Network (CNN) technique like SSD-Mobilenet is compared too. Performance evaluation can be further separated in (i) hardware: execution time, Frames per Second (FPS), CPU and RAM usage, and (ii) software: metrics indicating how good the classification was.

2   Related Works

Before Neural Networks (NN), other type of classification techniques were available in the context of Machine Learning. Take for example, SVM as described in [8], which uses standard sized vectors to perform classification. Chen in [6] uses this technique in the context of ITS, his work presents different steps of a system for counting and classification through SVM including: Background's subtraction through Gaussian Mixed Models, foreground mask with dilate and erode functions, Blob segmentation, classification using SVM and tracking with Kalman filter. Then, a Histogram of Gradients (HOG) function generates the standard sized vector to feed the SVM, reporting over 99% precision and recall. Nevertheless, all videos have the same quality and correspond to the same location and captures the front part of the vehicles. This means a specific training should be done for each location.

A similar work [19] generates an SVM classification system using a Raspberry Pi 3B and a web cam (640 × 480 pixels). In this case, the capture of vehicles and pedestrians is from the side of the road instead of from the front. Nonetheless, performance metrics are lower than those reported by Chen and there is no information about the consumption of CPU and RAM memory.

In the domain of Artificial Intelligence (AI) and Deep Learning the classification problem is a well studied topic, mainly for cars and pedestrians. Most of the studies assume that the information is already stored in a server, therefore the number of steps to perform the classification is reduced. When real-time object detection is required, these algorithms are designed to run on platforms with high processing capacities as those used by Lu and Chan in [11].

Interaction with vehicle monitoring systems requires a camera configuration, which can be arranged in different positions: top of the vehicle, side of the vehicle or back depending on the application or requirement, see for example [14] and [18]. In [14] a system is proposed for counting, detecting and tracking vehicles. There, authors implement an algorithm for detect the Region of Interest (ROI), clustering process, tracking, single-frame classification and counting. The testing platform was a PC with Intel Centrino Duo Processor (T7250@2.00 GHz), 4 GB DDR2 RAM and Windows Vista 32-Bits operating system, corresponding to a low capacity computer.

Roh performs in [16] the implementation of the Fast R-CNN algorithm with an improvement in the detection stage, which is argued to have poor performance in the detection of small objects. They show that the results achieved with the modification provide improvements in the detection of people and vehicles by reducing the detection of false positives (FP). An overall improvement of 14% in relation to Faster RCNN model is achieved.

In [12] a comparison is made between different CNN algorithms for object detection. Selected metrics include speed and accuracy for three different models: Single Shot Detector (SSD), Faster Region-based Convolutional Neural Networks (FR-CNN) and Region-based Fully Convolutional Networks (R-FCN). They analyze these meta architectures with different features extractors to evaluate the combination that provides the best results. They show that SSD and R-FCN models are faster than their counterparts: R-CNN, Fast R-CNN and Faster R-CNN, while the combination that provided the best precision was Faster R-CNN with Inception Resnet reaching mean Average Precision (mAP) values of around 34.2 with 300 proposals.

On the other hand in [15] and [16], authors analyze the performance of different algorithms for object detection by using Receiver Operating Characteristic (ROC) curves that present the recall based on false positives (complementary of specificity) for different cut points.

In [12] the authors use the time of GPU as a metric for measure the performance of the hardware used with the different algorithms, while in [13] the authors make an analysis of CPU/GPU performance and energy efficiency of CNN for object detection on an embedded platform and compare the results with a PC and a PC + GPU. The results show that using a PC + CPU + GPU, maximizes the number of images per second. Besides, results show extremely low processing when only an embedded device is used.

Different studies use data sets available on internet for the training and testing process of algorithms in object detection, the most used are: COCO data set [2], PASCAL VOC (Visual Object Classes) [1], ImageNet [3] and MNIST [10], which are free to use. These data sets include many images for the tests, the common resolution of the images varies between 3 and 30 Megapixels depending on the data set. Most data sets do not include videos with different resolutions or quality for tests.

3   Methods

3.1   Hardware

The implementation of algorithms for counting, classification and tracking (SVM and SSD) of vehicles and people are carried out in an embedded device (Raspberry Pi). The main characteristics of the device include: 4 ARM Cortex-A53, 1.2 GHz CPUs, a basic GPU not been able to be used for this application, 1 GB LPDDR2 (900 MHz) of RAM, camera for 5MP OmniVision 5647 module with Fixed image resolution of 2592×1944 pixels, and supports video 1080p @ 30 fps, 720p and 640×480 pixels.

Results of hardware performance allow to determine the feasibility of using an embedded device for real-time applications or if it is more suitable for applications in which the processing time is not critical.

3.2   Software

We take as reference two different approaches, SSD Neural Network framework and SVM (this method is not based on neural networks), both methods are widely used in object classification.

SVM IPHOG. To implement the SVM-based system, we take as reference the work done in [19] which implements a software based sensor for Intelligent Transportation Systems (ITS). Some processing stages involved in this algorithm are: KNN or GMM background learning, Background subtraction, Foreground extraction, Count and classification and data transmission. Figure 1 is taken from this study and presents all steps used in the implementation of the SVM algorithm.

CNN with SSD-Mobilenet. On the other hand we consider as reference the algorithm People Counter [4] and implemented the vehicle and people counter using the MobileNet architecture and the Single Shot Detector (SSD) framework. This combination was considered because in [12] authors determined that these methods can be used for super fast real-time object detection on resource constrained devices (including the Raspberry Pi, smart-phones, etc.). The model used in this publication is part of a Caffe version of the original implementation in TensorFlow [9] and was trained by chuanqi305 [7]. Figure 2 shows the methodology used to implement the vehicle counting system using the SSD/Mobilenet model.

MobileNet-SSD model was trained in the COCO (Common objects in context) data set and then adjusted with PASCAL's VOC reaching 72.7% of mean average precision (mAP). In this way, it is possible to detect 20 objects in images including airplanes, bicycles, birds, boats, bottles, buses, cars, cats, chairs, cows, dining tables, dogs, horses, motorbikes, people, potted plants, sheep, sofas, trains, and TV monitors. We use this implementation as default.

SVM Using Scale Invariant Features. As an alternative to the techniques proposed in Sect. 3.2 we additionally evaluated a method derived from the SVM classification. The proposed method is not based on the use of oriented gradient histograms (HOG) to perform image classification, instead consider the measures described in [5]. We consider measures that guarantee invariance with the scale and that allow adjusting to different video measurements. The measures considered are described below:

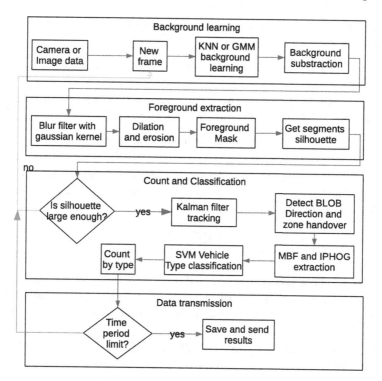

Fig. 1. SVM's workflow, taken from [19].

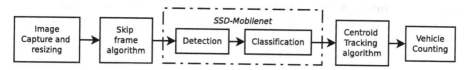

Fig. 2. SSD's workflow.

Percentage. Determine what percentage in terms of length has the minor axis of a bounding box relative to the major axis.

$$Percentage = ((100 * bounding\ box\ height)/bounding\ box\ width)) \quad (1)$$

Extension. The extent of a shape or contour is the relationship between the area of the contour and the area of the bounding box. In all cases, the extension will be less than 1.

$$extension = shape's\ area/bounding\ box's\ area \quad (2)$$

$$area\ bounding\ box = width\ bounding\ box\ x\ height\ bounding\ box \quad (3)$$

Solidity. The solidity of a shape is the area of contour of the blob divided by the area of the Convex Hull.

$$solidity = contour's\ area/\ convex\ hull's\ area \tag{4}$$

Appearance Ratio (proportion). The aspect ratio is simply the relationship between the width of the image and the height of the image.

$$aspect\ ratio = image's\ width/image's\ height \tag{5}$$

Eccentricity. Considers the absolute value of the quadratic difference of the major and minor semi axis. Where a and b are the major and minor semi axes of the ellipse adjusted to the blob.

$$e = \frac{\sqrt{|a^2 - b^2|}}{a}, \tag{6}$$

Comparison. This metric was created with the purpose of generating two categories of values that allow to distinguish a person from a car and a bus from a motorcycle, the width of the bounding box is compared with its height.

Number of Diagonals of Convex-Hull. Determines the number of lines that the Convex Hull algorithm uses to approximate the contours or silhouettes of an extracted blob.

Number of Sides (Approximation by the Polygon). Similar to the Convex Hull metric with the difference that this OpenCV function limits the number of lines with which a silhouette approaches. It usually approximates a polygon with a reduced number of sides. The classification scheme that follows the proposed method is detailed in the Fig. 3.

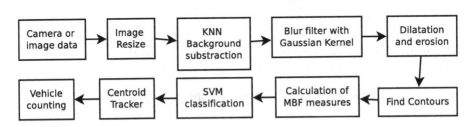

Fig. 3. Work flow for MBF scale invariant features' algorithm.

The calculated measures were grouped by their value and category (cars, people, motorcycles and trucks/buses), later this data set was trained with SVM. The measurements of 365 vehicles were used. These measurements were selected from a set of videos with similar characteristics to those of the real detection scenarios.

3.3   Skip Frame Algorithm

Through preliminary testing, we find very high processing times when all frames of a video are used on embedded devices. Thus, the number of objects to be detected by the CNN influence the processing time of each frame. We propose a technique to skip or jump a specific number of frames and reduce the work load in a CNN. Figure 4 shows the frame jump scheme when n is equal to five, which means skipping intervals of 5 frames.

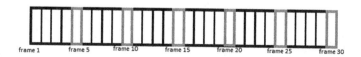

frame 1   frame 5   frame 10   frame 15   frame 20   frame 25   frame 30

Fig. 4. Schema to skip or jump n-frames.

3.4   Data Set

We use a set of 8 videos to calculate the quality and performance metrics of the proposed methods. Three different video resolutions were used (1920×1080, 1280×720 and 640×480 pixels). All the videos have a duration of 5 min and were captured in different lighting conditions (night and day). Table 1 presents the ground truth for each category of vehicles in the videos.

<table>
<tr><td></td><td colspan="5">Ground truth classes</td></tr>
<tr><td></td><td>C_1</td><td>C_2</td><td>$\cdots$</td><td>C_N</td><td>FP</td></tr>
<tr><td>C_1</td><td>$c_{1,1}$</td><td>$c_{1,2}$</td><td>$\cdots$</td><td>$c_{1,N}$</td><td>$c_{1,N+1}$</td></tr>
<tr><td>C_2</td><td>$c_{2,1}$</td><td>$c_{2,2}$</td><td>$\cdots$</td><td>$c_{2,N}$</td><td>$c_{2,N+1}$</td></tr>
<tr><td>$\vdots$</td><td>$\vdots$</td><td>$\vdots$</td><td>$\ddots$</td><td>$\vdots$</td><td>$\vdots$</td></tr>
<tr><td>C_N</td><td>$c_{N,1}$</td><td>$c_{N,2}$</td><td>$\cdots$</td><td>$c_{N,N}$</td><td>$c_{N,N+1}$</td></tr>
<tr><td>FN</td><td>$c_{N+1,1}$</td><td>$c_{N+1,2}$</td><td>$\cdots$</td><td>$c_{N+1,N}$</td><td>$c_{N+1,N+1}$</td></tr>
</table>

(Predicted classes)

Fig. 5. Extended confusion matrix.

3.5   Evaluation Metrics

In the analysis of performance of the SVM and SSD algorithms an extended confusion matrix is proposed with N classes, see Fig. 5. This matrix shows the current and predicted labels from a classification problem. The metrics used to evaluate the classification are: recall (REC), precision (PRE), and F1 Score

(F1) and are defined in Eq. 7. Where TP is True Positives and FP means false positives. False Negatives are represented with FN.

$$PRE = \frac{TP}{TP + FP}, REC = \frac{TP}{TP + FN}, F1 = \frac{2 * REC * PRE}{REC + PRE} \quad (7)$$

It is possible to obtain measures of Precision PRE_{ci} and Recall REC_{ci} for each class, these metrics are defined in Eq. 8.

$$PRE_{ci} = \frac{c_{i,i}}{\sum_{j=1}^{N+1} c_{i,j}}, REC_{ci} = \frac{c_{i,i}}{\sum_{j=1}^{N+1} c_{j,i}} \quad (8)$$

4   Results

We first took video sequences of intense vehicular flow from a side of the road. The manual counting of the mobility actors that appear in video was performed and statistics of each type of vehicle was generated. Four classes of vehicles are considered: cars, bicycle or motorcycle, bus and pedestrians. Table 1 presents the ground Truth from our videos.

Table 1. Ground truth for each category of vehicles in the videos.

Video	1	2	3	4	5	6	7	8
Cars	89	86	80	75	31	84	128	133
Bicycles	7	2	0	13	2	6	8	5
Buses	6	2	3	5	8	7	5	9
People	10	5	12	9	2	7	19	46
Total	114	96	97	104	43	106	163	194

4.1   Which Algorithm?

Table 3 shows a comparison in performance of the three methods grouped by the resolution of the video in terms of precision, recall and F1 score. With this information was possible to categorize and establish a quantitative analysis criteria.

Most successful counts are found in the class "cars" using a video resolution of 1280×720 pixels for SVM and SSD, while using a resolution of 640×480 pixels we observed that there was a difference with 32% in the REC parameter and 14% for PRE in the cars class using SVM.

In general, the method that provides the best results in terms of accuracy is SSD-Mobilenet, in second place is SVM-IPHOG and finally SVM-MBF. Additionally, Fig. 6 shows the relationship between PRE and REC graphically. We consider the two best methods in terms of PRE and REC (SSD and SVM-IPHOG). Each point is the average value of the metrics for each video category.

Table 2. Comparative SSD vs SVM-IPHOG vs SVM-MBF

	SVM								
Video	1(d)	2(n)	3(n)	4(d)	5(d)	6(d)	7(d)	8(d)	Average
FPS	8,05	8,71	9,15	8,98	11,40	8,87	4,18	5,70	8,13
Time	10,22	8,55	12,61	15,04	10,94	14,98	39,50	29,83	17,71
CPU	96,50	98,20	90,90	92,50	89,30	91,45	85,10	86,30	91,28
RAM	6,80	7,10	5,30	5,10	4,70	5,00	5,90	5,70	5,70
	SSD								
Video	1(d)	2(n)	3(n)	4(d)	5(d)	6(d)	7(d)	8(d)	Average
FPS	3,66	3,96	4,16	4,08	5,18	4,03	1,90	2,59	3,70
Time	20,45	17,11	25,22	30,08	21,89	29,97	78,99	59,67	35,42
CPU	99,20	98,30	89,20	89,30	90,30	91,40	97,90	99,10	94,34
RAM	29,40	31,40	21,20	22,60	23,90	20,20	29,20	28,50	25,80
	MBF								
Video	1(d)	2(n)	3(n)	4(d)	5(d)	6(d)	7(d)	8(d)	Average
FPS	5,41	4,96	6,45	6,01	14,51	6,32	3,24	3,87	6,34
Time	16,21	12,42	17,53	22,45	15,53	21,76	46,44	39,56	23,98
CPU	38,97	38,25	36,87	38,15	37,75	38,25	48,52	47,5	40,53
RAM	12,3	12,00	11,5	11,5	11,4	11,6	14,23	14,01	12,31

The x-axis represents the precision and the y-axis represents recall. The Fig. 6 shows that there are two cases: the results of the classification of SVM (squares) and SSD (circles), in this representation SSD groups a greater number of classes classified with values of precision and recall close to 1 in comparison to SVM which only has good results in the car class.

4.2 Performance and Platform

In terms of resources consumption Table 2 presents the percentage of CPU and RAM usage for SVM (IP-HOG and MBF) and SSD depending on the video resolution. The amount of FPS processed by the Raspberry Pi is also presented. The row called "Video" shows additional information about the time of the day, where **n** means night and **d** means day. Both methods consume similar CPU. However, SVM-IPHOG processes a greater amount of FPS, uses less RAM and is faster than SSD and SVM-MBF in all our scenarios. In Table 2 SVM-MBF has an intermediate resource consumption between SSD and SVM-IPHOG in terms of time, CPU and RAM. The Fig. 6 shows the number of minutes used by the device to process a video. SVM takes almost half the time than SSD but it can not reach the deadline of 5 min.

Table 3. Performance evaluation of SSD and SVM by video category.

		Cars			Bicycles			Buses			People		
		R1	R2	R3	R1	R2	R3	R1	R2	R3	R1	R2	R3
REC	SVM	0,54	0,86	0,69	0,08	0	0,10	0	0	0	0	0	0,03
	SSD	0,81	0,93	0,84	0,16	0	0	0,40	0,92	0,94	0,31	0,05	0,01
	MBF	0,62	0,37	0,66	0,88	0,90	0,63	0,72	0,76	0,83	0,41	0,81	0,62
PRE	SVM	0,91	0,94	0,89	0,13	0	0,50	0	0	0	0	0	0,25
	SSD	0,72	0,67	0,64	0,50	0	0	0,29	0,38	0,21	0,75	0,50	0,50
	MBF	0,76	0,97	0,56	0,69	0,18	0,50	0,39	0,16	0,47	0,71	0,77	0,97
F1	SVM	0,67	0,89	0,75	0	0	0,17	0	0	0	0	0	0,05
	SSD	0,71	0,65	0,65	0,24	0	0	0,25	0,34	0,34	0,43	0,02	0,02
	MBF	0,76	0,53	0,79	0,67	0,31	0,66	0,54	0,28	0,56	0,81	0,73	0,76

Note: R1 = 640 × 480, R2 = 1280 × 720 and R3 = 1920 × 1080

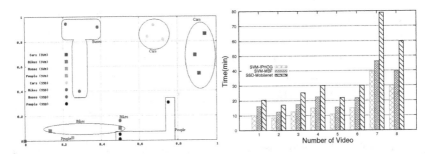

Fig. 6. Scheme of dispersion REC vs PRE for different classes and Processing times for SVM-IPHOG, SVM-MBF and SSD-Mobilenet algorithms.

4.3 Trade Off

From the Table 3, the Framework SSD provides better REC metrics in all video categories. However, this result is contrasted with the processing time, CPU and RAM memory consumption described in the Table 2. In this sense, it is evident that in applications that require real-time processing, like SSD-Mobilenet, it is not adequate since the delay is dependent on the processing power of the Raspberry Pi.

5 Discussion

In Fig. 6 processing times for a resolution of 1280 × 720 pixels is lower than for 640 × 480 pixels. It indicates that there is not relationship with resolution. However, for video 7 and 8 the processing time grows enormously almost by a factor of four when compared to other videos. We consider that this problem is because the video is recorded. Specifically, this behavior has led us to understand another important parameter of the video files called Bit rate. Even with a higher resolution, it is possible to have a low bit rate.

Therefore, the bit rate is the reason why a video with a resolution of 1280×720 pixels can be processed in a similar time or less than a video with a resolution of 640×480 pixels. The bit rate of the used videos was 1100 Kbps with resolution of 640×480 pixels, 3900 Kbps with 1920×1080 pixels and 900 Kbps with 1280×720 pixels. In addition, it is important to keep in mind that the proportion of time required between SSD and SVM is maintained.

For SVM IP-HOG and MBF all frames are processed, but in the case of SSD only a sub set of frames is used. Since SSD is a heavy model to be processed in the Raspberry Pi, we apply a skip frame technique described in the Sect. 3.3 considering a jump of 6 frames.

Another important aspect of Fig. 6 is the poor performance classifying buses. This is mainly due to poor segmentation with SVM-IPHOG and the similarity of the measures between the cars and buses category with SVM-MBF. When a bus appears, depending on the distance between the camera and the street a big area of the screen is used by the shape. This generates a problem for the segmentation algorithm in SVM-IPHOG.

On the other hand, the SSD model was trained with photos of scenarios in which the disposition of the vehicles is different to the test scenarios. To improve the results it is necessary to prepare a modified data set and compare the results. The photos from used scenarios capture vehicles from the side, while most of the data sets include photos of vehicles from the front.

6   Conclusions

We have presented a performance comparison of three different algorithms: SVM-IPHOG, SVM-MBF and SSD in a low-cost embedded platform like the Raspberry Pi 3B. We analyze the conditions in which a given algorithm provides higher values of recall (REC), precision (PRE) and F1 score depending on the resolution of video provided by different types of cameras and points of view.

With this work we determine if a low-cost embedded device is suitable for running classification and counting systems in real time and under which conditions it provides the highest performance. We conclude that algorithm from the Neural Networks, i.e SSD, is better than traditional algorithms, such as SVM, in all videos used for testing. However, this improvement in precision and recall demands higher consumption of resources inside the embedded device.

We continue to conduct tests on the accuracy of results in the video sensor. Future works include implementing additional hardware that allows to enhance the processing in the Raspberry Pi, such is the case of Intel Movidius Neural Computer Stick.

References

1. http://host.robots.ox.ac.uk/pascal/VOC/
2. Coco - common objects in context. http://cocodataset.org/
3. Imagenet. http://www.image-net.org/
4. Opencv people counter, August 2018. https://www.pyimagesearch.com/2018/08/13/opencv-people-counter/
5. Chen, Z., Ellis, T., Velastin, S.A.: Vehicle type categorization: a comparison of classification schemes. In: 2011 14th International IEEE Conference on Intelligent Transportation Systems (ITSC), pp. 74–79, October 2011. https://doi.org/10.1109/ITSC.2011.6083075
6. Chen, Z., Ellis, T., Velastin, S.A.: Vehicle detection, tracking and classification in urban traffic. In: 2012 15th International IEEE Conference on Intelligent Transportation Systems, pp. 951–956, September 2012. https://doi.org/10.1109/ITSC.2012.6338852
7. chuanqi305: chuanqi305/mobilenet-ssd, October 2018. https://github.com/chuanqi305/MobileNet-SSD
8. Cortes, C., Vapnik, V.: Support-vector networks. Mach. Learn. **20**(3), 273–297 (1995). https://doi.org/10.1007/BF00994018
9. Howard, A.G., et al.: Mobilenets: efficient convolutional neural networks for mobile vision applications. In: Computer Vision and Pattern Recognition, pp. 1–7, August 2017. https://doi.org/10.1109/CAIPT.2017.8555657
10. LeCun, Y., Cortes, C., Burges, C.: The mnist database. http://yann.lecun.com/exdb/mnist/
11. Lu, Z., Chan, K.S., Porta, T.L.: A computing platform for video crowdprocessing using deep learning. In: IEEE INFOCOM 2018 - IEEE Conference on Computer Communications, pp. 1430–1438, April 2018. https://doi.org/10.1109/INFOCOM.2018.8486406
12. Yadav, N., Binay, U.: Comparative study of object detection algorithms. Int. Res. J. Eng. Technol. (IRJET), 586–591 (2017). https://doi.org/10.23919/MVA.2017.7986913
13. Oh, S., Kim, M., Kim, D., Jeong, M., Lee, M.: Investigation on performance and energy efficiency of CNN-based object detection on embedded device. In: 2017 4th International Conference on Computer Applications and Information Processing Technology (CAIPT), pp. 1–4, August 2017. https://doi.org/10.1109/CAIPT.2017.8320657
14. Peña-González, R.H., Nuño-Maganda, M.A.: Computer vision based real-time vehicle tracking and classification system. In: 2014 IEEE 57th International Midwest Symposium on Circuits and Systems (MWSCAS), pp. 679–682, August 2014. https://doi.org/10.1109/MWSCAS.2014.6908506
15. Ren, X., Du, S., Zheng, Y.: Parallel RCNN: a deep learning method for people detection using RGB-D images. In: 2017 10th International Congress on Image and Signal Processing, BioMedical Engineering and Informatics (CISP-BMEI), pp. 1–6, October 2017. https://doi.org/10.1109/CISP-BMEI.2017.8302069
16. Roh, M., Lee, J.: Refining faster-RCNN for accurate object detection. In: 2017 Fifteenth IAPR International Conference on Machine Vision Applications (MVA), pp. 514–517, May 2017. https://doi.org/10.23919/MVA.2017.7986913
17. Ryus, P., et al.: NCHRP report 797. Guidebook on pedestrian and bicycle volume data collection. Transportation Research Board, Washington, DC (2014). ISSN: 0077–5614

18. Song, G.Y., Lee, K.Y., Lee, J.W.: Vehicle detection by edge-based candidate generation and appearance-based classification. In: 2008 IEEE Intelligent Vehicles Symposium, pp. 428–433, June 2008. https://doi.org/10.1109/IVS.2008.4621139
19. Torres-Espinoza, F., Barros-Gavilanes, G., Barros, M.J.: Computer vision classifier and platform for automatic counting: more than cars. In: Ecuador Technical Chapters Meeting 2017; 2nd ETCM Conference. pp. 1–6, October 2017. https://doi.org/10.1109/ETCM.2017.8247454, https://ieeexplore.ieee.org/document/8247454

Framework Comparison of Neural Networks for Automated Counting of Vehicles and Pedestrians

Galo Lalangui[2], Jorge Cordero[2], Omar Ruiz-Vivanco[2], Luis Barba-Guamán[2],
Jessica Guerrero[3], Fátima Farías[3], Wilmer Rivas[3], Nancy Loja[3],
Andrés Heredia[1(✉)] (iD), and Gabriel Barros-Gavilanes[1] (iD)

[1] LIDI, Universidad del Azuay, Av. 24 de Mayo 7-77, 010204 Cuenca, Ecuador
{andres.heredia,gbarrosg}@uazuay.edu.ec
[2] Universidad Técnica Particular de Loja, 1101608 Loja, Ecuador
{grlalangui,jmcordero,oaruiz,lrbarba}@utpl.edu.ec
[3] Universidad Técnica de Machala, Machala, Ecuador
{jguerrero_est,ffarias_est,wrivas,nmloja}@utmachala.edu.ec
http://www.uazuay.edu.ec, http://www.utpl.edu.ec,
http://utmachala.edu.ec

Abstract. This paper presents a comparison of three neural network frameworks used to make volumetric counts in an automated and continuous way. In addition to cars, the application count pedestrians. Frameworks used are: SSD Mobilenet re-trained, SSD Mobilenet pre-trained, and GoogLeNet pre-trained. The evaluation data set has a total duration of 60 min and comes from three different cameras. Images from the real deployment videos are included when training to enrich the detectable cases. Traditional detection models applied to vehicle counting systems usually provide high values for cars seen from the front. However, when the observer or camera is on the side, some models have lower detection and classification values. A new data set with fewer classes reach similar performance values as trained methods with default data sets. Results show that for the class cars, recall and precision values are 0.97 and 0.90 respectively in the best case, making use of a trained model by default, while for the class people the use of a re-trained model provides better results with precision and recall values of 1 and 0.82.

Keywords: Convolutional Neural Networks · Learning transfer · Automatic counter · Classification · Tracking · Single shot detector · Mobilenet

---

Thanks to the Ecuadorian Corporation for the Development of Research and Academia, CEDIA, for the financing provided to research, through the CEPRA projects, especially the CEPRA project - XII -2018; Clasificador-video para actores de la movilidad como alternativa a conteos volumetricos manuales.

A. D. Orjuela-Cañón et al. (Eds.): ColCACI 2019, CCIS 1096, pp. 16–28, 2019.
https://doi.org/10.1007/978-3-030-36211-9_2

1   Introduction

In Ecuador, large cities are suffering from serious traffic problems due to the increase in vehicular population. According to the INEC [15], the number of registered vehicles has increased by 8.8% in the last 3 years.

The vehicular and pedestrian count on the road is a process to gather information to evaluate traffic conditions. Then, data can be used for prediction of events such as traffic congestion, traffic accidents, improve future planning in traffic infrastructure, among others. To collect information on the use of public space, people are usually used to perform volumetric counts through polling. However, these samplings are very specific or short and involve high costs. In general, a paper and pencil are used and additional time is required to type the data in computer forms or spreadsheets. This methodology makes it difficult to observe the density of traffic though time and historic.

There are a lot of tools to capture videos of vehicular and pedestrian traffic such as surveillance cameras [29] or IP cameras recording video, mobile devices, web applications, sound sensors [28], laser sensors, drones, etc., see for example [6]. All these tools have utilities for traffic monitoring, however, a few occasions, the processing is performed on the collected information. The main parameter for the video flow is the physical installation of the camera, see for example [18]. Also, the quality of the video and its properties (e.g. Frames per Second, resolution, bit rate, encoding, etc.) are important.

Within a system that allows automatic and continuous counting, we have identified three parts or blocks: detection, classification, and tracking-counting. For detection, techniques are required to extract the bounding box from the objects that move. Then, these segmented objects pass to a classifier or object detector. The next step is to perform the previous step for each video frame and based on the proximity of the objects (relative distance), the movement of each object is estimated. Finally, the count is implemented by assigning an id in the objects to be detected, through the Centroid Tracker algorithm.

Nowadays, there are a lot of techniques based on Neural Networks (NN) which perform the task of detection and classification automatically, or as a black box. Due to the characteristics of these works, Convolutional Neural Networks (CNN) are used on most occasions. These methods have been involved in intelligent video surveillance applications, focusing mainly on the detection of vehicles. In general, these techniques depend on the amount of data and cases used for training. Classification rates are much higher than non-neuronal techniques.

This paper focuses on the techniques, platforms, and framework to analyze video flows for the application of automated counting. The research question is: Which of the existing models in the field of object detection and classification is the best for this application? To answer this question, we compare three models for object detection based on pre-trained and re-trained NN on three scenarios. Evaluation metrics are precision, recall, and F1 or reference value.

This paper is organized as follows: Sect. 2 presents similar works and metrics used for analysis in those works. Then, in Sect. 3, we select two frameworks and define experiments to measure the best framework. In Sect. 4, we present and analyze the results. Finally, we present our conclusions and future works in Sect. 5.

2   Related Works

Table 1. Comparison of frameworks on object detection and classification.

Authors	Method	Dataset	mAP	Learning rate	Video resolution	FPS
Biswas [4]	SSD-Mobilienet	4006 img-camera on highway	92.97% 79.30%	0.0004	1280 × 720	–
Han [11]	YOLO re-trained	3000 img	82.9%	0.001	1500 × 630	13
Ren [22]	RPN & Fast-RCNN	PASCAL VOC 2007–2012	73.2% 70.4%	0.001	500 × 375	5
Abouelnaga [1]	Inceptionv3	AUC Distracted Driver	95.17%	0.0001	1080 × 1920	72
Tran [27]	GoogLeNet	200.000 img	83%	0.0001	1280 × 720	–
Zmudzinski [31]	GoogLeNet	1098 img	87.15%	0.001	256 × 256	30

2.1   Historic Evolution of Techniques

An important research area in computer vision is the detection and classification of the objects. In the past, object detection using traditional computer vision methods included some techniques such as encode texture. [12,21], shape [13,16], and color [14]. Other methods of keypoint detectors [2,19,24] and local invariant descriptors [5,7,10] describe salient regions of an image.

The Histogram of Oriented Gradients algorithm (HOG) [7] proved to be very good at detecting objects in images when the viewpoint angle of the image did not change dramatically from what the classifier was trained on [23]. A great combination is the HOG algorithm and the Support Vector Machine (SVM) can be used to train highly accurate object classifiers, as those showed in [10].

Nowadays, there are a variety of techniques for classifying and detecting objects through artificial neural networks and deep learning. One of the primary benefits of deep learning and Convolutional Neural Networks is that it allows us to skip the feature extraction step and, instead, focus on the process of training our network, see [23].

In 1998, a basic architecture [17] was presented to recognize objects in images through a Deep NN. In other words, they did not have to extract characteristics, but the network learned from patterns of the images themselves. A great advance in neural networks with deep learning is evidenced in [26], where the use of several filters in their layers helped to classify the objects better.

2.2   Image Analysis of Video

Among the many existing articles that focus on video and deep learning of NN, Table 1 presents the more significant and recent works. The first column refers to the authors of each work. Column **Method** gives us a general idea of the models available in recent years. The comparison of these methods is out of the scope of this document. However, models differ in the number of layers and the number of neurons used in each layer. Another important aspect is the **Data set**. There exists a big number of data sets, and they are growing in the number of images that they contain. As a rule of thumb, bigger the data set, bigger the probability of including more cases in the training of the NN, and bigger detection and classification rate. The **mAP** is further explained in Sect. 2.3. Another parameter to list is the **Learning rate**, which gives an idea of the progress made by each step in the learning process. Usually, training consists of about 40 000 to 200 000 steps and depends on the method and the data set. Additionally, the **Video resolution** is also a determinant the number of Frames per Second (**FPS**) a system can reach. It is important not to confuse these FPS with those from the original video. The FPS presented in the Table 1 reflect the maximal value when the systems perform detection, classification, and tracking.

2.3   Metrics

Table 2. Number of classes and mAP in different frameworks.

Framework	Number of classes	mAP
SSD Mobilenet pre-trained	20	72.7
SSD Mobilenet trained	6	37.9
GoogLeNet pre-trained	1000	69.5

Mean Average Precision in Training. When evaluating object detector performance, we use an evaluation metric called mean Average Precision (mAP). This value indicates how accurate the detection is over the images, and is calculated using the evaluation set from all the labeled images.

Table 2 presents the number of classes available for each model, as well as the mAP. It is necessary to indicate that values listed for SSD Mobilenet pre-trained and GoogLeNet pre-trained are reported from their original's articles, and are only in the table for comparison with mAP's value from SSD Mobilenet trained data set. Table shows that even with a lower number of classes, mAP values are lower than those of the other models. Results produced by this model are in Sect. 4.

Table 3. Confusion matrix for model prediction, taken from [20]

		Prediction	
		Object detected	Object not detected
Observation	Object detected	True Positive (TP)	False Negative (FN)
	Object not detected	False Positive (FP)	True Negative (TN)

Confusion Matrix. Once the neural network is trained, the outputs are binary: true or false. True means that the object is present of the image, and False if it is not. Nevertheless, the system obtains a prediction and it should be contrasted against the Ground truth. For further details see [25]. Thus, to obtain the formulas based on the results, one must first understand the confusion matrix that shows True Positive (TP), True Negative (TN), False Positive (FP) and False Negative (FN) results. TP is the number of objects of the same class detected in the video correctly, TN is the number of objects that have not been detected by the NN. In the same way, FP is the number of objects that have been detected without having been trained in the network. Finally, FN indicates the number of objects not present in the detection, but that have been trained, see [20] for further details. Table 3 shows the confusion matrix to describe the performance of the object detection model.

System's Metrics. Finally, these model predictions are compared to the ground-truth labels from our testing set. As stated in Sect. 1, the metrics selected for evaluating the automatic counting system are:

– Precision (**PRE**) and is defined in Eq. 1.

$$PRE = \frac{TP}{TP + FP} \tag{1}$$

– Recall (**REC**) and is defined in Eq. 2.

$$REC = \frac{TP}{TP + FN} \tag{2}$$

– **F1** is defined in Eq. 3.

$$F1 = \frac{2 * REC * PRE}{REC + PRE} \tag{3}$$

These values are calculated per class and allow to generate a confusion matrix that includes all selected classes. Additionally, from the equations, it is understood that values close to 1 are the best for the three metrics.

In the next section, we describe our experiments.

Table 4. Ground Truth of the video data set.

Video	Motorcycles	Cars	Bikes	Trucks	Buses	Personas	Total
1	0	128	8	3	5	19	163
2	0	133	5	1	9	46	194
3	5	92	0	6	5	20	128
4	9	88	0	6	4	16	123
5	5	36	1	–	–	30	72
6	1	33	0	–	–	25	59
7	1	35	1	–	–	33	70
8	0	31	0	–	–	33	64
9	8	44	3	0	3	12	67
10	6	51	4	2	1	23	84
11	7	49	3	1	1	13	72
12	15	55	4	1	2	10	84

3   Methods

3.1   Video Data Set

The system tests are carried out on 12 videos, four for each scenario where there are available cameras. The standard resolution of the videos is 1920×1080 pixels, each video has a duration of 5 min with 30 FPS.

Of the twelve videos, the first four were taken from a Higher Educational Institution of the city of Cuenca, with the camera located in a building on the side of the road, the climatic conditions for the capture of the videos present good visibility (no rain) and are performed during daytime hours. The following four videos were taken from a downtown area of the city of Loja, where the camera has a frontal view with respect to the objects to be detected, the climatic condition in the videos presented good visibility (not rain) and were captured during the day, except for video 8 that was taken at night with presence of rain. Finally, the last four videos were taken from a central area of the city of Machala, with the camera located diagonally (15° approximately) with respect to the objects to be detected, the climatic conditions in the capture videos presented good visibility (not rain) and were captured during the daytime.

Table 4 presents the GroundTruth of the used videos. The selected classes are cars, bicycle, motorcycle, trucks, buses, and people. The table reports other classes that could be helpful when evaluating models and frameworks. Thus, these data can be used in future studies. Video five to eight do not report values for classes trucks and buses. This is due to the street used for recording the videos. It is in a downtown area and no buses nor trucks are allowed there.

3.2 Experiments

Videos listed and described in Sect. 3.1 are the input of a selected framework. Predictions obtained from the counting application are compared against the Ground Truth (see Table 4). The evaluation is done using the metrics defined in the previous section (Sect. 2.3). Namely, precision, recall, and F1. This general test of the system will help respond to the objectives outlined in Sect. 1.

3.3 Model Selection

As indicated in Sect. 1, the system is reduced to two phases: detection-classification and tracking-counting. For the first phase, we selected two pre-trained NN and then we train our own network. For the second phase, an object tracking algorithm was used (based on the centroid method). In addition to the counting, we use a specific region for each class. The selection of the pre-trained neural network was based on experimental research. For each experiment, several alternatives were tested considering the following: different models of pre-trained neural networks, parameters for the counting system, characteristics of the processing equipment. After all the experiments, the best one was selected based on the mAP of each NN.

Table 5 shows the selected frameworks (i.e. SSD Mobilenet and GoogLeNet). SSD Mobilenet reports faster detection and classification times. Thus, the data set is based on images from the highway. Additionally, the training process is simple and straight forward. This has shown useful to understand the process of generating a new data set or in the act of merging existing data sets. On the other hand, GoogLeNet reports a rich set of images for training.

In the context of tracking, these kinds of implementations (see for example [3,9]) use Euclidean distance from centroids of detected objects between frames. There exist more elaborated techniques using not only centroid's based tracking but also including prediction models, such as Kalman's filter [30]. However, these prediction techniques require considerable additional computation power. For this reason, in this work does not include prediction models for tracking.

Some scenarios have shown additional complexity (i.e. partial or complete occlusion between moving objects), hence, counting regions are selected. These regions allow controlling specific areas in the image where counting trajectories can be more predictable.

Table 5. Models used in the system.

Detection-classification	Tracking-counting
SSD Mobilenet re-trained	Centroid - counting region
SSD Mobilenet pre-trained	
GoogLeNet pre-trained	

3.4   Train and Validation

As described in Table 2 three models are used for vehicle detection: GoogLeNet, SSD Mobilenet pre-trained and SSD Mobilenet with own training. The training and validation process in the model was performed considering two data sets: one data set was developed by us with 1968 hand-labeled images which were obtained from two different mobility scenarios and a data set available in [8] which contains 67183 hand-labeled images. Both data sets were combined and the 30% of data was taken for validation and 70% for training. The training was performed using Tensorflow with a total of 80000 iterations reaching an error of around 0.3.

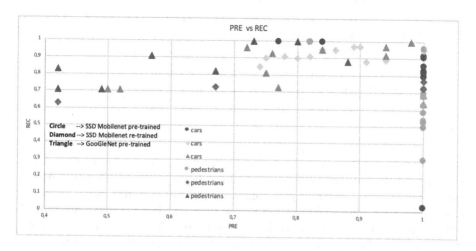

Fig. 1. REC vs PRE cars and pedestrians detection (Color figure online)

4   Results and Discussion

Table 6 presents system overall results for class cars for each model used. For the SSD Mobilenet model re-trained in video 8, values of REC and F1 are obtained close to zero. This is because said video was recorded at night and considering that the model was not re-trained with images in a night scenario detection is affected considerably in these scenarios, as seen in Tables 6 and 7.

Table 7 for the pre-trained SSD mobilenet model results in REC and F1 values close to zero in videos 1, 3 and 4, due to the high level of occlusion that prevents adequate detection of the analyzed class.

The recall parameter (REC) for the GoogLeNet framework in Table 7 presents an acceptable average of 81%, despite the fact that in the first four videos there is a distance with respect to the reference point. Besides that, you can not see the front of the cars, due to the capture of the cars in a lateral way.

Table 6. Counting results for the cars class.

| Video | SSD Mobilenet | | | | | | GoogLeNet | | |
| | Re-trained | | | Pre-trained | | | Pre-trained | | |
	PRE	REC	F1	PRE	REC	F1	PRE	REC	F1
1	1.00	0.86	0.92	0,97	0,90	0,93	0.71	0.52	0.60
2	1.00	0.82	0.90	0,97	0,89	0,93	0.71	0.50	0.59
3	0.82	1.00	0.90	0,95	0,86	0,90	0.73	0.77	0.75
4	1.00	0.80	0.89	0,95	0,84	0,89	0.81	0.75	0.78
5	0.84	1.00	0.91	0,95	1,00	0,97	0.96	0.72	0.83
6	1.00	0.91	0.95	0,88	0,91	0,90	0.69	1.00	0.81
7	1.00	0.83	0.91	0,89	0,94	0,92	0.64	1.00	0.78
8	1.00	0.03	0.06	0,85	0,74	0,79	0.97	0.94	0.95
9	1.00	0.82	0.90	0,90	0,80	0,84	0.95	0.84	0.89
10	0.77	1.00	0.87	0,90	0,75	0,82	0.93	0.76	0.84
11	1.00	0.92	0.96	0,91	0,82	0,86	0.92	0.94	0.93
12	1.00	0.82	0.90	0,91	0,78	0,84	1.00	0.98	0.99

While in Table 7 a low average of 43% is obtained in the value REC and F1. This happens because in the first four videos there is an enclosure, the camera captures the people behind it, which makes it difficult to detect them. In videos 6 and 7, the precision (PRE) has a value less than 70% because it is a pre-trained network and have a tracking id (if in a frame he loses it he recounts). These two situations allow false positives to be high, affecting the value of precision, for example, in these videos, it detects a kiosk (open premises) as a car.

Two of the 3 models are optimized for front-facing videos. For this reason, the group of videos taken from the side show inferior results when using the default models (SSD Mobilenet pre-trained and SSD Mobilenet re-trained). NN require large volumes of images to train. However, there is a different scenario that was not considered in training, in which it is possible to find that a pre-trained model can present very low results in terms of recall, see video 8 for people and cars. Night scenarios were not considered for training. Once the images of the videos are included, it improves detection and classification in all cases.

Table 8 shows the average values of the system by method, metric, and class. For class cars, overall values are close and high. All values are higher than .80 for precision, recall, and F1. On the other hand, for the class person, the results are lower. However, the re-trained model shows better results than the other two pre-trained models. This may imply that it is possible to generate better data sets by including more extreme scenarios in the training. Nevertheless, it is not evident how a measure of different cases a data set has.

Figure 1 shows that the SSD Mobilenet pre-trained framework has an average of 95% accuracy in cars (blue circle) and an average of 68% in pedestrians (yellow

Table 7. Counting results for the pedestrians class.

Video	SSD Mobilenet						GoogLeNet		
	Re-trained			Pre-trained			Pre-trained		
	PRE	REC	F1	PRE	REC	F1	PRE	REC	F1
1	0.70	1.00	0.83	0,25	0,05	0,09	1.00	0.05	0.10
2	0.59	1.00	0.74	0,79	0,24	0,37	1.00	0.02	0.04
3	0.31	1.00	0.47	0,25	0,05	0,08	1.00	0.05	0.10
4	0.68	1.00	0.81	0,40	0,13	0,19	1.00	0.06	0.12
5	0.73	1.00	0.85	0,50	0,04	0,07	0.88	0.88	0.88
6	0.96	1.00	0.98	0,75	0,27	0,40	0.82	0.67	0.73
7	1.00	0.82	0.90	0,81	0,32	0,46	0.71	0.49	0.58
8	1.00	0.03	0.06	0,57	0,11	0,19	0.91	0.57	0.70
9	0.63	1.00	0.77	0,73	0,67	0,70	0.71	0.42	0.53
10	0.53	1.00	0.70	0,73	1,00	0,85	1.00	0.73	0.84
11	0.54	1.00	0.70	0,63	0,42	0,50	0.83	0.42	0.56
12	0.50	1.00	0.67	0,77	1,00	0,87	1.00	0.80	0.89

Table 8. Average metric of all videos according to the method used.

Models	Metrics	Cars	Pedestrians
SSD-Mobilenet re-trained	REC	0,816	0,904
	PRE	0,953	0,681
	F1	0,839	0,706
SSD-Mobilenet pre-trained	REC	0,920	0,598
	PRE	0,852	0,358
	F1	0,883	0,396
GoogLeNet pre-trained	REC	0,811	0,429
	PRE	0,834	0,905
	F1	0,812	0,505

circle) recognition process. The SSD Mobilenet re-trained has an average of 85% and 35% in cars (orange diamond) and pedestrians (blue diamond) recognition. Finally, The GoogLeNet pre-trained has an average of 83% and 90% in cars (gray triangle) and pedestrians (green triangle) recognition process.

Limitations:

- There are limitations inside vehicle detection.
- Occlusion problems: The first and third group of videos are prone to present total or partial occlusion. This causes some problems with the tracking of the objects and can consequently alter the counts. In some cases, these problems make tracking inefficient and overcounting occurs.

5 Conclusions

This research presents the comparison of two detection and classification techniques using neural networks for a counting application of mobility actors in the public space. Groups of four videos from three different places were used to check the adaptability of the algorithms for this counting application. The new data set has a total duration of 60 min of video and was used for validation. The use of data from the deployment scenario in the training process makes detection and classification rate better for people. The results suggest that adding new scenarios for training improves detection values for classes not as frequent as, for example, people. However, all the methods present results on average over 80% for cars and much more variable results for the class person. Deep learning methods benefited from the augmented data set. However, since our augmented data set might be labeled inconsistently with the original training set, further inclusion of augmented data did not improve the results.

Future work includes performing load tests to find out how many simultaneous video streams a server can process when processing is done in the cloud. As well as comparing the speed of each method to perform the detection and classification.

References

1. Abouelnaga, Y., Eraqi, H.M., Moustafa, M.N.: Real-time distracted driver posture classification. CoRR abs/1706.09498. http://arxiv.org/abs/1706.09498, June 2017
2. Bay, H., Ess, A., Tuytelaars, T., Van Gool, L.: Speeded-up robust features (surf). Comput. Vis. Image Underst. **110**(3), 346–359 (2008)
3. Bhaskar, P.K., Yong, S.: Image processing based vehicle detection and tracking method. In: 2014 International Conference on Computer and Information Sciences (ICCOINS), pp. 1–5, June 2014. https://doi.org/10.1109/ICCOINS.2014.6868357
4. Biswas, D., Su, H., Wang, C., Stevanovic, A., Wang, W.: An automatic traffic density estimation using single shot detection (SSD) and MobileNet-SSD. Phys. Chem. Earth Parts A/B/C **110**, 176–184 (2018)
5. Calonder, M., Lepetit, V., Strecha, C., Fua, P.: BRIEF: binary robust independent elementary features. In: Daniilidis, K., Maragos, P., Paragios, N. (eds.) ECCV 2010. LNCS, vol. 6314, pp. 778–792. Springer, Heidelberg (2010). https://doi.org/10.1007/978-3-642-15561-1_56
6. Campo, W.Y., Arciniegas, J.L., García, R., Melendi, D.: Análisis de tráfico para un servicio de vídeo bajo demanda sobre recles HFC usando el protocolo RTMP. Información Tecnológica **21**(6), 37–48 (2010)
7. Dalal, N., Triggs, B.: Histograms of oriented gradients for human detection. In: International Conference on Computer Vision & Pattern Recognition (CVPR 2005), vol. 1, pp. 886–893. IEEE Computer Society (2005)
8. Dominguez-Sanchez, A., Cazorla, M., Orts-Escolano, S.: A new dataset and performance evaluation of a region-based cnn for urban object detection. Electronics **7**(11), 1–16 (2018). http://www.rovit.ua.es/dataset/traffic/?doi=10.1.1.79.6578
9. Farias, I.S., Fernandes, B.J.T., Albuquerque, E.Q., Leite, B.L.D.: Tracking and counting of vehicles for flow analysis from urban traffic videos. In: 2017 IEEE Latin American Conference on Computational Intelligence (LA-CCI), pp. 1–6, November 2017. https://doi.org/10.1109/LA-CCI.2017.8285724

10. Han, F., Shan, Y., Cekander, R., Sawhney, H.S., Kumar, R.: A two-stage approach to people and vehicle detection with hog-based SVM. In: Performance Metrics for Intelligent Systems 2006 Workshop, pp. 133–140 (2006)
11. Han, J., Liao, Y., Zhang, J., Wang, S., Li, S.: Target fusion detection of LiDAR and camera based on the improved YOLO algorithm. Sci. China, Ser. A Math. 6(10), 213 (2018)
12. Haralick, R.M., Shanmugam, K., et al.: Textural features for image classification. IEEE Trans. Syst. Man Cybern. 6, 610–621 (1973)
13. Hu, M.K.: Visual pattern recognition by moment invariants. IRE Trans. Inf. Theory 8(2), 179–187 (1962)
14. Huang, J., Kumar, S.R., Mitra, M., Zhu, W.J., Zabih, R.: Image indexing using color correlograms. In: CVPR, p. 762. IEEE (1997)
15. Instituto Nacional de Estadística y Censos: Transporte. http://www.ecuadorencifras.gob.ec/transporte/. Accessed 24 Feb 2019
16. Khotanzad, A., Hong, Y.H.: Invariant image recognition by zernike moments. IEEE Trans. Pattern Anal. Mach. Intell. 12(5), 489–497 (1990)
17. LeCun, Y., Bottou, L., Bengio, Y., Haffner, P., et al.: Gradient-based learning applied to document recognition. Proc. IEEE 86(11), 2278–2324 (1998)
18. Lee, S.C., Nevatia, R.: Robust camera calibration tool for video surveillance camera in urban environment. In: CVPR 2011 Workshops, pp. 62–67, June 2011
19. Lowe, D.G.: Object recognition from local scale-invariant features. In: ICCV, p. 1150. IEEE (1999)
20. Massiris, M., Delrieux, C., Fernández, J.Á.: Detección de equipos de proteccÓin personal mediante red neuronal convolucional yolo. http://eii.unex.es/ja2018/actas/JA2018_073.pdf. Accessed 25 Feb 2019
21. Ojala, T., Pietikäinen, M., Mäenpää, T.: Multiresolution gray-scale and rotation invariant texture classification with local binary patterns. IEEE Trans. Pattern Anal. Mach. Intell. 7, 971–987 (2002)
22. Ren, S., He, K., Girshick, R., Sun, J.: Faster R-CNN: towards real-time object detection with region proposal networks. In: Cortes, C., Lawrence, N.D., Lee, D.D., Sugiyama, M., Garnett, R. (eds.) Advances in Neural Information Processing Systems, vol. 28, pp. 91–99. Curran Associates, Inc. (2015)
23. Rosebrock, A.: Deep Learning for Computer Vision with Python: Starter Bundle. Pyimagesearch (2017)
24. Rosten, E., Drummond, T.: Fusing points and lines for high performance tracking. In: Null, pp. 1508–1515. IEEE (2005)
25. i Serrano, A.S., PeñaL, A.M.L.: YOLO object detector for onboard driving images. Enginyeria Informàtica 958 (2017). https://ddd.uab.cat/record/181557
26. Simonyan, K., Zisserman, A.: Very deep convolutional networks for large-scale image recognition. arXiv preprint arXiv:1409.1556 (2014)
27. Tang, P., Wang, H., Kwong, S.: G-MS2F: GoogLeNet based multi-stage feature fusion of deep CNN for scene recognition. Neurocomputing 225, 188–197 (2017)
28. Torres-Espinoza, F., Barros-Gavilanes, G.: Sound noise monitoring platform: Smart-phones as sensors. In: European Wireless 2017; 23th European Wireless Conference, pp. 1–6, May 2017. http://ieeexplore.ieee.org/document/8011287/
29. Torres-Espinoza, F., Barros-Gavilanes, G., Barros, M.J.: Computer vision classifier and platform for automatic counting: more than cars. In: 2nd ETCM Conference, Ecuador Technical Chapters Meeting 2017, pp. 1–6, October 2017. https://doi.org/10.1109/ETCM.2017.8247454. https://ieeexplore.ieee.org/document/8247454

30. Welch, G., Bishop, G.: An Introduction to the Kalman Filter. Technical Report 1. UNC, Chapel Hill, NC, USA, July 2006. https://www.cs.unc.edu/~welch/media/pdf/kalmanintro.pdf
31. Zmudzinski, L.: Deep learning guinea pig image classification using Nvidia DIGITS and GoogLeNet. In: Proceedings of the 27th International Workshop on Concurrency, September 2018

Retail Traffic-Flow Analysis Using a Fast Multi-object Detection and Tracking System

Richard Cobos⬤, Jefferson Hernandez⬤, and Andres G. Abad$^{(\boxtimes)}$⬤

Industrial Artificial Intelligence (INARI) Research Lab,
Escuela Superior Politecnica del Litoral (ESPOL),
Campus Gustavo Galindo Velasco, 09-01-5863, Guayaquil, Ecuador
{ricgecob,jefehern,agabad}@espol.edu.ec

Abstract. Traffic-flow analysis allows to make critical decisions for retail operation management. Common approaches for traffic-flow analysis make use of hardware-based solutions, which have major drawbacks, such as high deployment and maintenance costs. In this work, we address this issue by proposing a Multiple-Object Tracking (MOT) system, following the tracking-by-detection paradigm, that leverages on an ensemble of detectors, each running every f frames. We further measured the performance of our model in the MOT16 Challenge and applied our algorithm to obtain heatmaps and paths for customers and shopping carts in a retail store from CCTV cameras.

Keywords: Multi-object tracking · Shopping-carts detection · Indoor localization and tracking · Kalman filters

1 Introduction

Traffic-flow analysis allows to make critical decisions and predictions for retail-scene applications, such as, hot zones estimation, dwell time calculation, and conversion rate inference. Common hardware-based solutions include Wireless Sensor Networks (WSN) [5] and Radio Frequency Identification Devices (RFID) [7]. Implementation of such devices have major drawbacks, such as high deployment and maintenance costs.

Our focus is on obtaining customers trajectories in a retail store from video data using the tracking-by-detection paradigm for the Multiple-Object Tracking (MOT) problem [1–3,26], which is comprised of two steps: (1) obtaining potential locations of objects of interest using an object detector—deep-learning-based object detectors, such as [18,19], have been proposed for this step, but they are often the computational bottleneck of modern tracking-by-detection systems, limiting their use for real-time applications—and (2) associating these detections to object trajectories—this has been done using Kalman filters, k-shortest paths optimization and other combinatorial optimization approaches [2,3,28]. The present work is an extended version of our previous paper [6].

© Springer Nature Switzerland AG 2019
A. D. Orjuela-Cañón et al. (Eds.): ColCACI 2019, CCIS 1096, pp. 29–39, 2019.
https://doi.org/10.1007/978-3-030-36211-9_3

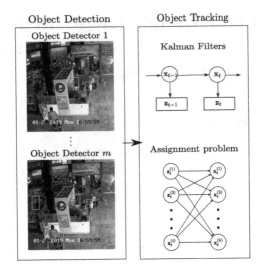

Fig. 1. Proposed multi-object tracking system with an object detector ensemble.

In this work, we present a tracking-by-detection system for path analysis (Sect. 2) leveraging on an ensemble of detectors, each running every f frames; the detections are combined using a variation of the soft non-maximum suppression (Soft-NMS) algorithm. Our system incorporates the following advantages: (1) it is able to run in real time (or even faster, for offline video post processing), while mitigating a significant drop in its accuracy; (2) it associates detections with tracks using a simple and fast algorithm devised in [3] (using Kalman filters and solving an assignment optimization problem), since the ensemble of object detectors further relaxes the constraints of the tracking pipeline (see Fig. 1); and (3) it takes uncertainty into account, unlike [3], by using a statistical-based distance measure. We measured the performance of our model in the MOT16 Challenge [15] (Sect. 2), a popular benchmark for MOT algorithms. Finally, we applied our algorithm to obtain heatmaps and paths for customers and shopping carts in a retail store from video data (Sect. 3).

2   Proposed Tracking-by-Detection System

We begin by reviewing the tracking-by-detection formulation of the MOT problem, which follows closely the formulation used in [27].

We assume the existence of $z_t^{(i)}$, corresponding to detection i at time t. Here we do not specify the form of the detection (e.g., bounding box, feature vector, optical-flow traces) or its origin (single detector or an ensemble of detectors). We denote the set of all detections in a video as $\hat{Z}$.

We further define a track $x^{(k)}$ as a time series of states containing elements $x_t^{(k)}$ with all information necessary to track an object including, but not limited to, its current location. These tracks encode the changes that object k undergoes from the moment of its first effective detection to its last one, providing the necessary notion of persistance to distinguish objects from one another within a video. We define the collection of all K tracks as $\mathbf{X} = \{\mathbf{x}^{(1)}, \cdots, \mathbf{x}^{(K)}\}$.

Using the tracking-by-detection formulation of MOT, we aim to maximize the posterior probability of $\mathbf{X}$ given $\hat{\mathbf{Z}}$, as

$$\max_{\mathbf{X}} p(\mathbf{X}|\hat{\mathbf{Z}}) = \max_{\mathbf{X}} p(\hat{\mathbf{Z}}|\mathbf{X})p(\mathbf{X})$$

$$= \max_{\mathbf{X}} \underbrace{\prod_{i,t} p(\mathbf{z}_t^{(i)}|\mathbf{X})}_{\text{detection likelihood}} \underbrace{\prod_{k} p(\mathbf{x}^{(k)})}_{\text{tracking transitions}} , \qquad (1)$$

where we assumed conditional independence between detections given a collection of tracks; and independence between tracks. We further assume that track transitions follow a first order Markov model $p(\mathbf{x}^{(k)}) = p(x_0^{(k)}) \prod_t p(x_t^{(k)}|x_{t-1}^{(k)})$, where $x_0^{(k)}$ is the initial state of the track and t ranges from the second to the last frame where object k has been tracked.

Equation (1) shows that the MOT problem can be decomposed into two sub-problems: assessing the likelihood of detections $p(\hat{\mathbf{Z}}|\mathbf{X})$ (e.g., ignoring detections that show unlikely movement, evaluating the need for new tracks) and modelling state transitions $p(x_t^{(k)}|x_{t-1}^{(k)})$.

2.1 Object Detection System

Object detection is the first step of any tracking-by-detection system constituting, in most cases, the computational bottleneck of the system.

To increase prediction performance, one technique is to use an ensemble of models which optimizes over the hypothesis space $\mathcal{H}$, to choose the most likely prediction. Under certain specific independence assumptions, ensembles are more accurate than their individual models [10]. Here, we propose an ensemble of object detectors skipping f frames. This aims to reduce the computational demand of the detectors, while avoiding a significant decrease in overall accuracy.

In the optimal case, the models should be combined in an ensemble to form an object detector $p(\hat{\mathbf{Z}}; \mathbf{Z})$ where $\hat{\mathbf{Z}}$ are the detections at some particular frame fed to the tracking system, and $\mathbf{Z}$ are the ground-truth detections at frame t. This is based on the bayesian framework $\int_{\mathbf{h}\in\mathcal{H}} p(\hat{\mathbf{Z}}|\mathbf{h}; \mathbf{Z})p(\mathbf{h}; \mathbf{Z})d\mathbf{h}$, where $\mathbf{h}$ is the hypothesis of the model. Note that such treatment becomes mathematically intractable. Our ensemble aims to approximate this theoretical framework.

We combine m independently trained object detectors, each operating every f frames. Detector i proposes its bounding boxes predictions $\mathbf{B}^{(i)} = \{\mathbf{b}_1^{(i)}, \ldots, \mathbf{b}_{n^{(i)}}^{(i)}\}$ and their associated scores $\mathbf{S}^{(i)} = \{s_1^{(i)}, \ldots, s_{n^{(i)}}^{(i)}\}$; score $s_j^{(i)} \in \mathbb{R}_{[0,1]}$ corresponds to a measure of the confidence of object detector i about the detection j.

Algorithm 1. Object Detection Ensemble

Input: Detections bounding boxes $\mathbf{b}_j^{(i)}$, Detections scores $s_j^{(i)}$, β, Detectors score thresholds $c^{(i)}$
Output: Conciliated predictions of the m detectors
1: $\hat{\mathbf{Z}}_t \leftarrow \emptyset$
2: **while** $\mathbf{B} \neq \emptyset$ **do**
3:      Find the object with highest score $\mathbf{b}_{j*}^{(i^*)}$
4:      **for all** $\mathbf{b}_j^{(i)} \in \mathbf{B}; i \neq i^*$ **do**
5:          $g_j^{(i)} \leftarrow \exp(-\beta \mathrm{IoU}(\mathbf{b}_{j*}^{(i^*)}, \mathbf{b}_j^{(i)}))$
6:          $\tilde{s}_j^{(i)} \leftarrow g_j^{(i)} s_j^{(i)}$
7:          **if** $\tilde{s}_j^{(i)} < c^{(i)}$ **then**
8:              $\mathbf{B} \leftarrow \mathbf{B} \setminus \mathbf{b}_j^{(i)}$
9:              $\mathbf{S} \leftarrow \mathbf{S} \setminus s_j^{(i)}$
10:      $\mathbf{B} \leftarrow \mathbf{B} \setminus \mathbf{b}_{j*}^{(i^*)}$
11:      $\mathbf{S} \leftarrow \mathbf{S} \setminus s_{j*}^{(i^*)}$
12:      $\hat{\mathbf{Z}}_t \leftarrow \hat{\mathbf{Z}}_t \cup \{\mathbf{b}_{j*}^{(i^*)}\}$
13: **Return** $\hat{\mathbf{Z}}_t$

At the beginning of the algorithm, all predictions are joined into set $\mathbf{B} = \bigcup_{i=1}^m \mathbf{B}^{(i)}$; a similar definition is given to $\mathbf{S}$. Each iteration begins by extracting the detection with highest confidence $s_{j*}^{(i^*)}$. An exponential decay is used for correcting the overlapping bounding boxes scores by measuring the *Intersection over Union* (IoU) between $\mathbf{b}_{j*}^{(i^*)}$ and $\mathbf{b}_j^{(i)}$. Here $g_j^{(i)} = \exp(-\beta \mathrm{IoU}(\mathbf{b}_{j*}^{(i^*)}, \mathbf{b}_j^{(i)}))$ is a function bounded in $[0, 1]$ for any non-negative β and IoU, being β a free parameter used for scaling. Function g is used to update scores as $\tilde{s}_j^{(i)} = g_j^{(i)} s_j^{(i)}$ and, thus, it can be seen as a variation of the Soft-NMS algorithm [4].

After each iteration, the prior and final detections are updated as $\mathbf{B} = \mathbf{B} \setminus \{\mathbf{b}_{j*}^{(i^*)}\}$, $\mathbf{S} = \mathbf{S} \setminus \{s_{j*}^{(i^*)}\}$, and $\hat{\mathbf{Z}}_t = \hat{\mathbf{Z}}_t \cup \{\mathbf{b}_{j*}^{(i^*)}\}$, respectively. To reduce computational load, detections whose scores are below their detector confidence threshold $c^{(i)}$, are dropped after each iteration. The detailed procedure is provided in Algorithm 1.

2.2 Multi-object Tracking System

The term $p(\tilde{\mathbf{Z}}|\mathbf{X})$ in Eq. (1), has been previously used in [17,23,24] as a mechanism to model short-term occlusion using the sensitivity and specificity of the detector. Here we overcome short-term occlusion using an ensemble of detectors. This allows us to relax more the tracking problem by assuming conditional independence between detections given states

$$p(\tilde{\mathbf{Z}}_{1:t}|\mathbf{X}_t) = \prod_{k,\tau} p(\mathbf{z}_\tau^{(k)}|\mathbf{x}_\tau^{(k)}). \tag{2}$$

We argue that these assumptions, while restrictive, are justified given the deep-learning powered advancements in object detection made in the last few years. The assumptions made in Eq. (2) allow us to write Eq. (1) in the following recursive form

$$p(\mathbf{X}|\tilde{\mathbf{Z}}_{1:t}) = p(\mathbf{X}|\tilde{\mathbf{Z}}_{1:t-1}) \prod_k p(\mathbf{z}_t^{(k)}|\mathbf{x}_t^{(k)})p(\mathbf{x}_t^{(k)}|\mathbf{x}_{t-1}^{(k)}), \tag{3}$$

providing a way to maximize the posterior at time t given the current detections and the posterior at time $t-1$ (i.e., solving the MOT problem in a frame-to-frame basis).

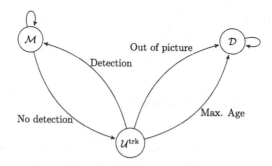

Fig. 2. State transition diagram for a track.

A natural sequential algorithm to maximize the posterior follows from Eq. (3). To approximate the posterior, this algorithm uses Kalman filters and a $\{0,1\}$-assignment problem, where at frame t, cost c_{ij} corresponds to the Mahalanobis distance $(\mathbf{z}_t^{(i)}-\mathbf{x}_t^{(j)})^\mathsf{T}\Sigma_t^{-1}(\mathbf{z}_t^{(i)}-\mathbf{x}_t^{(j)})$ between detections and tracks. Here, matrix Σ is the uncertainty matrix obtained from the Kalman filter and its incorporation is advantageous for two reasons: (1) the assignment of tracks to far detections becomes unlikely; and (2) short-term occlusion can be handled when motion uncertainty is low. These properties are important to our application since we assume that object motion does not change rapidly in short periods of time.

The states that a track might undergo are depicted in Fig. 2. Track dynamics are as follows: a track can stay in the matched state $\mathcal{M}$ (or return to it from the unmatched state) if it was assigned a detection; a track can be in the unmatched state $\mathcal{U}^{\mathrm{trk}}$ if it became unassigned; and a tracker can be in the deleted state $\mathcal{D}$ if it has remained unassigned for a time longer than "Max. Age" or if it is predicted to be "Out of Picture" (OOP). The detailed procedure of our MOT system is presented in Algorithm 2.

Algorithm 2. MOT system algorithm

Input: Video; and defined parameters $\beta, f, \text{Max.Age}$
Output: Object's IDs and their corresponding bounding boxes
1: **while** Duration of video, frame-skip of f frames **do**
2:      $\mathbf{B} \leftarrow$ Detections from every Object detector
3:      $\mathbf{S} \leftarrow$ Confidence scores from every Object detector
4:      $\tilde{\mathbf{Z}} \leftarrow$ Soft-NMS$(\mathbf{B}, \mathbf{S}, \beta)$ as described in algorithm 1
5:      Obtain sets $\mathcal{M}, \mathcal{U}^{\text{trk}}, \mathcal{U}^{\text{det}}$ by solving the $\{0,1\}$-assignment problem
6:      **for** Track in $\mathcal{M}$ **do**
7:          Update Track using detections $\tilde{\mathbf{Z}}$
8:      **for** Detections in $\mathcal{U}^{\text{det}}$ **do**
9:          Initialize a new Track
10:     **for** Track in $\mathcal{U}^{\text{trk}}$ **do**
11:         Predict the next state of Track
12:     Delete tracks older than Max.Age or OOP
13: **Return** Object's IDs, bounding boxes.

2.3   Numerical Results and Analysis

Table 1. Results on the MOT16 Challenge [15]. For a fair comparison, we chose only methods that use their own detections. All methods are *online* (i.e., they perform frame to frame associations). *SORT [3] does not report IDF1.

	MOTA	IDF1	MT	ML	FP	FN	ID Sw.	Hz
DeepSORT [25]	61.4	62.2	32.8%	**18.2%**	12,852	56,668	781	17.4
TAP [28]	64.8	**73.5**	**40.6%**	22.0%	13,470	49,927	794	39.4
EAMTT [21]	52.5	53.3	19.0%	34.9%	4,407	81,223	910	12.2
CNNKCF [22]	40.4	44.6	13.4%	44.3%	14,052	93,651	920	84.6
FMOT_BL [11]	59.4	58.8	24.5%	28.9%	7,454	65,825	798	49.3
CNNMTT [14]	65.2	62.2	32.4%	21.3%	6,578	55,896	946	11.2
RAR16wVGG [9]	63.0	63.8	39.9%	22.1%	13,663	53,248	**482**	1.6
SORT [3]*	33.4	–	11.7%	30.9%	7,318	**32,615**	1,001	**260.0**
GM_PHD_N1T [1]	33.3	25.5	5.5%	56.0%	**1,750**	116,452	3,499	9.9
POI [26]	**66.1**	65.1	34.0%	20.8%	5,061	55,914	805	9.9
OURS ($f = 1$)	43.7	47.1	23.2%	18.7%	15,728	45,152	1,289	249.6
OURS ($f = 5$)	34.3	43.0	12.6%	29.4%	2,932	10,568	1,007	**1,431.5**
OURS ($f = 10$)	28.3	55.2	10.7%	34.5%	1,352	5,919	729	**3,000.1**

We assessed the performance of our MOT system in the MOT16 benchmark[1] [15], where tracking performance is evaluated on seven challenging test sequences (containing both moving and static cameras). We used the detections provided by

---

[1] Evaluation codes were downloaded from https://github.com/cheind/py-motmetrics. git as recommended by the MOT16 challenge.

our ensemble running with a frame-skip of f frames. Our ensemble is composed of two object detectors based on the YOLOv3 [18] (a one-stage detector) and Light-head R-CNN [12] (a two-stage detector) architectures. The detectors were trained on the COCO [13] and PASCAL [8] datasets, respectively. The ensemble was arranged in this manner to increase detectors independence, favoring the performance of the ensemble. Our tracking system ran at 249.6 Hz on a single core of an Intel i9 3.3 GHz processor with 48 GB of RAM memory. Likewise, the detector ensemble ran on an Nvidia GTX 1080 Ti with 12 GB of vRAM using the PyTorch deep-learning framework [16].

Evaluation was carried out according to the following metrics:

- Multi-object tracking accuracy (MOTA): summarizes tracking accuracy in terms of false positives, false negatives and identity switches (more is better).
- ID F1 Score (IDF1): ratio of correctly identified detections over the average number of ground-truth and computed detections (more is better).
- Mostly tracked (MT): ratio of ground-truth tracks that have the same label for at least 80% of their respective life span (more is better).
- Mostly lost (ML): ratio of ground-truth trajectories that are tracked at most 20% of their respective life span (less is better).
- Identity switches (ID Sw): number of times the ID of a ground-truth changes (less is better).
- False positives (FP) (less is better).
- False negatives (FN) (less is better).
- Speed (Hz): processing speed in frames per second excluding the detector (more is better).

For a detailed explanation of these metrics the reader is referred to [15] and [20].

Our results are shown in Table 1 together with other reported relevant approaches on the same dataset. Our proposed model achieved the highest speed among the considered entries in the MOT16 challenge, which have a tendency to aim for accuracy (MOTA). While this is fine for offline implementations, we argue that real-time performance is necessary for many applications (e.g., people counting and path analysis). Figure 3 shows the performance of various entries in the challenge. This figure shows a trend: methods with high accuracy are the slowest (bottom right of figure), and very fast methods tend to have a lower accuracy (top left of figure); few methods are able to achieve high accuracy and speed (FMOT_BL [11], TAP [28]). We note that detection time is not considered in the values reported at the MOT16 challenge, which could make some entries unsuitable for real-time use. Our application (considering tracking and detection time) was able to run with real-time performance using $f = 5$ frames with a drop of 9 points in accuracy as reported in Table 1, thus, our model expands the Pareto-optimality frontier between accuracy and speed. Most entries with MOTA higher than 50% employ some sort of person re-identification, which decreases their speed. For further comparisons between our approach and other methods, the reader is referred to [6].

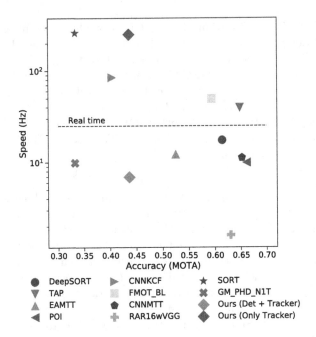

Fig. 3. Accuracy vs Speed of different entries of the MOT16 challenge.

3 Applications

We applied our model to find trajectories of customers and shopping carts in a retail store, using videos from CCTV cameras. We augmented the object detectors in the ensemble to include the shopping-cart class. Shopping-carts images used in the training process were composed by a mixture of ideal and challenging pictures, including images from CCTV cameras, which were taken from different angles and had significant occlusion; all these images were labeled by ourselves. Heatmaps were created by placing a gaussian kernel in the lower segment of each detection bounding box and then obtaining the multi-modal distribution by kernel addition. On the other hand, paths were generated interpolating between missing detections of a track using B-splines.

Following the described procedure, our model is able to obtain customers and shopping-carts heatmaps to locate spots with greatest traffic activity; these can be used, for example, to design store layouts for optimal product placement and to evaluate the effectiveness of visual merchandising. Likewise, obtained paths can be used to analyze customer behavior with respect to merchandise displays and group-activity dynamics, or to estimate high dwell times and their locations. Figure 4 shows trajectories and heatmaps obtained by our model, corresponding to customers and shopping carts.

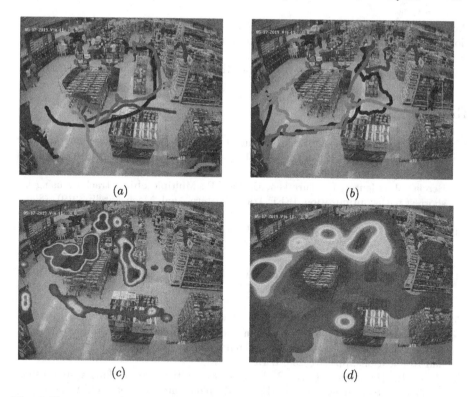

Fig. 4. Heatmaps and trajectories of different IDs in a grocery store. (a) Shopping-carts trajectories. (b) Customers trajectories. (c) Shopping-carts heatmap. (d) Customers heatmap.

4 Conclusion and Future Work

This work proposes a traffic-flow analysis method using the fast implementation of the multi-object tracking system presented in [6]. The proposed model expands the Pareto-optimality frontier of the MOT16 challenge, both in speed and accuracy; making it appropriate for real-time applications. The presented ensemble enhances the tracking system significantly by reducing the false negatives of each detector. The whole system reaches real-time performance (or faster in offline implementations). Two applications of our MOT system are obtaining heatmaps and path trajectories for customers and shopping carts that can be used to optimize the store layout and to discover customers interests.

Future work directions include incorporating person re-identification in the tracking system to calculate average sales per customer or localized *conversion rates*; and implementing homography to obtain heatmaps and trajectories on a global frame of reference.

Acknowledgment. The authors would like to acknowledge the stimulating discussions and help from Victor Merchan, Joo Wang Kim and Ricardo Palacios, as well as Tiendas Industriales Asociadas Sociedad Anonima (TIA S.A.), a leading grocery retailer in Ecuador, for providing funding for this research effort.

References

1. Baisa, N.L., Wallace, A.: Development of a N-type GM-PHD filter for multiple target, multiple type visual tracking. J. Vis. Commun. Image Represent. **59**, 257–271 (2019)
2. Berclaz, J., Fleuret, F., Turetken, E., Fua, P.: Multiple object tracking using k-shortest paths optimization. IEEE Trans. Pattern Anal. Mach. Intell. **33**(9), 1806–1819 (2011)
3. Bewley, A., Ge, Z., Ott, L., Ramos, F., Upcroft, B.: Simple online and realtime tracking. In: 2016 IEEE International Conference on Image Processing (ICIP), pp. 3464–3468. IEEE (2016)
4. Bodla, N., Singh, B., Chellappa, R., Davis, L.S.: Soft-NMS–improving object detection with one line of code. In: 2017 IEEE International Conference on Computer Vision (ICCV), pp. 5562–5570. IEEE (2017)
5. Cheng, Q.J., Ng, J.K.Y., Shum, K.C.Y.: A wireless LAN location estimation system using center of gravity as an algorithm selector for enhancing location estimation. In: 2012 IEEE 26th International Conference on Advanced Information Networking and Applications, pp. 261–268. IEEE (2012)
6. Cobos, R., Hernandez, J., Abad, A.G.: A fast multi-object tracking system using an object detector ensemble. In: IEEE 2nd Colombian Conference on Applications in Computational Intelligence (ColCACI) (2019)
7. Contigiani, M., Pietrini, R., Mancini, A., Zingaretti, P.: Implementation of a tracking system based on UWB technology in a retail environment. In: 2016 12th IEEE/ASME International Conference on Mechatronic and Embedded Systems and Applications (MESA), pp. 1–6. IEEE (2016)
8. Everingham, M., Van Gool, L., Williams, C.K., Winn, J., Zisserman, A.: The pascal visual object classes challenge 2007 (voc2007) results (2007)
9. Fang, K., Xiang, Y., Li, X., Savarese, S.: Recurrent autoregressive networks for online multi-object tracking. In: 2018 IEEE Winter Conference on Applications of Computer Vision (WACV), pp. 466–475. IEEE (2018)
10. Kuncheva, L.I., Whitaker, C.J.: Measures of diversity in classifier ensembles and their relationship with the ensemble accuracy. Mach. Learn. **51**(2), 181–207 (2003)
11. Kurkova, V., Manolopoulos, Y., Hammer, B., Iliadis, L., Maglogiannis, I. (eds.): Artificial Neural Networks and Machine Learning ICANN 2018: 27th International Conference on Artificial Neural Networks, Rhodes, Greece, 4–7 October 2018, Proceedings, Part I. Theoretical Computer Science and General Issues. Springer International Publishing (2018)
12. Li, Z., Peng, C., Yu, G., Zhang, X., Deng, Y., Sun, J.: Light-head R-CNN: In defense of two-stage object detector. arXiv preprint arXiv:1711.07264 (2017)
13. Lin, T.-Y., et al.: Microsoft COCO: common objects in context. In: Fleet, D., Pajdla, T., Schiele, B., Tuytelaars, T. (eds.) ECCV 2014. LNCS, vol. 8693, pp. 740–755. Springer, Cham (2014). https://doi.org/10.1007/978-3-319-10602-1_48
14. Mahmoudi, N., Ahadi, S.M., Rahmati, M.: Multi-target tracking using CNN-based features: Cnnmtt. Multimedia Tools and Applications, pp. 1–20 (2018)

15. Milan, A., Leal-Taixé, L., Reid, I., Roth, S., Schindler, K.: Mot16: A benchmark for multi-object tracking. arXiv preprint arXiv:1603.00831 (2016)
16. Paszke, A., et al.: Automatic differentiation in pytorch. In: NIPS-W (2017)
17. Pirsiavash, H., Ramanan, D., Fowlkes, C.C.: Globally-optimal greedy algorithms for tracking a variable number of objects. In: 2011 IEEE Conference on Computer Vision and Pattern Recognition (CVPR), pp. 1201–1208. IEEE (2011)
18. Redmon, J., Divvala, S., Girshick, R., Farhadi, A.: You only look once: Unified, real-time object detection. In: Proceedings of the IEEE Conference on Computer Vision and Pattern Recognition, pp. 779–788 (2016)
19. Ren, S., He, K., Girshick, R., Sun, J.: Faster R-CNN: towards real-time object detection with region proposal networks. In: Advances in Neural Information Processing Systems, pp. 91–99 (2015)
20. Ristani, E., Solera, F., Zou, R., Cucchiara, R., Tomasi, C.: Performance measures and a data set for multi-target, multi-camera tracking. In: Hua, G., Jégou, H. (eds.) ECCV 2016. LNCS, vol. 9914, pp. 17–35. Springer, Cham (2016). https://doi.org/10.1007/978-3-319-48881-3_2
21. Sanchez-Matilla, R., Poiesi, F., Cavallaro, A.: Online multi-target tracking with strong and weak detections. In: Hua, G., Jégou, H. (eds.) ECCV 2016. LNCS, vol. 9914, pp. 84–99. Springer, Cham (2016). https://doi.org/10.1007/978-3-319-48881-3_7
22. Stillman, S., Tanawongsuwan, R., Essa, I.: Tracking multiple people with multiple cameras, January 1999
23. Tang, S., Andres, B., Andriluka, M., Schiele, B.: Subgraph decomposition for multi-target tracking. In: Proceedings of the IEEE Conference on Computer Vision and Pattern Recognition, pp. 5033–5041 (2015)
24. Tang, S., Andres, B., Andriluka, M., Schiele, B.: Multi-person tracking by multicut and deep matching. In: Hua, G., Jégou, H. (eds.) ECCV 2016. LNCS, vol. 9914, pp. 100–111. Springer, Cham (2016). https://doi.org/10.1007/978-3-319-48881-3_8
25. Wojke, N., Bewley, A., Paulus, D.: Simple online and realtime tracking with a deep association metric. In: 2017 IEEE International Conference on Image Processing (ICIP), pp. 3645–3649. IEEE (2017)
26. Yu, F., Li, W., Li, Q., Liu, Y., Shi, X., Yan, J.: POI: multiple object tracking with high performance detection and appearance feature. In: Hua, G., Jégou, H. (eds.) ECCV 2016. LNCS, vol. 9914, pp. 36–42. Springer, Cham (2016). https://doi.org/10.1007/978-3-319-48881-3_3
27. Zhang, L., Li, Y., Nevatia, R.: Global data association for multi-object tracking using network flows. In: IEEE Conference on Computer Vision and Pattern Recognition, CVPR 2008, pp. 1–8. IEEE (2008)
28. Zhou, Z., Xing, J., Zhang, M., Hu, W.: Online multi-target tracking with tensor-based high-order graph matching. In: 2018 24th International Conference on Pattern Recognition (ICPR), pp. 1809–1814. IEEE (2018)

Accelerating Video Processing Inside Embedded Devices to Count Mobility Actors

Andrés Heredia[1]([⊠]) [iD] and Gabriel Barros-Gavilanes[1,2] [iD]

[1] LIDI, Universidad del Azuay, Av. 24 de Mayo 7-77, 010204 Cuenca, Ecuador
{andres.heredia,gbarrosg}@uazuay.edu.ec
[2] tivo.ec Research, Don Bosco 2-07, 010205 Cuenca, Ecuador
http://www.uazuay.edu.ec

Abstract. The actual number of surveillance cameras and the different methods for counting vehicles originate the question: What is the best place to process video flows? This work analyze techniques to accelerate a counting system for mobility actors like cars, pedestrians, motorcycles, bicycles, buses, and trucks in the context of an Edge computing application using deep learning. To solve this problem this study presents the analysis and implementation of different techniques based on the use of an additional hardware element as is the case of a Vision Processing Unit (VPU) in combination with methods that affect the resolution, bit rate, and time of video processing. For this purpose we consider the Mobilenet-SSD model with two approaches: a pre-trained model with known data sets and a trained model with images from our specific scenarios. Additionally, we compare an optimized model using OpenVINO toolkit and overclock of hardware. The use of SSD-Mobilenet's model generates different results in terms of accuracy and time of video processing in the system. Results show that the use of an embedded device in combination with a VPU and video processing techniques reach 18.62 Frames per Second (FPS). Thus, video processing time is slightly superior (5.63 min) for a video of 5 min. Optimized model and overclock show improvements too. Recall and precision values of 91% and 97% are reported in the best case (class car) for the vehicle counting system.

Keywords: Computer vision · Raspberry Pi · Mobilenet · Single shot detection · Convolutional Neural Network · Vision Processing Unit · OpenVino · Overclock

1 Introduction

Integrated Transportation Systems (ITS) involve the processing and collection of a large amount of data in relation to public infrastructures. While it is true

Thanks to the Ecuadorian Corporation for the Development of Research and Academia, CEDIA, for the financing provided to research, through the CEPRA projects, especially the CEPRA project - XII - 2018; Clasificador-video para actores de la movilidad como alternativa a conteos volumetricos manuales.

that there are numerous types of sensors (e.g. inductive loop, pneumatic, etc.), we focus our attention only on video or surveillance cameras and in sensors able to differentiate between mobility actors (i.e. cars, people, motorcycles, buses, etc). Therefore, our goal is to reduce human intervention to perform the process of vehicle counting. This counting application includes detection, classification, tracking and counting of mobility actors and could include traditional Machine Learning techniques (see for example [14]) or more recent techniques like Convolutional Neural Networks (CNN).

This raises the question about the right place to process video flows. If a fast network connection is available, it is possible to send video for further processing on the Cloud or a local server like in Fog computing applications. This type of processing demands a continuous transmission of the video streams from the capture site to the servers. However, Edge processing could be an alternative for processing video "in situ". The use of CNN seems feasible using embedded devices and hardware accelerators like a Vision Processing Unit (VPU). However, it is not possible to process video in real time while using a simple detection model like SSD-Mobilenet, as presented in [8].

Specifically our contributions include: (i) performance comparison of CNN techniques on a Raspberry Pi 3B, with and without a VPU like the Movidius Neural Computer Stick (NCS). Performance include software (accuracy) and hardware (processing times and Frames Per Second (FPS)), according to different parameters of the video such as bit rate and resolution. (ii) a comparison between default and retrained models. (iii) benefits of using specialized optimization toolkits and overclok.

2   Related Works

In the context of Deep Neural Networks (DNN) there are a great variety of models that allow the implementation of systems using object detection through deep learning. For example, in [9] three different models for object detection are analyzed: Single Shot Detector (SSD), Faster Region-based Convolutional Neural Networks (R-CNN) and Region based-Fully Convolutional Networks (R-FCN). These models are combined with different feature extractors like VGG, Resnet-101, and Mobilenet to determine the best combination in terms of performance and speed. The authors report that the combination of Faster R-CNN with Resnet-101 provide the best accuracy for the object detector with a 33.7% of mean Average Precision (mAP) and 396ms of GPU time, while the SSD-MobileNet model provides a mAP of 19% with a GPU time of 40ms. The hardware configurations include an Nvidia Titan X GPU card running on a 32 GB RAM device with an Intel Xeon E5-1650 v2 processor, this implies a trade off between the mAP and the GPU time.

Other studies seek to improve the available object detector models. In [13] for example the performance of traditional Faster R-CNN method is optimized by mixing blocks with Fast R-CNN model in a single network, this new network is called RF-RCNN. The traditional method Faster R-CNN has a precision of around 0.61 and with RF-RCNN this value improves to 0.75.

In relation to the deployment of a convolutional neural networks (CNN) in a low capacity embedded device the number of publications that propose a unified detection, tracking and counting system is small. Most studies are limited to a single field of application like detection, classification or counting using traditional techniques like Background Subtraction and SVM (see for example [5,12,14]).

In [10], an analysis is made in terms of power and computational capability of an inference model based on CNN for an object detection system. The implementation uses an embedded device platform with support for GPU and the results are compared with a traditional PC-based platform. Authors report a frame rate of 53.355 (images/s) for the embedded device (CPU + GPU) and 0.383 (images/s) with CPU only. The support provided by embedded devices to Convolutional Neural Networks is affected by the processing capacity of these platforms. To solve this problem in [11] Movidius Neural Computer Stick is used for the deployment of an object detection system in real time on a low power embedded device (RPi 3B). The results show that Movidius reaches 3.5 FPS versus 0.5 FPS without the device.

The authors cited previously in most cases use the detection models in advanced computers that have a GPU, the reason is that models like Faster R-CNN, R-FCN or GoogleLenet demand high processing which can not be satisfied by an embedded device or even with the use of an extra VPU. In this context the most suitable model for the deployment with embedded devices and extra graphic processing elements is SSD-Mobilnet which is strictly designed for devices with low processing capacities [11].

Table 1 summarizes the main characteristics of models implemented by the authors in this section. First columns shows the models, then, training parameter such as: mAP and GPU's training time. Next column presents reported FPS of the system. Column Hardware provides insights about the physical set up. From the table, SSD-Mobilenet is the only CNN model used in RPi and have faster trainning time with acceptable mAP. We use this model for this reason.

Table 1. Characteristics used in various models for object detection.

Model	mAP	GPU (training time)	FPS	Hardware	Author
SSD-Mobilenet	19.0	40 ms	–	GPU	[9]
	72.7	–	0.5	RPi (CPU)	[11]
		–	3.5	RPi + VPU	
Faster R-CNN	33.0	396 ms	–	GPU	[9]
R-FCN	30.5	386 ms	–	GPU	
RF-RCNN	75.0	–	–	GPU	[13]
GoogleLenet	68.0	–	53.33	CPU + GPU	[10]
		–	0.383	CPU	

3   System Architecture

Figure 1 illustrates the structure of the vehicle counting system. In first stage, input images change to a standard size of 600 × 600 pixels. Then, according to the number of frame the image is skipped or considered by a jump frame algorithm. Afterwards, counting and tracking is performed inside a Region of Interest (RoI). This is mainly to avoid occlusion and extra processing in the tracking algorithm. Each stage is described in detail in Sects. 3.2, 3.3, and 3.4. Figure 2 presents the workflow required for using Movidius NCS [3] inside an embedded machine. The file containing the CNN as a graph or "Graph file" is used to deploy the SSD-Mobilenet model in the embedded device. Graph file must be created in a computer with at least 2 GB of RAM and in the embedded device the Movidius API must be configured. This API allows sending the Graph file to the NCS and request predictions on images.

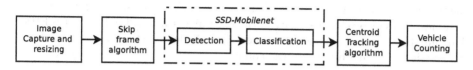

Fig. 1. Structure of the vehicle counting system.

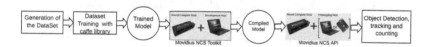

Fig. 2. Workflow of the vehicle counting system.

3.1   Data Set Description and Training Model

Our data set is composed by 13 videos of 5 min each with different resolutions. The SSD-Mobilenet model was implemented in two ways: We generate our own training set with their respective annotations, using LabelImg [4] software, gathering different traffic mobility actors, according to the reference guide of Chuanqi305 [6]. 1968 hand labeled images which were captured with different resolutions (640 × 480, 1280 × 720, and 1920 × 1080 pixels) in two different scenarios. Then, the SSD-Mobilenet model was trained with Caffe deep learning library, with a total of 30000 iterations reaching an error of around 0.07. Training and validation process was considering 30% of data for validation and 70% for training. The number of vehicles considered for the data set and their respective mAP after training, are described in Table 2.

In addition, we considered the pre-trained SSD Mobilenet model [6] which uses other data sets such as: MS-COCO [2] (91 classes and 164000 images) and VOC0712 [1] (20 classes and 11530 images), and reaches a mAP of 0.727 with 21 different classes.

Table 2. Number of annotations and mAP values for each class.

	Type of object				
	Cars	Pedestrians	Motorcycles	Buses	Trucks
Number of objects	982	826	125	90	50
mAp	0.84	0.79	0.69	0.46	0.35

3.2 Skip Frame Algorithm and Bit Rate-Resolution of Video

Skip Frame Algorithm: Through preliminar testing, we find very high processing times when all frames of a video are used on embedded devices. Thus, the number of objects to be detected by the CNN influence the processing time of each frame. For this reason, we propose a technique to selectively skip or jump a specific number of frames and reduce the work load of the CNN. Figure 3 shows the frame jump scheme when n is equal to five, which means skipping intervals of 5 frames. If a video contains 30 FPS, then the algorithm will only select 6 FPS. This number of frames is enough to feed the vehicle detection and the tracking model without losing quality in the count.

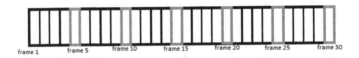

Fig. 3. Schema to skip or jump n-frames.

Bit Rate and Resolution: We considered videos with different bit rate and three types of resolution (1920 × 1080, 1280 × 720, and 640 × 480 pixels) to identify relations between these parameters. By default, a high performance camera is configured to provide a bit rate higher than 8000 kbps, but it was modified to consider a bit rate in the range of 800 kbps to 4500 kbps. With this modification the processing on the RPi improved by around 20%. However, bit rate below 700 kbps generated videos with low size in memory but with poor image quality. Section 5 presents how resolution and bit rate affect the processing time in the RPi.

3.3 Object Detection Method

The main objective of this work is to design a system that allows the detection, tracking and counting of vehicles and pedestrians on the road using an embedded device. To satisfy this requirement, we have chosen SSD-Mobilenet [8] model to detect the main objects within driving environments. SSD-Mobilenet is designed to provide fast execution on mobile platforms, as described in [15]. This model matches objects with default boxes of different aspect ratios and uses multi-scale feature maps to perform object detection. This feature provides better precision at different scales [11].

3.4 Tracking and Counting

Tracking algorithm is based on the centroid detection in the object of interest (car, person, motorcycle, bus, etc) in each frame. The algorithm is called "centroid tracking" since it is based on the Euclidean distance between the centroids of existing objects and the new centroids of objects between subsequent frames in a video. This object tracking algorithm does not require high computational processing, especially for embedded devices.

Each time that the object detector (SSD-Mobilenet) returns a bounding box its centroid is determined and an ID is assigned, this ID identifies the movement of the object in the video sequence. The centroid is useful in the calculation of the Euclidean distance that involves frames f_i and f_{i-1}. The Tracking is done within a specific region called "Counting Region", this allows to reduce the computational processing in the RPi. Red box in Fig. 4 determines the "Counting Region" for a specific scenario.

Fig. 4. Counting Region for one analyzed scenario.

3.5 OpenVino and Overclock

As an improvement to the scheme in Fig. 2, we propose a parallel workflow that takes advantage in the development of OpenVino, an Intel library for hardware optimized computer vision. In addition, the operation frequency in the Raspberry Pi 3B was modified to speed up the processing of images in the embedded device.

The use of the two optimization methods generates a new work scheme which can be seen in Fig. 5. The configuration of the overclock for modify the operating frequency in the Raspberry Pi 3B was made under the following parameters: arm_freq=1400, gpu_freq=500, sdram_freq=500 y over_voltage=5.

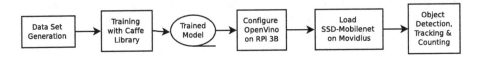

Fig. 5. Workflow: OpenVino + Overclock.

4   Experimental Setup

4.1   Metrics for the Object Detector Model (SSD-Mobilenet)

To evaluate the accuracy of the trained SSD-Mobilenet model with our own data set we use the mean Average Precision (mAP) described in [7].

Calculation of mAP in the trained object detector is as follows: First, Average Precision (AP) is calculated considering the Intersection over Union (IoU) greater than 50% (see Eq. 1) for each class present in the ground truth. Then, an average of all AP values in each class is calculated.

$$IoU = \frac{Area of Overlap}{Area of Union} \tag{1}$$

4.2   Metrics for the Counting and Classification System

To evaluate the accuracy of the vehicle counting process, we use metrics such as: precision (PRE), recall (REC) and F1 Score (F1) as presented in [5]. These metrics are defined in Eqs. 2.

Where **TP** is True Positives, **FP** means False Positives and False Negatives are represented by **FN**.

$$PRE = \frac{TP}{TP+FP}, REC = \frac{TP}{TP+FN}, F1 = \frac{2*REC*PRE}{REC+PRE} \tag{2}$$

It is possible to obtain measures of Precision PRE_{ci} and Recall REC_{ci} for each class, as defined in Eqs. 3.

$$PRE_{ci} = \frac{c_{i,i}}{\sum_{j=1}^{N+1} c_{i,j}}, REC_{ci} = \frac{c_{i,i}}{\sum_{j=1}^{N+1} c_{j,i}} \tag{3}$$

Where: $C_{i,i}$, $C_{i,j}$ and $C_{j,i}$ are defined in the confusion matrix for N classes, see Fig. 6.

Ground truth classes

		C_1	C_2	$\cdots$	C_N	FP
	C_1	$c_{1,1}$	$c_{1,2}$	$\cdots$	$c_{1,N}$	$c_{1,N+1}$
	C_2	$c_{2,1}$	$c_{2,2}$	$\cdots$	$c_{2,N}$	$c_{2,N+1}$
	$\vdots$	$\vdots$	$\vdots$	$\ddots$	$\vdots$	$\vdots$
	C_N	$c_{N,1}$	$c_{N,2}$	$\cdots$	$c_{N,N}$	$c_{N,N+1}$
	FN	$c_{N+1,1}$	$c_{N+1,2}$	$\cdots$	$c_{N+1,N}$	$c_{N+1,N+1}$

(Predicted classes)

Fig. 6. Extended confusion matrix.

4.3   Tests Definition

For the performance analysis of vehicle detection and counting system, we designed four stress tests, as described in Table 3.

Table 3. Tests carried out (Hardware + object detection models)

	Type of training (SSD-Mobilenet)	
Hardware	Own trained model	Pre-trained model
Rpi + NCS	Test A	Test B
Rpi	Test C	Test D

We consider the use of Movidius NCS in combination with RPi and the SSD-Mobilenet model pre-trained and trained by us. Likewise, we omitted the use of Movidius NCS in Test C and D to determine the influence of this device in the performance of quality measures and execution times.

5   Results

In a first step, video sequences of intense vehicular flow are taken from a side view of the road, then a manual counting of the actors or vehicles that appear on video was performed and statistics of each type of class are generated. Table 4 presents the ground truth values from the captured videos in the system.

5.1   Accuracy of SSD-Mobilenet Trained Model

The analysis of the trained detector model with our own data set is performed. For this purpose we use the Mean Average Precision (mAP) metric which is widely accepted in different object detection challenges like PASCAL VOC, ImageNet and COCO. The mAP values for each class are presented in Table 2 and the general mAP of the model is calculated by using the average mAP considering each class. For five classes it is 62.6% (Table 6).

Table 4. Ground truth and detected vehicles for each category.

Mobility actor	Number of video												
	1	2	3	4	5	6	7	8	9	10	11	12	13
Car	92	77	19	80	77	31	84	71	61	62	92	88	128
Person	10	5	0	14	13	3	7	11	8	11	20	16	23
Motorcycle or bicycle	7	2	0	0	12	2	6	3	6	11	5	9	8
Bus	6	3	0	3	5	8	7	3	8	3	5	4	5
Truck	1	1	0	2	2	0	2	1	3	0	6	3	3

Table 5. Number of FPS, bit rate, and processing time in minutes for different tests.

Resolution	Video	Test A		Test B		Test C		Test D		Bit rate (kbps)
		FPS	Time	FPS	Time	FPS	Time	FPS	Time	
1280 × 720	1	11.74	6.38	9.99	7.50	0.77	194.81	0.68	220.59	1041
	2	10.41	6.51	10.15	6.68	0.65	230.77	0.54	277.78	921
	3	10.6	7.08	10.26	7.32	0.79	189.87	0.55	272.73	890
640 × 480	4	18.62	5.63	16.71	6.27	1.12	133.93	0.95	157.89	3700
	5	16.79	7.31	17.41	7.06	1.07	140.19	0.86	174.42	3967
	6	18.68	6.01	17.13	6.61	1.02	147.06	0.81	185.19	3476
	7	17.06	7.08	17.01	7.11	0.96	156.25	0.79	189.87	4061
	8	17.05	7.63	17.74	7.34	0.9	166.67	0.86	174.42	3242
	9	17.03	7.80	16.93	7.85	0.85	176.47	0.77	194.81	3013
	10	17.86	7.34	16.48	7.95	0.82	182.93	0.78	192.31	2820
1920 × 1080	11	8.64	17.43	8.89	19.01	1.32	113.64	0.93	161.29	2074
	12	8.35	17.99	7.73	19.40	1.1	136.36	0.92	163.04	2002
	13	8.69	17.28	7.11	21.10	1.38	108.70	0.98	153.06	1888

Table 6. Improvements in processing times using OpenVino and Overclock (Test B).

		Video resolution												
		1280 × 720			640 × 480							1920 × 1080		
Number of video		1	2	3	4	5	6	7	8	9	10	11	12	13
OpenVino	FPS	13,26	13,29	14,05	18,91	19,61	19,33	19,21	19,94	19,13	18,68	13,91	12,11	12,01
.	Time	5,65	5,11	5,34	3,79	4,58	4,13	4,63	4,86	5,37	5,47	9,02	10,23	10,45
OpenVino +	FPS	14,41	14,29	15,20	19,59	20,29	20,01	19,89	20,62	19,81	19,36	14,35	12,61	12,51
Overclock	Time	5,20	4,75	4,89	3,29	4,08	3,63	4,13	4,36	4,87	4,97	8,75	9,93	10,15

5.2 Which Combination is the Best?

Table 5 shows that **Test A** provides better results in terms of time and number of processed frames in comparison to Test B, C and D. In the best case processing times of 1.12 times (5.63 min) are reached for video 4 and 3.59 times in the worst scenario for video 12.

Comparing Test C and D, the number of FPS processed without the use of Movidius NCS is less than 1 FPS in most videos, this generates large and unfeasible processing times for vehicle counting applications.

In Test A for videos with higher resolution (1920 × 1080 pixels) and bit rate around 2000 kbps the processing times are more than 3 times the duration of the original video (5 min), while for videos with reduced resolution (640 × 480 pixels) and bit rate around 3500 kbps the best processing times are reached. The videos with resolution of 1280 × 720 pixels show the influence of bit rate (around 900 kbps) in the processing time of the system, in this case despite its high resolution a value of 11 FPS is reached on average. The same analysis is performed in Test B, C and D with the difference that the factor of delay in video processing increases drastically according to the test.

Table 7. Quality metrics for the counting and classification system.

	Test A			Test B			Test C			Test D		
	REC	PRE	F1	REC	PRE	F1	REC	PRE	F1	REC	PRE	F1
Car	0.91	0.97	0.94	0.92	0.87	0.89	0.89	0.95	0.92	0.86	0.68	0.71
Person	0.99	0.68	0.79	0.56	0.89	0.59	0.97	0.66	0.77	0.12	0.58	0.18
Motorcycle	0.81	0.93	0.83	0.34	0.75	0.43	0.79	0.91	0.81	0.05	0.17	0.08
Bus	0.91	0.87	0.86	0.88	0.64	0.68	0.89	0.85	0.84	0.75	0.29	0.34
Truck	0.55	0.64	0.56	–	–	–	0.53	0.62	0.54	–	–	–

5.3 Performance Analysis for the Parallel Workflow (OpenVino + Oveclock)

The results of the FPS number and video processing times obtained with the workflow of Fig. 2 show that there are not videos in the data set that can be processed in real time, the best case reaches a processing time of 5.63 min.

With the alternative workflow in Fig. 5 and taking Test B as a reference, processing times and number of FPS reached are evaluated. Results show remarkable improvements in all video categories. Especially, the combination of overclock + OpenVino allows to reduce the video processing time by 34.2% in the best case. The videos with resolution of 640 × 480 pixels are those reporting best processing times. In this test, all videos report a processing time of less than 5 min.

6 Discussion

Table 5 offers a comparison for the results obtained in Test A, B, C and D, this table shows that the SSD-Mobilenet model trained by us (with own data set) in comparison with a pre-trained model (SSD-Mobilenet with MS COCO and VOC0712 data sets) generates a reduction in the processing time of the videos. For example, in video 1-Test A 6.38 min are reached and in video 1-Test B the time increases to 7.50 min, the model with own training accelerates the processing in 1.12 min. The same happens for the remaining videos in Test A and B. If we perform a similar analysis on Test C and D, the difference in processing times for each video is notorious, for example in video 1 for Test C and Test D presents a difference of 25.78 min.

On the other hand, the use of OpenVino library and the overclocking process in the device produce notable improvements in the processing times without affecting the results of vehicle counting. Comparing the workflows in Figs. 2 and 5, it is evident that the later scheme is the better than the former in terms of performance and speed. Another aspect that influences in the processing times and quality metrics of the counting system is the number of skipped frames applied. A jump of 5 frames was used as detailed in Sect. 3.2, this jump value was chosen based on empirical tests which showed that a frame jump of less than 5 frames caused large increases in the processing times but a great accuracy in the detection and tracking of vehicles. On the other hand, with a jump of frame higher than 5 frames processing times decreased considerably (even less than 5 min) but vehicular detection and tracking are affected causing bad count results. This suggests a trade off should be made to obtain the best results.

Table 7 presents classification and counting measures. For the case of Test A and Test C, SSD-Mobilenet model trained with our own data set provides the best metrics in all classes with Movidius NSC and without the device, it is important to note that the pre-trained model does not have the "truck" class and for this case the metrics are omitted.

7   Conclusions

In the context of an automatic counting application, we demonstrate the feasibility of using embedded devices in conjunction with additional graphic processing elements and CNN models for the execution of tasks that demand processing speeds close to those required by a real-time application.

To satisfy this requirement we work with two schemes: the first scheme based on the use of Movidius with its native API and a second scheme in which Movidius is used with Openvino's optimized library plus a configuration to the processor of the Raspberry Pi to accelerate its operation (overclock). We conclude that the scheme used by OpenVino + overclock is the best in terms of precision and speed. Additionally, results present the impact of parameters like video resolution, bit rate and CNN models in the processing time of videos.

Future works include improvements of the vehicle counting system specifically in the block of tracking. These improvements would allow a correct vehicle tracking even with an increase in the number of skip frames.

References

1. http://host.robots.ox.ac.uk/pascal/VOC/

2. Coco - common objects in context. http://cocodataset.org/
3. Intel, January 2019. https://www.movidius.com/
4. Tzutalin/Labelimg: Labelimg, code (2015). https://github.com/tzutalin/labelImg
5. Chen, Z., Ellis, T., Velastin, S.A.: Vehicle detection, tracking and classification in urban traffic. In: 2012 15th International IEEE Conference on Intelligent Transportation Systems, pp. 951–956, September 2012. https://doi.org/10.1109/ITSC.2012.6338852
6. chuanqi305: chuanqi305/mobilenet-ssd, October 2018. https://github.com/chuanqi305/MobileNet-SSD
7. Li, K., Huang, Z., Cheng, Y., Lee, C.: A maximal figure-of-merit learning approach to maximizing mean average precision with deep neural network based classifiers. In: 2014 IEEE International Conference on Acoustics, Speech and Signal Processing (ICASSP), pp. 4503–4507, May 2014. https://doi.org/10.1109/ICASSP.2014.6854454
8. Liu, W., et al.: SSD: single shot MultiBox detector. In: Leibe, B., Matas, J., Sebe, N., Welling, M. (eds.) ECCV 2016. LNCS, vol. 9905, pp. 21–37. Springer, Cham (2016). https://doi.org/10.1007/978-3-319-46448-0_2
9. Nikhil Yadav, U.B.: Comparative study of object detection algorithms. Int. Res. J. Eng. Technol. (IRJET). 586–591 (2017). https://doi.org/10.23919/MVA.2017.7986913
10. Oh, S., Kim, M., Kim, D., Jeong, M., Lee, M.: Investigation on performance and energy efficiency of CNN-based object detection on embedded device. In: 2017 4th International Conference on Computer Applications and Information Processing Technology (CAIPT), pp. 1–4, August 2017. https://doi.org/10.1109/CAIPT.2017.8320657
11. Othman, N.A., Aydin, I.: A new deep learning application based on movidius NCS for embedded object detection and recognition. In: 2018 2nd International Symposium on Multidisciplinary Studies and Innovative Technologies (ISMSIT), pp. 1–5, October 2018. https://doi.org/10.1109/ISMSIT.2018.8567306
12. Peña-González, R.H., Nuño-Maganda, M.A.: Computer vision based real-time vehicle tracking and classification system. In: 2014 IEEE 57th International Midwest Symposium on Circuits and Systems (MWSCAS), pp. 679–682, August 2014. https://doi.org/10.1109/MWSCAS.2014.6908506
13. Roh, M., Lee, J.: Refining faster-RCNN for accurate object detection. In: 2017 Fifteenth IAPR International Conference on Machine Vision Applications (MVA), pp. 514–517, May 2017. https://doi.org/10.23919/MVA.2017.7986913
14. Torres-Espinoza, F., Barros-Gavilanes, G., Barros, M.J.: Computer vision classifier and platform for automatic counting: more than cars. In: Ecuador Technical Chapters Meeting 2017; 2nd ETCM Conference, pp. 1–6, October 2017. https://doi.org/10.1109/ETCM.2017.8247454, https://ieeexplore.ieee.org/document/8247454
15. Wang, R.J., Li, X., Ling, C.X.: Pelee: a real-time object detection system on mobile devices. In: Bengio, S., Wallach, H., Larochelle, H., Grauman, K., Cesa-Bianchi, N., Garnett, R. (eds.) Advances in Neural Information Processing Systems, vol. 31, pp. 1967–1976. Curran Associates, Inc. (2018). http://papers.nips.cc/paper/7466-pelee-a-real-time-object-detection-system-on-mobile-devices.pdf

Biomedical Systems

Influences of the Trained State Model into the Decoding of Elbow Motion Using Kalman Filter

E. Y. Veslin[1(✉)] ⓘ, M. S. Dutra[1], L. Bevilacqua[1], L.S.C. Raptopoulos[2],
W. S. Andrade[2], and J. G. M. Soares[1]

[1] Federal University of Rio de Janeiro, Rio de Janeiro, RJ, Brazil
elkinveslin@ufrj.br
[2] Federal Center of Technological Education Celso Suckow da Fonseca –
CEFET/RJ, Rio de Janeiro, RJ, Brazil

Abstract. The properties of the Kalman Filter to decode elbow movement from non-invasive *EEG* are analyzed in this article. A set of configuration parameters using cross-validation are tested in order to find the ones that reduce the estimation error. Found that selecting correctly the number of channels and the time step used to configure the signal, it is possible to improve the filter estimation capabilities. As there was an apparent incidence of the variations in the recorded data used to train the model, an investigation of how those alterations affect the estimation precision in various data sets was made. The presented results showed that significant variations in the velocity and acceleration of the data set trains filters with lower accuracy than the ones built from a more uniform set.

Keywords: Electroencephalography · Kalman Filter · Brain-machine interfaces · Decoding

1 Introduction

The interpretation and use of brain patterns related to cognitive tasks is the basis of the Brain-Computer Interfaces (*BCI*) and Brain-Machine Interfaces (*BMI*). Neural patterns related to motor control, imagination and movement intention have been identified, and, integrated through *BCI* systems to control mechanisms destined to movement assistance in disabled persons with a partial or total restriction on the movement of their limbs. Examples of such devices are: exoskeletons [9,16], prosthetic apparatus [5], wheelchairs [20] or robotic manipulators [15].

Previous studies had demonstrated the possibility to decode kinematics from *EEG* signals [7] and, consequently, achieve a continuous motion reconstruction. The first attempts to create a model to reconstruct continuous motion are found in [2], where was demonstrated that *M1* cells firing rates are related to the

© Springer Nature Switzerland AG 2019
A. D. Orjuela-Cañón et al. (Eds.): ColCACI 2019, CCIS 1096, pp. 55–68, 2019.
https://doi.org/10.1007/978-3-030-36211-9_5

movement direction in center-out hand movements. These firing rates were more intense with executed movements in a preferred direction, gradually decreasing as they went far. Mathematical models that establish a relationship between the tuning of the cell and the direction were developed in [2,3]. Subsequently, a model that includes the hand velocity was introduced by [11]. Also, a linear model that relates the firing rate and hand position based on fitting coefficients through training was introduced by [8].

In [18], a method for decoding 2-D hand movement from primates neural activity through a generative model in a Bayesian approach using a Kalman Filter was introduced. This approach allowed to decode multiple kinematic variables from invasive *EEG*, enhancing the estimation performance in comparison with works that decoded kinematics from linear filters [1,9,17]. Thereupon, in [14], the experiment was replied in humans models using surface-level *EEG* obtaining similar results.

Kalman Filter was successfully applied to decode hand movement trajectories using Electrocorticography (*ECoG*) [13], hand velocity [10], position and velocity of a cursor in a screen [6], and control of a robotic arm by patients with tetraplegia [4]. Those experiments achieved the reconstruction of Cartesian movements and did not explore the use of the Kalman Filter to decode specific kinematic parameters in the joint dimension.

This work proposes to apply the Kalman Filter to decode the right elbow flexion/extension movement using non-invasive *EEG* recordings. The filter model is tested through cross-validation techniques determining a set of configuration parameters optimizing the signal decoding result. Also, the response is analyzed in a new group of data, evaluating the response according to the used data set.

2   Materials and Methods

2.1   Experimental Paradigm

This study was conducted by the protocol approved by the Ethics Committee of *Federal University of Rio de Janeiro* (Approbation number: 851.521). Six healthy right-handed volunteers (2 females and four males), without previous training in similar procedures, were studied. During the test, the volunteer is seated on a chair, with his arms in the rest position in a conditioned room (Fig. 1-left).

A screen was used to present the cue for the action, and the instructions were randomly generated to avoid any anticipation in action (Fig. 1-center). The experiment consisted of two actions indicated by a arrow (black for arm movement and white for non-movement), being formed each one by 60 trials of 10 s. Afterwards, the data was selected, extracting information for those time intervals were movement was executed. Non-movement data set was not used in this test. A movement consisted of the right elbow flexion and their return to rest position (an action on the interval of 90°to 150° approximately).

2.2   *EEG* Recording and Signal Processing

The *EEG* was recorded continuously from scalp electrodes using the *Neuron-Spectrum* system and software (Neurosoft Ltd., Ivanovo, Russia). A total of 32 passive *Ag-AgCl* electrodes were distributed around the scalp using a *MCScap* (Medical Computer Systems Ltd., Moscow, Russia) with removable electrodes according to a 10-10 modified system (Fig. 1-right). An additional *EMG* electrodes monitored the muscular activity in the biceps. A *MPU6050* accelerometer located in the forearm was used to read the angular position.

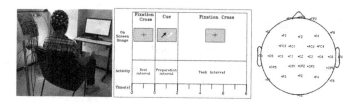

Fig. 1. (Left) Volunteer disposition in front of the command screen. (Center) Description of the trial, referencing the on-screen image during the interval and the activity developed by the volunteer. (Right) Location of the 32 channels around the scalp.

The signals were amplified, digitized with a sampling rate of 1000 Hz and band-pass filtered in the 0.5–100 Hz frequency band. *EEG* data were processed using the *EEGLAB* Matlab toolbox. Artifacts, as eye blinking and head movements presented as components with homogeneous contributions, were removed using the *ICA* algorithm of the *EEGLAB* toolbox. The signals were removed using *runica* as decomposition method through the 10 s test in all the recorded trials. Segments with high signal interference or disturb were also removed.

Due to their relationship to motor control, *EEG* signals in the mu band were considered, thus, a fourth-order pass-band filter in the 8 to 13 Hz band was applied. To obtain the movement time interval in each trial was used a muscle activation detector in the *EMG* signal, utilizing the algorithm described in [19].

3   The Kalman Filter

The decoding model has as purpose to estimate the state $\mathbf{x}_k$ in the time instant t_k. The states represent right elbow angular position, velocity and acceleration. As a measured signal, the notation $\mathbf{z} \in \Re^C$ is used, where C stands for the number of *EEG* electrodes used to decode the elbow kinematic.

According to [18] the filter is determined assuming a linear relationship between the state $\mathbf{x}_k$ and the observations $\mathbf{z}_k$ in the instant of time t_k. The generative model is then stated as:

$$\mathbf{z}_k = \mathbf{H}_k \mathbf{x}_k + \mathbf{v}_k \tag{1}$$

Where $\mathbf{H}_k \in \Re^{C \times 3}$ is a matrix that linearly relates the neural activity captured from the *EEG* electrodes with the kinematics. A Gaussian noise

$\mathbf{v}_k$ described as a normal distribution whit zero mean and covariance matrix $\mathbf{R}_k \in \Re^{C \times C}$, $\mathbf{v}_k \sim (0, \mathbf{R}_k)$.

The state $\mathbf{x}_k$ propagates in time according to the model:

$$\mathbf{x}_{k+1} = \mathbf{A}_k \mathbf{x}_k + \mathbf{w}_k \tag{2}$$

Where $\mathbf{A}_k \in \Re^{3 \times 3}$ is a matrix that linearly relates the kinematics between times k and $k+1$. The noise term $\mathbf{w}_k$ is assumed to have a normal distribution with zero mean and covariance $\mathbf{Q}_k \in \Re^{3 \times 3}$, $\mathbf{w}_k \sim (0, \mathbf{Q}_k)$.

3.1 Training Process

To train $\mathbf{A}_k, \mathbf{H}_k, \mathbf{R}_k$ and $\mathbf{Q}_k$ it was assumed that the models of Eqs. 1 and 2 are invariant along time. Considering that the signals $\mathbf{x}_k$ and $\mathbf{z}_k$ have a length $k = 1 \ldots M$. Using least squares [18], the solutions for matrix $\mathbf{A}$ and $\mathbf{H}$ are expressed as:

$$\begin{aligned} \mathbf{A} &= \mathbf{X}_2 \mathbf{X}_1^T (\mathbf{X}_1 \mathbf{X}_1^T)^{-1} \\ \mathbf{H} &= \mathbf{Z} \mathbf{X}^T (\mathbf{X} \mathbf{X}^T)^{-1} \end{aligned} \tag{3}$$

Using the learned values of $\mathbf{A}$ and $\mathbf{H}$ the noise covariance are then determined:

$$\begin{aligned} \mathbf{Q} &= \frac{(\mathbf{X}_2 - \mathbf{A}\mathbf{X}_1)(\mathbf{X}_2 - \mathbf{A}\mathbf{X}_1)^T}{(M-1)} \\ \mathbf{R} &= \frac{(\mathbf{Z} - \mathbf{H}\mathbf{X})(\mathbf{Z} - \mathbf{H}\mathbf{X})^T}{M} \end{aligned} \tag{4}$$

Where the matrix $\mathbf{X} \in \Re^{3 \times M}$ correspond to the state values, matrix $\mathbf{X}_1 \in \Re^{3 \times M-1}$ represents the state values from time interval $k = 1 \ldots M-1$, the matrix $\mathbf{Z} \in \Re^{C \times M}$ is the *EEG* signals from the C channels, and the matrix $\mathbf{X}_2 \in \Re^{3, M-1}$ stands for the state values taken from the time interval $k = 2 \ldots M$.

Matrices $\mathbf{A}, \mathbf{H}, \mathbf{R}$ and $\mathbf{Q}$ coefficients, are dependents of the training data. They could be configured according to a set of parameters, being, the number of channels C and the step time Δ_t. Different combinations of such parameters were tested using cross-validation in a 6-folds configuration, the responses where measured with Mean Squared Error *MSE* (Eq. 5) and the Correlation Coefficient *CC* (Eq. 6).

$$\mathbf{MSE} = \frac{1}{M} \sum_{k=1}^{M} (\mathbf{x}_k - \hat{\mathbf{x}}_k)^2 \tag{5}$$

$$\mathbf{CC} = \frac{\sum_k (\mathbf{x}_k - \bar{\mathbf{x}})(\hat{\mathbf{x}}_k - \bar{\hat{\mathbf{x}}})}{\sqrt{\sum_k (\mathbf{x}_k - \bar{\mathbf{x}})^2 \sum_k (\hat{\mathbf{x}}_k - \bar{\hat{\mathbf{x}}})^2}} \tag{6}$$

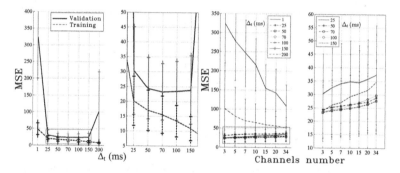

Fig. 2. Error curve across volunteers according to Δ_t (left) and the number of channels C (right) for ascending tasks. (Color figure online)

4   Results

4.1   Cross-validation

In the beginning, the channels were reorganized according to the coherence respect to C_3. In Fig. 2 the error curves obtained for ascending movements are presented, testing Δ_t values from 1 to 200 ms, and a set of channels C from 3 to 34. The left graphics illustrate the validation (black line) and training (dashed line) response according to the time step. Meanwhile, the right graphic presents the MSE in training according to the number of channels considering the Δ_t value. The horizontal lines present the variance through volunteers. The red square shows a low MSE zone that is augmented at the right.

According to the results, the parameters $\Delta_t = 70$ ms and $C = 3$ channels were selected. This choosing was generalized in all the volunteers.

4.2   State Estimation

A new 6-fold cross-validation was performed to evaluate the filter response according to the selected parameters. The compiled results in this section show the response of the validation set in Fig. 3 a decoding example is presented for an ascending (a), and a descending (b) task.

The mean response for each volunteer decoding respect to position x_1, velocity x_2 and acceleration x_3 in ascending and descending tasks are presented in Tables 1 and 2. The mean Frobenius norm value $\|\mathbf{A}\|$ of the trained state matrix $\mathbf{A}$ is introduced to give an insight of the relationship between the matrix coefficients and the decoding response.

Was observed that lower values in $\|\mathbf{A}\|$ gives decoding responses with low mean MSE and high mean CC. To illustrate this assertion, a dispersion graphic collecting all volunteers MSE against their respective $\|\mathbf{A}\|$ was built in Fig. 4 for ascending (a) and descending (b) tasks. When $\|\mathbf{A}\|$ (horizontal axis) is raising

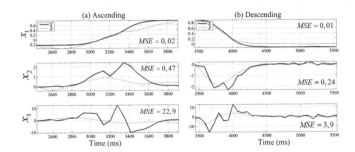

Fig. 3. Decoding for ascending (a) and descending (b) movements. The bold line indicates the real value for position x_1, velocity x_2, and acceleration x_3, and the dashed line is the state estimation $\hat{\mathbf{x}}$.

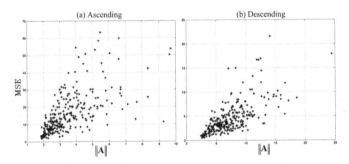

Fig. 4. Dispersion graphics of MSE against $\|\mathbf{A}\|$ for ascending (a) and descending (b) movements in the 6 volunteers.

up, their respective MSE (vertical axis), grown proportionally with minimal and maximal limits that increases along x-axis forming a cone-shape across the plane.

Due to $\mathbf{A}$ was resultant from states signals x_n, both magnitudes were analyzed through a dispersion graphic. In Fig. 5 are compared the norm of $\mathbf{A}$ against the standard deviation of the training set states used to build it. Was observed that in sets with higher speed and acceleration variance, the resultant $\|\mathbf{A}\|$ increased in a quasi-exponential form. However, the position state not presented similar behavior, due to it had a lower standard deviation.

4.3   Decoding Imposed Movement

The results in the previous section showed that those volunteers whose data set allowed to train state models with lower $\|\mathbf{A}\|$ value presents better decoding results. To validate the decoding capabilities according to the data set, kinematic patterns that trained a state model matrix with $\|\mathbf{A}\| < 3$ were selected. This value was chosen as it seems to present a high decoding accuracy according to the dispersion graphic in Fig. 5.

Thus, a proposed motion was trained with the collected data and was used as a reference trajectory for decoding movement in a new test group. This group

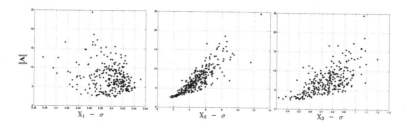

Fig. 5. Dispersion graphics comparing the Standard Deviation (σ) of the estimated states and their resultant $\|\mathbf{A}\|$ in ascending movements.

Table 1. MSE and CC of each x_n state for all the V_n volunteers for ascending movements.

Volunteer		V_1	V_2	V_3	V_4	V_5	V_6
MSE	x_1	0,45	0,23	0,24	0,23	0,67	1,18
	x_2	2,33	1,22	1,69	1,17	2,31	10,41
	x_3	115,5	38,88	74,77	39,41	93,13	436,69
	μ	*39,43*	*13,44*	*25,57*	*13,60*	*32,04*	*149,43*
CC	x_1	0,56	0,53	0,51	0,75	0,54	0,33
	x_2	0,09	0,32	0,24	0,18	0,15	0,15
	x_3	−0,06	0,22	0,16	0,19	0,06	0,12
	μ	*0,20*	*0,36*	*0,30*	*0,37*	*0,25*	*0,20*
$\|\mathbf{A}\|$		4,5	2,5	3,59	2,18	3,31	12,35

Table 2. MSE and CC of each x_n state for all the V_n volunteers for descending movements.

Volunteer		V_1	V_2	V_3	V_4	V_5	V_6
MSE	x_1	0,02	0,04	0,04	0,02	0,02	0,02
	x_2	0,34	0,25	0,12	0,3	0,25	0,24
	x_3	21,87	27,74	7,38	22,28	15,27	23,33
	μ	*7,41*	*9,34*	*2,51*	*7,53*	*5,18*	*7,86*
CC	x_1	0,97	0,98	0,98	0,97	0,98	0,98
	x_2	0,8	0,79	0,84	0,75	0,79	0,83
	x_3	0,65	0,54	0,5	0,49	0,57	0,58
	μ	*0,81*	*0,77*	*0,77*	*0,74*	*0,78*	*0,80*
$\|\mathbf{A}\|$		8,9	9,4	3,87	7,66	6,74	8,84

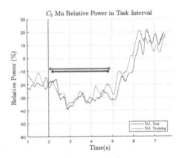

Fig. 6. Grand Average Relative Power for Training (orange) and Test (blue) groups when the movement was executed. (Color figure online)

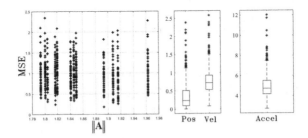

Fig. 7. (Left) Is presented the dispersion graphics of *MSE* against norm of $\|\mathbf{A}\|$ using regulated trajectories. (Right) bar plot describes the *MSE* variation for each state.

consisted of a set of signals from 12 volunteers who developed the same experiment without motion sensor. The proposed movement was adjusted for each volunteer according to their mean interval of movement, that action allowed to eliminate inter-trial variations.

Before initiating the test, *EEG* signals from both groups were compared to analyze equivalence respect to the cognitive response and the movement in Fig. 6 had presented a grand average Relative Power over C_3 channel in the analyzed band from both the training (orange) and test (blue) groups in the task interval when a motion was executed. This analysis was done according to [12], using a relative signal the time interval $t < 0$ s, when the non-task cognitive state was expected. The horizontal bars represent the movement average time interval.

In both cases, a de-synchronization in the band (ERD) was presented before the movement onset and continues until it ends near to 5 s. Then, a synchronization *ERS* was presented on the band, increasing the signal energy around 20%. In both circumstances, this response was expected according to the literature.

In Fig. 7 is presented the decoding response for ascending trajectories. Due to variations on each volunteer, the adjusted trajectory norm vary their magnitude. The decoding capabilities leads to a maximum mean *MSE* of 2.5. Selecting an adequate set of trajectories allowed the filter to estimate motion in all three states with a minor error over the tested volunteers. In the right part of the figure,

MSE variations for each state are presented. Acceleration continues presenting the worst response over all the decoded states.

The proposed model was compared with a second test, here, trajectories with $\|A\| > 5$ from the first data set were selected to conform the imposed trajectory, this value was chosen as it presented lower decoding precision in Fig. 4. The response of this group is presented in Fig. 8. Due to the selection of an intended movement composed with non-homogeneous data set, the decoding error increased in all three states.

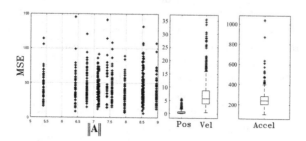

Fig. 8. (Left) Is presented the dispersion graphics of *MSE* against norm of $\|A\|$ using non-regulated trajectories. (Right) bar plot describes the *MSE* variation for each state.

In the Table 3 is presented a resume of the experiment. In it is described the *MSE* variation across volunteers according to $\|A\|$.

Table 3. *MSE* response with respect to the 12 volunteers.

	$\|A\| > 5$						$\|A\| < 3$					
	x_1		x_2		x_3		x_1		x_2		x_3	
Vol.	μ	σ	μ	σ	μ	σ	μ	σ	μ	σ	μ	σ
V_1	0,75	0,98	8,80	6,37	268,9	73,00	0,31	0,36	0,80	0,36	5,04	1,51
V_2	0,71	0,76	11,22	7,65	336,4	200,81	0,30	0,29	0,84	0,31	5,28	1,63
V_3	0,56	0,65	6,04	2,91	234,5	55,94	0,42	0,37	0,77	0,27	4,70	0,83
V_4	0,60	0,66	6,42	2,94	249,0	50,39	0,51	0,43	0,87	0,25	5,22	1,26
V_5	0,64	0,76	8,48	5,11	270,0	58,74	0,32	0,39	0,73	0,33	4,90	0,92
V_6	0,28	0,36	4,80	3,16	232,6	64,06	0,30	0,28	0,64	0,32	4,72	1,09
V_7	0,57	0,56	5,76	3,36	235,3	82,26	0,34	0,29	0,71	0,32	4,82	1,24
V_8	0,50	0,82	6,46	5,87	238,9	68,83	0,21	0,29	0,67	0,38	4,80	1,19
V_9	0,70	0,94	8,28	7,59	249,6	77,24	0,38	0,41	0,77	0,50	4,70	1,34
V_{10}	0,79	0,78	8,24	3,72	268,8	47,22	0,59	0,28	0,84	0,17	5,16	0,76
V_{11}	0,75	1,06	6,93	6,07	242,6	84,72	0,41	0,45	0,86	0,40	5,00	1,07
V_{12}	0,53	0,87	7,16	5,57	237,5	52,89	0,25	0,31	0,70	0,27	4,62	0,92

5 Discussion

The results of the previous section showed that the Kalman Filter presented a variate capability to decode the elbow motion from non-invasive EEG, this variability was dependent on both the configuration parameters used to configure the signals that trained the propagation model and the data set variability.

The error curve in Fig. 2 showed an optimal interval of $50 \leq \Delta_t \geq 150$ ms around the 6 volunteers. Also, it was found that increasing the number of channels for that specific interval, a decreasing of the decoding accuracy was presented. Thus, with EEG channels C_3, C_5 and C_1 it was possible to achieve an optimal decoding response. The selected readings had in common their proximity to the contra-lateral right arm control region. This results also were found for descending movements. Presumably, the decoding algorithm required a set of channels with a strong coherence among them; hence, tests with a major number of electrodes may require a high-density configuration.

The error curves gave us an insight of parameter Δ_t influence into the state estimation. When its values increased, it led to a diminution in the decoding error for both ascending and descending movements. This result was similar to the found in [18] were decoding response increased with an augment of the time step, indicating that movements described with fewer points are closer to the linear consideration done for the propagation model. However, decoding with high Δ_t values could affect the movement control when fast response BMI systems are required.

The results after the parameter selection showed that acceleration is the state with the worst decoding response presenting a mean MSE up to 400 in one of the volunteers. This result also was coincident with [18], who considered that this state appears not to be encoded in neural firing rates. Following results in the imposing motion decoding test showed that trained $\mathbf{A}$ matrix with high value into the acceleration coefficients led to wrong responses, minimizing the precision of the a $priori$ prediction. Therefore, we argue that the incapacity of the filter to estimate acceleration is more related to the state model than the biological response of the neural firing rates, where noise caused by the derivation of the signal is higher, and it is intensified as the movement augments their speed, having difficulty the state model to propagate an adequate response.

The result in Tables 1, 2 and Fig. 4 showed that volunteers who presented lower mean MSE and higher mean CC, also had lower $\mathbf{A}$ matrix norm value, this result repeated in descending tasks. The relationship between both magnitudes was linear with positive inclination, but points disperse in the plane forming a cone, this shape is related with $\|\mathbf{A}\|$ as the dispersion plane increased along with the value coefficients.

The results in Fig. 5 showed that increments in $\|\mathbf{A}\|$ are related to movement variability, specifically, with an increase in the motion's velocity and acceleration during the test. Consequently, when matrix $\mathbf{A}$ was trained with high variance trials, the resulted model in Eq. 2 will not estimate the state value correctly, to verify this, the mean σ of the three states, the mean $\|\mathbf{A}\|$ and the mean MSE in each volunteer are compared in Table 4, observing that volunteers who presented a high variation in the movement's velocity and acceleration during the training, presented high mean *MSE*. However, the algorithm response was more accurate for decoding descending movements, even in the acceleration state, whose worst *MSE* was of 27,74 for Volunteer 3.

Table 4. Mean Standard Deviation of each state compared with their respective mean norm of matrix **A** and mean *MSE*.

Volunteer	V_1	V_2	V_3	V_4	V_5	V_6
$x_1(\sigma)$	0,42	0,42	0,43	0,42	0,43	0,42
$x_2(\sigma)$	1,19	0,86	1,15	0,85	1,16	1,88
$x_3(\sigma)$	10,02	5,88	9,14	5,77	9,23	20,80
$\|\mathbf{A}\|$	4,70	2,87	4,02	2,44	3,45	12,91
MSE	39,43	13,44	25,57	13,60	32,04	149,43

According to these results, we believe that movement estimation had a higher dependence of the propagation model. Through all the volunteers, was found that the **A** matrix trained from movements with high variability achieved the worst estimation values. Indeed, the optimal value of $\Delta_t = 70$ ms, built **A** matrix with more difficulties to propagate fast movements. Arguably, the experimental conditions were dependent on the physical and mental conditions of the volunteers, as the ascending movements presented worst decoding estimations through volunteers than the descending ones, thus, factors like the volunteer's reaction to the visual stimulus, fatigue, and the gravity effects during the flexion could cause a high variation in the executed movement. Volunteers, as V_2 in Table 1 presented a better signal decoding for ascending movements than, for example, V_6, being the major differences in the acceleration and velocity, that indicates a lower regularity in the task execution by V_6 as the trained filters fail to estimate the movement.

Hence, the optimal encoding parameters searching led to finding a value set fitted in conditions specified by the regularity of the volunteer during the experiment. The proposed linear models, therefore, are not suited for high movement variations, and, presumably, coefficients related to velocity and acceleration estimation were trained to specific movement conditions.

In order to test this assessment, a state matrix from trajectories with higher and lower regularity was built and used to decode motion from a new data set. The results showed that a non-regulated motion led to training a model which high decoding inaccuracy and also, presenting an increment in the *MSE* dispersion on all the tested volunteers over all states. This dispersion was analogous to the cone shape distribution found in the posterior group, being less significant as $\|\mathbf{A}\|$ decreases.

Consequently, a wrong state prediction during the *a priori* step makes the filter more dependent of the measurement value in the *a posteriori* step, which discordance with the estimated value led the filter to avoid the convergence in the **K**-gain, resulting in a reduced decoding precision. Therefore, we theorized that models originated from non-regulated data are more sensitive to the inter-trial *EEG* variance, increasing dramatically the *MSE* as the resulting matrix **A** got higher coefficients values, making the filter unstable as it obtains larger **K**-gain values.

6   Conclusion

In this work, the Kalman filter was tested to decode the elbow movement using non-invasive *EEG* signals. The experimental result showed us that it is possible to decode this movement with relative precision. An optimal configuration for the state and measurement signals was made through a set of parameters (number of channels and time step), allowing us to find the best estimation through cross-validation. Were found that the decoded movement presented a precision variation around the volunteers and that the filter decodes better the descending task than the ascending ones.

A set of analysis was made using the optimal set of parameters and was found that the capability to estimate different movements by the filter appears to be affected by the trained state model. Being that, when the resultant matrix **A** coefficient presented higher values, the resultant decoding error in the valida-tion group increased. Subsequently, when propagation models were trained from data with significant variance, it means, movements with higher variation in the acceleration and velocity, the resultant **A** matrix presented high values coeffi-cients, that subsequently, occasioned low precision estimation in the validation data sets.

Was found that those volunteers who executed movements with high irreg-ularity presented the worst estimation results in comparison of those that per-formed a set of movements with low variance. Regardless, due to the form that the experiment was conducted, is possible that the resulted propagation model was a generalization of the most common actions executed by the volunteers, therefore, parameters selected from cross-validation, were the ones that fitted the most regular actions, with an estimation capability related to a specific region inside the set of possibilities made during the experiment.

The presented results gave us an insight into how Kalman filter works and how the training set could be configured through a rigorous selection of trials to improve decoding results. Therefore, the information could be removed according to the response of the volunteer, if it does not cope with the task regularity. On the other hand, it is possible to integrate them with clustering algorithms that detect different ranges of movement, and therefore, to allow us to train a set of filters according to the mean speed of each range, adapting them to decode a significant set of movements with minor estimation error.

Acknowledgment. The authors would like to thank FINEP, CNPq, FAPERJ, Fundação COPPETEC, and DIPPG/CEFET-RJ for supporting our work. As well, the students Edwiges Beatriz Coimbra de Souza, Aline Macedo Rocha Rodriguez e Andre Silva for their helping in the *EEG* data acquisition, and Marco Vinicio Chiorri for technical assistance.

References

1. Bradberry, T.J., Gentili, R.J., Contreras-Vidal, J.L.: Reconstructing three-dimensional hand movements from noninvasive electroencephalographic signals. J. Neurosci. **30**(9), 3432–3437 (2010)
2. Georgopoulos, A., Kalasa, J., Caminiti, R., Massey, J.: On the relations between the direction of two-dimensional arm movements and cell discharge in primate motor cortex. J. Neurosci. **2**, 1527–1537 (1982)
3. Georgopoulos, A.P., Schwartz, A.B., Kettner, R.E.: Neuronal population coding of movement direction. Science **233**(4771), 1416–1419 (1986)
4. Hochberg, L.R., et al.: Reach and grasp by people with tetraplegia using a neurally controlled robotic arm. Nature **485**(7398), 372 (2012)
5. Hochberg, L.R., et al.: Neuronal ensemble control of prosthetic devices by a human with tetraplegia. Nature **442**(7099), 164–171 (2006)
6. Homer, M.L., et al.: Mixing decoded cursor velocity and position from an offline Kalman filter improves cursor control in people with tetraplegia. In: 2013 6th International IEEE/EMBS Conference on Neural Engineering (NER), pp. 715–718. IEEE (2013)
7. Jerbi, K., et al.: Inferring hand movement kinematics from MEG, EEG and intracranial EEG: from brain-machine interfaces to motor rehabilitation. IRBM **32**(1), 8–18 (2011)
8. Kettner, R.E., Schwartz, A.B., Georgopoulos, A.P.: Primate motor cortex and free arm movements to visual targets in three-dimensional space. iii. positional gradients and population coding of movement direction from various movement origins. J. Neurosci. **8**(8), 2938–2947 (1988)
9. Lalitharatne, T.D., Yoshino, A., Hayashi, Y., Teramoto, K., Kiguchi, K.: Toward EEG control of upper limb power-assist exoskeletons: a preliminary study of decoding elbow joint velocities using EEG signals. In: 2012 International Symposium on Micro-NanoMechatronics and Human Science (MHS), pp. 421–424. IEEE (2012)
10. Lv, J., Li, Y., Gu, Z.: Decoding hand movement velocity from electroencephalogram signals during a drawing task. Biomed. Eng. Online **9**(1), 1 (2010)
11. Moran, D.W., Schwartz, A.B.: Motor cortical activity during drawing movements: population representation during spiral tracing. J. Neurophysiol. **82**(5), 2693–2704 (1999)
12. Pfurtscheller, G., da Silva, F.L.: Event-related EEG/MEG synchronization and desynchronization: basic principles. Clin. Neurophysiol. **110**, 1842–1857 (1999)
13. Pistohl, T., Ball, T., Schulze-Bonhage, A., Aertsen, A., Mehring, C.: Prediction of arm movement trajectories from ECoG-recordings in humans. J. Neurosci. Methods **167**(1), 105–114 (2008)
14. Robinson, N., Guan, C., Vinod, A.: Adaptive estimation of hand movement trajectory in an EEG based brain-computer interface system. J. Neural Eng. **12**(6), 066019 (2015)
15. Roy, R., Mahadevappa, M., Kumar, C.: Trajectory path planning of EEG controlled robotic arm using GA. Procedia Comput. Sci. **84**, 147–151 (2016)

16. Soekadar, S.R., Witkowski, M., Vitiello, N., Birbaumer, N.: An EEG/EOG-based hybrid brain-neural computer interaction (BNCI) system to control an exoskeleton for the paralyzed hand. Biomed. Tech. **60**(3), 199–205 (2015)
17. Ubeda, A., et al.: Single joint movement decoding from EEG in healthy and incomplete spinal cord injured subjects. In: 2015 IEEE/RSJ International Conference on Intelligent Robots and Systems (IROS), pp. 6179–6183. IEEE (2015)
18. Wu, W., Black, M., Gao, Y., Bienenstock, E., Serruya, M., Donoghue, J.: Inferring hand motion from multi-cell recordings in motor cortex using a Kalman filter. In: SAB 2002-Workshop on Motor Control in Humans and Robots: On the Interplay of Real Brains and Artificial Devices, pp. 66–73 (2002)
19. Xu, L., Adler, A.: An improved method for muscle activation detection during gait. In: Canadian Conference on Electrical and Computer Engineering, 2004, vol. 1, pp. 357–360. IEEE (2004)
20. Zhang, R., et al.: Control of a wheelchair in an indoor environment based on a brain-computer interface and automated navigation. IEEE Trans. Neural Syst. Rehabil. Eng. **24**(1), 128–139 (2016)

Building Dengue Sensors for Brazil Using a Social Network and Text Mining

Josimar Edinson Chire Saire[(⊠)] (ID)

Institute of Mathematics and Computer Science (ICMC),
University of São Paulo (USP), Sao Carlos, SP, Brazil
jecs89@usp.br

Abstract. The increasing use of Social Networks to share personal information has opened many resources to analyze the behaviour of one city, state or country. Topics related to politics, science, health alarms and others are shared by users everyday to monitor an prevent events. Natural Language Processing is the tool to analyze this text and get some insight using Machine Learning Techniques. In this work, *Twitter* is analyzed to detect social events because users are considered sensors. The analysis is performed over Brazilian tweets to detect dengue. The results show the utility of the proposal to recognize dengue epidemics in the Brazilian territory.

Keywords: Natural Language Processing · Dengue · Social network · Machine Learning · Crossover operator

The interest for Dengue increased during the last decade because a continuous growing every year. In spite of the information, it is no possible to estimate world distribution for many reasons: governmental actions, cost of the monitoring. The estimation of risk is up to 54.7% [1], approximated to 3.74 billion of global population.

For the previous reasons, Dengue is the main concern for Brazilian Government [6] because the number of incidences is higher every year. At the same time, following, there is an influence of the climate on the spread of dengue, [2] found the relationship of the low transmission in United States in contrast [4] concluded the influence of the hot weather in dengue incidences in Sao Paulo state. Besides, a disordered growth of Brazilian cities opens the possibility to have more incidences because the lack of sanitation and inadequate housing. Only in 2016, more than 1.5 million cases of dengue were identified in Brazil and about 700 patients died.

Social Networks (SN) have been studied to find behaviour of the population [3,18]. Twitter is used for the open access to get data and the size of tweets (max. 140 characters). In the specific case of health, studies reveal the tendency of users of posting symptoms before seeking medical care even [12]. Considering [11], the social network with the third largest growth in number of users between 2015 and 2016 was Brazil.

A. D. Orjuela-Cañón et al. (Eds.): ColCACI 2019, CCIS 1096, pp. 69–77, 2019.
https://doi.org/10.1007/978-3-030-36211-9_6

In this work is presented a proposal to evaluate Brazilian tweets to monitor dengue cases in Brazil territory to test the possibility of building sensors of dengue occurrence from knowledge extracted from text (tweets).

The paper is organized as follows. Section 1 presents the related work and Sect. 2 describes the methodology. Section 3 details the proposed study. Finally, the conclusions are presented in Sect. 4.

1   Related Work

Many research projects have investigated methods of extracting knowledge of digital content from the Internet, especially textual data, to understand and monitor phenomena occurring in the real world. For example, there are studies that use the Web to monitor the emergence and spread of epidemics [7], analyze voting trends in elections [5], monitor consumer behavior regarding products, goods and services [9], as well as building smart indicators to support various areas such as agriculture and medicine [15].

The variety of applications that can be developed through the extraction and sensing of knowledge published on the Web has made this research topic become a trend in an area known a *"Web Science"* [8,13,16,17]. There are several new specific challenges related to this topic, such as the large volume of textual data, the high speed in which new texts become available, and the heterogeneity of information sources, which has led to the development of more appropriate approaches to this scenario.

One of the first works based on the concept of web data sensing was proposed by [7] for the detection of epidemics. It was developed by Google researchers and the spread of influenza virus (flu) was used as the basis of studies. The authors performed an analysis of data from Google's search engine related to the period from March 11, 2007 to September 28, 2013. For each search expression a score was given. Still, the searches were organized according to the user's region. From these data, a time series was obtained based on the search expressions and such series used to predict the next influenza epidemics by linear regression. The results were promising concerning they had low prediction error. The highlight of this work is to emphasize the concept of mapping information from the Web (virtual world) to interpret or predict phenomena that occur in the physical world.

Based on analysis of the 22-year base of the New York Times newspaper from 1986 to 2008, [14] proposed a method to identify in the news possible alerts of epidemics, catastrophes, among other types of events. The biggest challenge for this method is an event prediction strategy. To that end, the authors have developed a network of causality between news stories, in which they identify which news are the cause of each other. For this, time and location information was used, as well a training set labeled by humans. An interesting result was real preventive action for a cholera epidemic, in which the system detected its future occurrence.

The study proposed in this paper involves analyzing to what extent social networks information can contribute to the improvement of the knowledge already available about certain subject.

2   Methodology

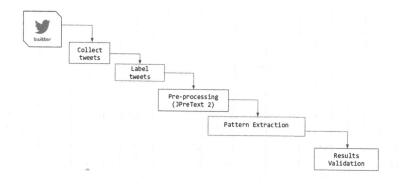

Fig. 1. Methodology

This section explains every step of the methodology presented in Fig. 1.

2.1   Event Collection and Preprocessing

To create the dataset of tweets for a posterior labeling, a search using Twitter API (Application Program Interface) was performed from the period of January 2009 to October 2017. As the keyword dengue has the same writing in many languages different to Portuguese, an extra field for searching was considered: geographical position. Each tweet contains one or more events, the tweets are unstructured data then a pre-processing step is necessary. This step structures the data to get meaningful set of terms (*e.g.* keywords and expressions). Next, the pre-processing process was done using *Pretext2*[1]. Each tweet corresponds to the JSON object. The structure of a JSON object is presented in Fig. 2.

There are terms (*stopwords*) with any contribution to the understanding or meaning to the text then those must be eliminated. These words are terms that do not add representativeness to the collection of documents, or when isolated are indiscriminate, such as articles, pronouns and adverbs. This technique significantly reduces the number of terms by decreasing the computational cost of the next steps.

Subsequently, the normalization of words is performed with *stemming* process. This method reduces a word to the root word. In summary, the aim is to identify the morphological variations and synonyms of a word and transform it

---

[1] The tool is available on http://sites.labic.icmc.usp.br/pretext/.

```
{
  "created_at":"Thu Apr 06 15:24:15 +0000 2017",
  "id": 850006245121695744,
  "id_str": "850006245121695744",
  "text": "eu acho q to com dengue, tem condições não",
  "user": {},
  "entities": {}
}
```

Fig. 2. Json structure

into an unambiguous representation for these variations. For example, the terms "diagnosis", "diagnostic", "diagnosed" can be reduced to the "diagnos" radical.

The meaning of isolated words is simple or not enough to express other concepts composes of two or more words then the use of n-grams is necessary, which are words that appear in sequence in the collection of documents and have a relationship between them.

Statistical measures such as Term Frequency (TF) and Frequency of Documents (DF) can be used to select terms. Terms with high frequency are considered insignificant because they are common in most texts, not adding value to the information of the text. Therefore, a cut-off value was assumed with the rule $DF \leq 0.9N$, that is, the amount of documents in which a term t can appear is a maximum of 90%, considering the total number of documents is N. Low-frequency terms are regarded as occasional and are not used. In this sense, a cut-off value was accepted based on the rule $DF \geq 2$, in which each term must appear in at least two documents.

After the selection of the most relevant terms from the data, the structuring of the documents is necessary. The most used model is the vector space, where each document is a vector in a multidimensional space and each dimension is a collection term. Thus, the terms were arranged in a bag-of-words, or table document-term, where each d_i corresponds to the i document, t_{ij} represents the j-term of d_i. In the vector space, each document is defined as a vector $d_i = (t_{i1}, t_{i2}, \ldots, t_{im})$. The value of the measure t_{ij} indicates the importance of the term j in the document i. For example, if the value of t_{ij} was calculated based on the term frequency, it would be counted how many times a given term appeared in a certain document.

Considering the documents differ in size, it is common that a term appears more often in larger documents than in smaller ones. In addition, it is known that some terms appear many times but have little importance. For the previous reason, the Inverse of Frequency by Document (IDF) can be incorporated to ponder terms contribution. Then the terms that occur in many documents will have decreased weight, whereas the weight of those that occur rarely will be increased. This criterion is called TF-IDF [19] and was adopted in this work.

2.2   Tweets Labeling

After the analysis of the tweets, other indicators of interest (categories) can be found in addition to *dengue* and *non dengue*, as in the case of *dengue combat* and *dengue information* indicators. For this work, 667 tweets were labeled according to the categories mentioned previously, Fig. 3 presents the distribution of the classes.

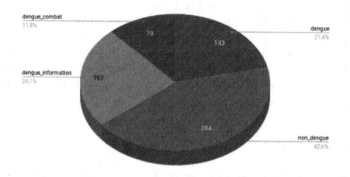

Fig. 3. Dataset

Each category is detailed as follows:

- Dengue: 143 tweets that represent confirmed cases of dengue, whether done by the person himself or by reference to a case. Example *"The doctor said I'm with dengue fever"*.
- Non Dengue: 284 ambiguous tweets that references dengue of other concepts, as metaphors for people lives. Example *"It can not be true, my life is more stationary than the focus of dengue"*.
- Dengue Information: 161 tweets that depict some statistics or official information on dengue. Example: *In 2015, 30% of dengue cases were recorded in February*.
- Dengue Combat: 79 tweets that represent combat actions taken to prevent or combat dengue. Example: *The state of Sao Paulo reinforced dengue prevention measures and invested 20% more in campaigns than last year.*

2.3   Event Classification

In this work, we used supervised algorithms to build the sensors. Supervised algorithms learn from the input dataset to generalize after with new data.

The supervised algorithms used in the study were: Naive Bayes, Multinomial Naive Bayes and J48 Decision Tree. An explanation of such algorithms [10] is given below:

- Naive Bayes (NB) is a classifier based on the Bayes theorem and consists in a statistical approach, in which the classification of instances is based on probability calculations and the domain knowledge is also expressed in a probabilistic way. It is considered naive because assumes the independence between pairs of characteristics. Basically, the classifier estimates the probability of each event being pertaining to a given class.
- Multinomial Naive Bayes (MNB) is a variation of the Naive Bayes algorithm. The point is that MNB is more appropriate for text classification, where the data are typically represented as words vectors.
- Decision Trees (DT) is an approach that aims to divide a complex decision into a set of simpler decisions, where the final answer is similar to the one intended. The Decision Tree algorithm used in this work is the J48, which applies entropy to choose the attributes that best represent the dataset. If there is no amount of uncertainty in the data, the entropy is 0, but if all values are equally probable, the entropy becomes 1.

3   Proposed Study

Four experiments will be described below. The objective is to analyze the different possible variations mentioned in the Sect. 2 and to decide which is more appropriate for our purpose. In other words, we intend to discover which configuration has the greater *F-measure*. *F-measure* is a measure that combines precision and recall of a given classifier results. Its range varies from 0 to 1, considering that the closer to 1 certain value is, the better is the classifier performance.

Experiment 1. The first experiment had the following configuration:

- **N-grams:** 1, 2, 3 n-grams.
- **Weigh Construction:** Term Frequency as measure to the weight construction in the bag-of-words.
- **Selection of Terms:** Selection of terms with a lower limit of 2% and maximum of 90%.
- **Stopwords:** This analyse did not consider stopwords removal.
- **Test Approach:** Cross-validation with 10-folds.

The results presented in Table 1 states the MNB classifier had higher f-measure score in most of the classes, except in the *dengue combat* class. Besides, the *non dengue* class had better performance in the classification task.

Table 1. Results of Experiment 1

	NB	MNB	DT
dengue	0.561	**0.642**	0.635
non_dengue	0.738	**0.775**	0.759
dengue_info	0.573	**0.613**	0.538
dengue_combat	**0.717**	0.698	0.713

Experiment 2. The second experiment had the following configuration:

- **N-grams:** 1, 2, 3 n-grams.
- **Weigh Construction:** Term Frequency Inverse Document Frequency (TF-IDF) as measure to the weight construction in the bag-of-words.
- **Selection of Terms:** Selection of terms with a lower limit of 2% and maximum of 90%.
- **Stopwords:** This analyse did not consider stopwords removal.
- **Test Approach:** Cross-validation with 10-folds.

The results presented in Table 2 demonstrate that the MNB classifier had higher f-measure in all classes. In addition to, the change in the measurement of construction of the weights improved the results.

Table 2. Results of Experiment 2

	NB	MNB	DT
dengue	0.561	**0.656**	0.65
non_dengue	0.738	**0.781**	0.763
dengue_info	0.573	**0.623**	0.538
dengue_combat	0.717	**0.725**	0.713

Experiment 3. The third experiment had the following configuration:

- **N-grams:** 1, 2, 3 n-grams.
- **Weigh Construction:** Term Frequency Inverse Document Frequency (TF-IDF) as measure to the weight construction in the bag-of-words.
- **Selection of Terms:** Selection of terms with a lower limit of 2% and maximum of 90%.
- **Stopwords:** This analyze considered stopwords removal.
- **Test Approach:** Cross-validation with 10-folds.

The results presented in Table 3 states that the inclusion of the stopwords removal decreased the quality of the results. Therefore, the removal of stopwords is not useful for our purpose.

Table 3. Results of Experiment 3

	NB	MNB	DT
dengue	0.56	0.58	**0.676**
non_dengue	0.761	**0.77**	0.761
dengue_info	0.59	**0.623**	0.596
dengue_combat	0.703	**0.737**	0.628

Experiment 4. Lastly, the fourth experiment aims to compare the mean result of previous experiments. The results are presented in Table 4.

Table 4. Results of Experiment 4

	NB	MNB	DT
Exp 1	0.658	**0.698**	0.674
Exp 2	0.658	**0.709**	0.678
Exp 3	0.686	**0.701**	0.678

In conclusion, the MNB classifier had better performance for all cases and that the best configuration is to use tf-idf as a measure for building weights and not removing stopwords.

4   Conclusion

In this paper we present the use of tweets as social sensors for dengue detection in Brazilian territory based on Text Mining and Machine Learning algorithms. Experiments were conducted to analyze the accuracy of our methodology with enough results to demonstrate the potential of the analysis from Twitter, besides the results confirm that it is possible to extract pertinent information.

In spite of noise and the lack of data structure, it was possible to build indicators using Artificial Intelligence techniques.

For future work, we intend to expand the classes to perform a deep analysis.

Besides this study can be the basement to perform other studies related to social behaviour of people of an specific country related to politics, health and other.

References

1. Brady, O.J., et al.: Refining the global spatial limits of dengue virus transmission by evidence-based consensus. PLoS Negl. Trop. Dis. **6**(8), 1–15 (2012). https://doi.org/10.1371/journal.pntd.0001760

2. Butterworth, M.K., Morin, C.W., Comrie, A.C.: An analysis of the potential impact of climate change on dengue transmission in the southeastern united states. Environ. Health Perspect. **125**(4), 579–585 (2017). https://doi.org/10.1289/EHP218
3. Carlos, M.A., Nogueira, M., Machado, R.J.: Analysis of dengue outbreaks using big data analytics and social networks. In: 2017 4th International Conference on Systems and Informatics (ICSAI). pp. 1592–1597 (November 2017). https://doi.org/10.1109/ICSAI.2017.8248538
4. Carneiro, M.A.F., et al.: Environmental factors can influence dengue reported cases. Rev. Assoc. Med. Bras. **63**(11), 957–961 (2017). http://www.scielo.br/scielo.php?script=sciarttext&pid=S0104-42302017001100957&nrm=iso
5. Contractor, D., Chawda, B., Mehta, S., Subramaniam, L.V., Faruquie, T.A.: Tracking political elections on social media: applications and experience. In: Proceedings of the 24th International Conference on Artificial Intelligence, pp. 2320–2326. AAAI Press (2015)
6. G1: 2016 already had more than 1.9 million cases of dengue, chikungunya and zika. in portuguese: (2016) já teve mais de 1,9 milhão de casos de dengue, chikungunya e zika (2016)
7. Ginsberg, J., et al.: Detecting influenza epidemics using search engine query data. Nature **457**(7232), 1012–1014 (2009)
8. Hall, W.: 10 years of web science. In: Proceedings of the 8th ACM Conference on Web Science, p. 7. ACM (2016)
9. Liu, B.: Sentiment analysis and opinion mining. Synth. Lect. Hum. Language Technol. **5**(1), 1–167 (2012)
10. Mitsa, T.: Temporal Data Mining, 1st edn. Chapman & Hall/CRC, Boca Raton (2010)
11. Newspaper, S.P.: Brazil has the third highest growth of twitter in number of users. in portuguese: Brasil tem o 3° maior crescimento do twitter em número de usuários (2017)
12. Now, I.: Ministry of health wants to monitor social networks to combat dengue. in portuguese: Ministério da saúde quer monitorar redes sociais para combater a dengue (2011)
13. Phethean, C., Simperl, E., Tiropanis, T., Tinati, R., Hall, W.: The role of data science in web science. IEEE Intell. Syst. **31**(3), 102–107 (2016)
14. Radinsky, K., Horvitz, E.: Mining the web to predict future events. In: Proceedings of the Sixth ACM International Conference on Web Search and Data Mining, pp. 255–264. ACM (2013)
15. Rivera, S.J., Minsker, B.S., Work, D.B., Roth, D.: A text mining framework for advancing sustainability indicators. Environ. Modell. Softw. **62**, 128–138 (2014)
16. Shadbolt, N., Berners-Lee, T.: Web science emerges. Sci. Am. **299**(4), 76–81 (2008)
17. Tiropanis, T., et al.: The web science observatory. IEEE Intell. Syst. **28**(2), 100–104 (2013)
18. Villanes, A., Griffiths, E., Rappa, M., Healey, C.G.: Dengue fever surveillance in india using text mining in public media. Am. J. Trop. Med. Hyg. **98**(1), 181–191 (2018). https://doi.org/10.4269/ajtmh.17-0253. http://www.ajtmh.org/content/journals/10.4269/ajtmh.17-0253
19. Zhang, W., Yoshida, T., Tang, X.: A comparative study of TF*IDF, LSI and multiwords for text classification. Expert Syst. Appl. **38**(3), 2758–2765 (2011). https://doi.org/10.1016/j.eswa.2010.08.066. http://www.sciencedirect.com/science/article/pii/S0957417410008626

Prediction of Diabetic Patient Readmission Using Machine Learning

Juan Camilo Ramírez$^{(\boxtimes)}$ and David Herrera

Universidad Antonio Nariño, Bogotá, Colombia
juan.ramirez@uan.edu.co

Abstract. Hospital readmissions pose additional costs and discomfort for the patient and their occurrences are indicative of deficient health service quality, hence efforts are generally made by medical professionals in order to prevent them. These endeavors are especially critical in the case of chronic conditions, such as diabetes. Recent developments in machine learning have been successful at predicting readmissions from the medical history of the diabetic patient. However, these approaches rely on a large number of clinical variables thereby requiring deep learning techniques. This article presents the application of simpler machine learning models achieving superior prediction performance while making computations more tractable.

Keywords: Diabetes · Hospital readmission · Neural network · Random forest · Logistic regression · Support vector machines

1   Introduction

Hospital readmissions are a health care quality metric, given their associated costs both to the patient and the clinical institution, and thus are one indicator of inefficiency in the healthcare system [1,3,19,21]. A readmission is generally defined as the event where the patient must be admitted again after discharge for the same health condition within a short time interval, usually 30 days. The term *index admission* is frequently used to denote the original hospital stay whereas the readmission is any subsequent stay. Research on this topic occasionally contemplates time frames other than 30 days, including 90 days or one year. Sometimes the time interval before readmission is not measured from the discharge date but from a procedure practiced during the index admission [4,22,25].

The underlying causes and risk factors leading to hospital readmissions are still a matter of academic investigation. This is true for readmissions associated to both health disorders and surgical procedures. A topic of interest is the relationship between the readmission causes and complications occurred during a surgical procedure or if the readmission is associated to a new issue occurred after discharge [23]. Some studies researching this causality have shown, for instance, that post-surgery readmissions have been associated to post-discharge

© Springer Nature Switzerland AG 2019
A. D. Orjuela-Cañón et al. (Eds.): ColCACI 2019, CCIS 1096, pp. 78–88, 2019.
https://doi.org/10.1007/978-3-030-36211-9_7

events and not complications occurred during the index admission [23]. This causality, in the context of different health disorders and surgical procedures, has been investigated using different statistical and computational approaches. These are normally conducted using different possible determining factors, such as patients' demographic and social data as well as clinical variables (*e.g.*, treatments, procedures, *etc.*) [8] and administrative data (*e.g.*, information related to health insurance claims) [15]. Computational methods include logistic regression, association rules, support vector machines and deep learning, among others [6,16,17,32]. Hospital readmissions are amply studied in a variety of medical conditions, however, they only recently have started to attract attention of researchers in the study of healthcare policies for diabetic patients [27]. Different machine learning approaches, including deep learning, have been attempted in order to predict a diabetic patient's risk of readmission based on their medical history with varying results [6,11,14,24,29,30].

The present investigation evaluates several machine learning models aimed at predicting readmission from clinical data recorded in previous visits by the diabetic patient. The techniques used include logistic regression, support vector machines, neural networks and random forests. The models are trained and evaluated over a publicly available dataset comprising patient data from a hospital network in the United States collected over the course of nearly ten years [29]. The performance of all the models tested is evaluated using several metrics, including F1 and ROC AUC (Area Under the Curve in Receiver Operating Characteristic analysis). Random forests is shown to outperform all the models under evaluation and to exhibit comparable or superior prediction rates than the other models trained over the same data and previously reported in the literature, including deep learning, while requiring significantly less computing power.

2   Related Work

Different studies can be found in the literature attempting to achieve a prediction of hospital readmissions in the context of various health conditions using machine learning or statistical approaches. These methods normally are forced to search for an appropriate trade-off between the resulting model's predictability and interpretability, since it is desired to not only obtain a statistically significant prediction but to identify the most determinant risk factors associated to this situation. For the prediction of pneumonia-related readmissions, for instance, high-performance generalised additive models with pairwise interactions have been applied to healthcare data in order to obtain interpretable models, something that is normally not possible with traditional but powerful approaches such as neural networks [6]. Readmissions related to heart failure have been investigated through the application of support vector machines, logistic regression and random forests, with the latter exhibiting the best predictive power of the techniques evaluated [26]. However, related investigations considering different data sources have yielded more modest prediction metrics [12]. Random forests have also been obseved to exhibit good predictive performance in other frameworks in comparison to logistic regressions and deep neural networks, for instance [13].

In addition to the above, various investigations can be found in the literature seeking a reliable prediction of diabetic patient readmission using a variety of machine learning models and patient data sources. [29], for instance, use multi-variable logistic regression in order to show that there is a decreased risk of 30-day readmission in diabetic inpatients who have their hemoglobin A1c (HbA1c) measured and that this association is true only for patients whose only primary diagnosis is diabetes. This model is trained over a preprocessed dataset derived from electronic health records and comprising several pieces of information from inpatient visits including demographic data, prescriptions and diagnoses coded using the ICD-9 (*International Statistical Classification of Diseases and Related Health Problems*, ninth revision) convention, which is the standard for classification of health conditions maintained by the World Health Organization (WHO). The dataset has been made public on the UCI Machine Learning Repository[1] and has subsequently been reused in related studies employing different prediction models and preprocessing methods, all evaluated with different measures. These metrics, derived from the model's exhibited number of true positives (TP), true negatives (TN), false positives (FP) and false negatives (FN), include accuracy (Eq. 1), precision (Eq. 2), recall (Eq. 3), specificity (Eq. 4), F1 (Eq. 5) and the area under the ROC curve (ROC AUC score) obtained after plotting the model's recall (Eq. 3) against the fall-out (Eq. 6).

$$\text{Accuracy} = \frac{TP + TN}{TP + TN + FP + FN} \tag{1}$$

$$\text{Precision} = \frac{TP}{TP + FP} \tag{2}$$

$$\text{Recall} = \frac{TP}{TP + FN} \tag{3}$$

$$\text{Specificity} = \frac{TN}{TN + FP} \tag{4}$$

$$\text{F1} = \frac{2TP}{2TP + FP + FN} \tag{5}$$

$$\text{Fall-out} = 1 - \text{Specificity} = \frac{FP}{FP + TN} \tag{6}$$

These metrics can be further explained and interpreted as follows. Accuracy (Eq. 1) provides the ratio of correct predictions made by the model. However, this figure provides an incomplete evaluation when working with datasets where the distribution of the class is imbalanced, *e.g.*, when training a binary classification model and there is a significant discrepancy in the dataset between the number of positive instances and their negative counterparts. In such cases the model may just 'learn' to always predict the majority class, regardless of the

---

[1] UCI Machine Learning Repository (https://archive.ics.uci.edu/ml/).

independent variables, as this strategy would blindly lead to correct predictions for the most part. Precision (Eq. 2) can be defined as the fraction of relevant instances among the retrieved instances, and thus can be interpreted as the model's positive predictive value. A high precision indicates that the model has a low false positive rate and thus measures how many of the instances classified by the model as positive are actually positive. Recall (Eq. 3) provides the ratio of relevant instance successfully retrieved by the model out of the number of relevant instances in the dataset (including those the model failed to retrieve). That is to say, recall measures how many of all the instances that are truly positive are labelled as such by the model. Specificity (Eq. 4) provides the ratio of true negatives, *e.g.*, the percentage of non-readmitted patients who are correctly identified as such by the model. F1 (Eq. 5) considers both the precision and the recall and provides the harmonic average of the two, with its maximum value (1) being indicative of perfect precision and recall. Finally, the ROC curve illustrates the predictive power of a binary classification model as the discrimination threshold is varied. It is obtained by plotting the sensitivity as a function of the fallout (Eq. 6), which is also known as the false positive rate or probability of false alarm.

Random forests models trained on the dataset compiled by [29] have exhibited good precision-recall scores (0.65) [2] whereas other classifiers fine-tuned through evolutionary algorithms (EA) have yielded good performance in terms of accuracy, recall and specificity (0.97, 1.00, 0.97, respectively) [9]. While the aforementioned traditional approaches are good at identifying key features and achieving high prediction accuracy, they do not capture more complex patterns between features that may be hidden in the data. With this in mind, hybrid approaches, such as in [30], combine meta-heuristic methods, such as evolutionary simulated annealing, and sparse logistic Lasso regression to improve feature selection. Very briefly, the model optimises coefficients of Logistic Regression using evolutionary strategies and simulated annealing algorithms and use Lasso regularization to prevent over-training, a drawback of Logistic Regression when applied to unbalanced data. Simulated annealing (SA) is a probabilistic technique for approximating the global optimum of a function, particularly in a large search space of discrete values. To prevent getting stuck in local optima, an evolutionary strategy (ES) is used to select a good starting point for the SA algorithm and optimise the coefficients of the model. LASSO or least absolute shrinkage and selection operator is a regression analysis method used for feature selection that uses regularization to improve prediction accuracy and interpretability. It achieves this by selecting a subset of the features rather than using all of them. The proposed hybrid classification framework called Evolutionary Simulating Annealing LASSO Logistic Regression (ESALOR) selects features using correlation, information gain and decision trees, and refine these parameters using LASSO. They then use ES and SA to optimise those coefficients and use the optimal solution to predict patient readmission. ELASOR improves accuracy, precision, recall and F1 measures (0.76, 0.77, 0.77, 0.86, respectively) over conventional classification methods including support vector machines (SVM), artificial neural networks (ANN), naive bayes (NB) and logistic regression (LR). While the improvements of the first three indicators are slight, ELASOR shows a marked improvement in the F-measure, which provides a better estimate of algorithm performance when testing on an imbalanced data set as it takes both false positives and false negatives into account. Various classifiers have shown varying performance metrics when patients in this dataset are grouped by age [24]. High ROC AUC (0.95) and F1 (0.92) scores have been achieved with deep learning models, including convolutional networks [14]. The same dataset has been used along with others in order to evaluate novel data mining and deep learning methods [7,18,28]. In other, related studies, risk factors for readmission have also been found by training other machine learning models on different clinical datasets collected in India and the United States [5,11,20]. Motivated by striking a balance between accuracy and interpretability, [16] proposes two novel methods: K-LRT, a likelihood ratio test-based method, and a joint clustering and classification (JCC) method, that combines clustering and classification to identify hidden clusters and adapts classifiers to each accordingly. They compare their approach to traditional machine learning methods, such as sparse support vector machines (SVM), sparse logistic regression and random forests, using them as baseline methods, and validate their algorithm on large datasets from the Boston Medical Center.

The K-LRT method identifies the K most significant features of each patient and the JCC method creates classifiers per each positive clusters. It achieves this by alternately training a classification model and then re-clustering positive samples, resulting in an algorithm that scales well and provides interpretable characteristics. Their proposed methodology first identifies diabetes-related diagnoses from the records, using ICD-9 [31] and CPT [10] coding systems, removing non-related procedures. They then form four time blocks of one, two, three years before the target year, and a fourth time block of all earlier records, producing a vector of just over 9,400 dimensions of features to characterise each patient. They then remove features that account for less than 1% of the patients, leaving 320 medical and 3 demographic features. Again, using the ICD-9 codes that identify type I or II diabetes and uncontrolled or unspecified state, they merge these 4 types per the four time blocks to create 16 more features. To better balance the data, they set a policy for target year based on hospitalization records to produce a ratio of 17% of hospitalised patients in the dataset, producing over 33,000 patients to split into training and testing datasets. As their primary goal is to assist and alert patients and doctors to prevent hospitalizations, the baseline random forests classifier is based on commonly used features such as age, race, gender hemoglobin A1c, which measures average blood sugar concentration, and number of emergency room visits. They also compare their algorithm to alternating clustering and classification (ACC) and SVMs (linear and radial basis function) as well as two hierarchical approaches that combine clustering and classification. Results are reported in AUC (0.7924) which fare better than conventional methods but does not surpass random forests (0.8453). However, their method allows for interpretation and identifying key features.

3   Methods

The dataset, originally compiled by [29] and publicly available in CSV format,[2] is composed of electronic records spanning ten years (1999 through 2008) with various demographic and clinical variables per patient. The most salient aspects of the dataset can be summarised very briefly as follows: each row corresponds to a hospital visit by a patient and each patient may have more than one visit, *i.e.*, several rows may be associated to the same patient. Demographic information of the patient is stored as categorical variables, including `gender` and `race` as well as `age`, which appears as labels describing intervals measured in years (*e.g.*, [0, 10), [10, 20), [20, 30), *etc.*). Columns `diag_1`, `diag_2`, and `diag_3` contain ICD-9 codes indicating the diagnoses made during the visit. Missing values in any feature are identified by a '?' label. Each row includes also 24 features associated to different medications against diabetes, each one indicating if the drug, or a change in its dosage, was prescribed. The possible values for all these 24 columns are 'NO' (not prescribed), 'Steady' (no change in dosage), 'Up' (increased dosage) and 'Down' (decreased dosage). The class attribute indicates if the patient was readmitted after the visit and its possible values are 'NO' (*i.e.*, no readmission), '<30' (*i.e.* readmission occurred within 30 days) '>30' (*i.e.*, readmission occurred after 30 days). Full details of the dataset, including detailed descriptions of the features mentioned earlier and others that have been omitted for brevity, can be found in the original study by [29].

Prior to training the models proposed in this paper, this dataset was preprocessed as follows: for all patients only the first visit was retained, *i.e.*, second and subsequent visits from the same patient were removed in order to ensure independence of the data. Eight columns were removed because most of the values in them were unknown or missing or because they do not pertain to the medical state of the patient (namely `encounter_id`, `patient_nbr`, `weight`, `admission_type_id`, `discharge_disposition_id`, `admission_source_id`, `payer_code` and `medical_specialty`). After this, numerical features were kept intact whereas categorical variables were mapped to numerical representations as follows: class labels 'NO' and '>30' were merged into one, representing *'no 30-day readmission'* (encoded numerically as 0), while keeping the third class '<30' intact (encoded numerically as 1), representing *'30-day readmission.'* This way the problem is reduced to one of binary classification.

The remaining categorical columns were transformed as follows: ICD-9 codes representing the diagnoses of the patient in each visit were grouped by their ICD-9 Chapter,[3] thus reducing the number of possible values in columns `diag_1`, `diag_2`, and `diag_3` to only 19. Thereafter, these three categorical attributes were transformed to numerical ones by replacing them with dummy variables. That is to say, `diag_1` was replaced with new, binary columns, one for each ICD-9 Chapter code, in such a way that a value of 1 in one of these new columns indicates that a diagnosis of a disease or condition from this ICD-9 category was

---

[2] Diabetes 130-US hospitals for years 1999–2008 Data Set (https://bit.ly/2kqU73b).
[3] ICD-9-CM Chapters (https://icd.codes/icd9cm).

made and recorded in the original diag_1 whereas a value of 0 indicates otherwise. For instance, a value of 1 in dummy variable diag_1_ICD-9_9 would indicate that the patient's first diagnosis pertains to a condition in ICD-9 Chapter 9, namely a disease of the digestive system, and a value of 0 would indicate otherwise. Variables diag_2 and diag_3 were replaced with dummy counterparts in the same manner. An analogous procedure was followed in order to replace other non-ordinal, categorical columns, such as race and gender, with dummy variables.

Ordinal, categorical values in column age were replaced directly with numerical values, with higher values reflecting higher age groups (e.g., [0, 10) was encoded as 0, [10, 20) was encoded as 1, etc.). Finally, all 24 columns referring to medication prescriptions were converted to binary features by merging values 'Steady,' 'Up,' and 'Down' into one single value representing 'Drug prescribed' while value 'NO' was kept intact to represent 'Drug not prescribed.' Subsequently, each one of these 24 medication prescription features was replaced with a binary dummy variable, in a manner analogous to that described earlier for diagnosis attributes.

After all these feature transformations the resulting dataset comprises 100 columns, including the class column. In order to reduce the dimensionality of the data prior to training the prediction models, principal component analysis was conducted in order to reduce the number of features from 100 to 45 while preserving 98% of the variance. Thereafter, all features were normalised to a common scale, with unit variance and zero mean. After this, prediction models with logistic regression (LR), single layer perceptron (SLP), multilayer perceptron (MLP), random forests (RF) and support vector machines (SVM), the latter with various kernels, were individually trained on the selected features using 10-fold cross-validation. Before doing this, the training data were balanced through oversampling since the original dataset was found to be highly unbalanced, with 63, 417 'no 30-day readmission' visits against only 6, 152 '30-day readmission' visits. Several performance metrics were calculated for each trained model, including ROC AUC and F1. Overfitting was prevented by the use of cross-validation during training and evaluation as well as by the application of oversampling only on the training data and not the testing data.

All the models were implemented in Python (2.7.15) using the library scikit-learn (0.20). The LR model was trained using the stochastic average gradient (SAG) solver implementation provided by scikit-learn. The rectified linear unit (ReLU) function was used as the activation function in the SLP and MLP models, with the latter having one 23-neuron hidden layer, whose size was chosen as a middle point between that of the input (45) and the output (1) layers. The RF model was trained with 100 trees in order to improve the estimates from the out-of-bag predictions without increasing the computational cost of training. The SVM model was implemented using the linear kernel. During experimentation the models were observed to exhibit the best predictive and computational performance with these parameters and the results are presented in the following section of this article. Nevertheless, other parameter choices were also considered for each model during experimentation, *e.g.*, a larger hidden layer for MLP and logistic regression as an activation function for SLP, other kernels for the SVM models (*e.g.*, polynomial, sigmoidal and radial basis function (RBF)) among others. However, the predictive performance of these was found to be inferior and thus these were omitted from this article for brevity.

4   Results

The performance metrics obtained with each one of the models trained are listed in Table 1. These metrics show that the least performing model was the single layer perceptron whereas the best prediction scores were achieved, by far, by the random forest model. These even exceed those reportedly obtained through deep learning techniques, listed in Sect. 2, while requiring significantly less computing power. Notably, Table 1 also shows that none of the other models evaluated managed to obtain performance scores near those achieved by the random forest model, instead obtaining rather modest scores, mostly just over 0.5.

Table 1. Performance metrics of models logistic regression (LR), single layer perceptron (SLP), multilayer perceptron (MLP), support vector machines (SVM) and random forests (RF).

Model	ROC AUC	F1	Precision	Recall	Accuracy
LR	0.5783	0.5550	0.5599	0.5515	0.5566
SLP	0.5229	0.5484	0.5129	0.5929	0.5147
MLP	0.6548	0.6164	0.6100	0.6095	0.6083
SVM	0.5053	0.5126	0.4578	0.6574	0.5941
RF	0.9999	0.9974	0.9950	0.9999	0.9974

5   Conclusions

This research article presents a machine learning approach for the identification of diabetic patients at risk of requiring hospital readmissions. A reduction of these statistics should be expected to contribute towards the improvement of patients' well-being as well as towards a reduction in financial and reputational costs to healthcare institutions. This is particularly critical for patients of chronic conditions, such as diabetes. This creates the need for policies and strategies to reduce these statistics, especially methods to predict when a patient is at high risk of requiring readmission in the future. The best prediction rates reported in the recent literature have been achieved only through the use of deep learning on the patient clinical data collected by [29]. However, the present research article describes a novel method for efficiently managing the same dataset for the training of machine learning models, allowing better prediction rates without requiring deep learning. The best-performing model trained in this study, namely random forest, exceeds the prediction metrics reported by others in the recent literature using the same base dataset. This includes the precision-recall scores (0.65) reported by [2] as well as the ROC AUC (0.95) and F1 (0.92) scores reported by [14] through the use of convolutional networks, while also exceeding or closely approximating the accuracy, recall and specificity (0.97, 1.00, 0.97, respectively) reported by [9]. To the best knowledge of the authors of the present study, no prediction models reported in the literature achieve the same performance metrics obtained by the RF model presented in this paper.

The main contributing factor to this result is the preprocessing of the patient data, which is achieved through a method not previously explored in the related literature using the same dataset. This method contemplates the simplification of the data in various ways, one being the reduction of several variables' domain with the intent of allowing the prediction models to generalise more easily. This includes the grouping of patients' diagnoses codes by their corresponding ICD-9 Chapters, thus reducing the domain of these variables to only 19 possible values. This simplification was completed with application of a similar strategy on some of the other dataset's features, including the class attribute whose domain was adjusted from three to two possible values, thus transforming the original problem, *i.e.*, the prediction of a future readmission, into one of binary classification. This simplification of the problem, paired with the dimensionality reduction achieved through principal component analysis as well as the class balancing achieved through oversampling, results in a much more compact dataset from which generalisations can be learned by the prediction models presented. This, without requiring deep learning techniques and also achieving higher performance metrics than those reported previously in related literature using the same original dataset.

With the main exception of the domain reduction of some features described earlier, the data preprocessing procedure used in the present study and the methodology described in previous, related studies share some aspects, such as consideration of only first patient visits, feature selection and data balancing [9,14]. As stated before, this simplification of the data is arguably a contributing factor to the predictive power of the models proposed. Nevertheless, interpretability of the prediction is still limited despite this simplification of the dataset, given the complexity of the random forest technique. Furthermore, the proposed data preprocessing clearly comes at the cost of reduced granularity. It can be reasonably hypothesised, though evidently not guaranteed, that these results could be further improved with larger datasets, *i.e.*, with higher numbers of patient visits with the same features. This investigation is focused on diabetes, however, this type of approach could be further evaluated in the context of other chronic conditions, such as heart disease.

References

1. Axon, R.N., Williams, M.V.: Hospital readmission as an accountability measure. JAMA **305**(5), 504–505 (2011)
2. Bhuvan, M.S., Kumar, A., Zafar, A., Kishore, V.: Identifying diabetic patients with high risk of readmission. arXiv preprint arXiv:1602.04257 (2016)
3. Boulding, W., Glickman, S.W., Manary, M.P., Schulman, K.A., Staelin, R.: Relationship between patient satisfaction with inpatient care and hospital readmission within 30 days. Am. J. Managed Care **17**(1), 41–48 (2011)
4. Breen, T.J., Patel, H., Purga, S., Fein, S.A., Philbin, E.F., Torosoff, M.: Effects of index admission length of stay on readmission interval in patients with heart failure. Circ.: Cardiovasc. Qual. Outcomes **11**(suppl_1), A275–A275 (2018)
5. Brisimi, T.S., Xu, T., Wang, T., Dai, W., Adams, W.G., Paschalidis, I.C.: Predicting chronic disease hospitalizations from electronic health records: an interpretable classification approach. Proc. IEEE **106**(4), 690–707 (2018)
6. Caruana, R., Lou, Y., Gehrke, J., Koch, P., Sturm, M., Elhadad, N.: Intelligible models for healthcare: predicting pneumonia risk and hospital 30-day readmission. In: Proceedings of the 21th ACM SIGKDD International Conference on Knowledge Discovery and Data Mining, pp. 1721–1730. ACM (2015)
7. Chou, E., Nguyen, T., Beal, J., Haque, A., Fei-Fei, L.: A fully private pipeline for deep learning on electronic health records. arXiv preprint arXiv:1811.09951 (2018)
8. Choudhry, S.A., Li, J., Davis, D., Erdmann, C., Sikka, R., Sutariya, B.: A public-private partnership develops and externally validates a 30-day hospital readmission risk prediction model. Online J. Publ. Health Inform. **5**(2), 219 (2013)
9. Choudhury, A., Greene, D., Christopher, M.: Evaluating patient readmission risk: a predictive analytics approach. arXiv preprint arXiv:1812.11028 (2018)
10. CPT: Current Procedural Terminology (CPT) American Medical Association (2014). https://www.ama-assn.org/amaone/cpt-current-procedural-terminology
11. Duggal, R., Shukla, S., Chandra, S., Shukla, B., Khatri, S.K.: Predictive risk modelling for early hospital readmission of patients with diabetes in India. Int. J. Diab. Dev. Countries **36**(4), 519–528 (2016)
12. Frizzell, J.D., et al.: Prediction of 30-day all-cause readmissions in patients hospitalized for heart failure: comparison of machine learning and other statistical approaches. JAMA Cardiol. **2**(2), 204–209 (2017)
13. Futoma, J., Morris, J., Lucas, J.: A comparison of models for predicting early hospital readmissions. J. Biomed. Inform. **56**, 229–238 (2015)
14. Hammoudeh, A., Al-Naymat, G., Ghannam, I., Obied, N.: Predicting hospital readmission among diabetics using deep learning. Procedia Comput. Sci. **141**, 484–489 (2018)
15. He, D., Mathews, S.C., Kalloo, A.N., Hutfless, S.: Mining high-dimensional administrative claims data to predict early hospital readmissions. J. Am. Med. Inform. Assoc. **21**(2), 272–279 (2014)
16. Hosseinzadeh, A., Izadi, M., Verma, A., Precup, D., Buckeridge, D.: Assessing the predictability of hospital readmission using machine learning. In: Twenty-Fifth IAAI Conference (2013)
17. Kansagara, D., et al.: Risk prediction models for hospital readmission: a systematic review. JAMA **306**(15), 1688–1698 (2011)
18. Kaschel, H., Rocco, V., Reinao, G.: An open algorithm for systematic evaluation of readmission predictors on diabetic patients from data warehouses. In: 2018 IEEE International Conference on Automation/XXIII Congress of the Chilean Association of Automatic Control, pp. 1–6. IEEE (2018)

19. Kassin, M.T., et al.: Risk factors for 30-day hospital readmission among general surgery patients. J. Am. Coll. Surg. **215**(3), 322–330 (2012)

20. King, C., et al.: Identifying risk factors for 30-day readmission events among American Indian patients with diabetes in the four corners region of the southwest from 2009 to 2016. PLoS ONE **13**(8), e0195476 (2018)

21. Kripalani, S., Theobald, C.N., Anctil, B., Vasilevskis, E.E.: Reducing hospital readmission rates: current strategies and future directions. Ann. Rev. Med. **65**, 471–485 (2014)

22. Krumholz, H.M., et al.: Readmission after hospitalization for congestive heart failure among medicare beneficiaries. Arch. Intern. Med. **157**(1), 99–104 (1997)

23. Merkow, R.P., et al.: Underlying reasons associated with hospital readmission following surgery in the United States. JAMA **313**(5), 483–495 (2015)

24. Mingle, D.: Predicting diabetic readmission rates: moving beyond Hba1c. Curr. Trends Biomed. Eng. Biosci. **7**(3), 555707 (2017)

25. Moore, B.J., White, S., Washington, R., Coenen, N., Elixhauser, A.: Identifying increased risk of readmission and in-hospital mortality using hospital administrative data. Med. Care **55**(7), 698–705 (2017)

26. Mortazavi, B.J., et al.: Analysis of machine learning techniques for heart failure readmissions. Circ. Cardiovasc. Qual. Outcomes **9**(6), 629–640 (2016)

27. Rubin, D.J.: Hospital readmission of patients with diabetes. Curr. Diab. Rep. **15**(4), 17 (2015)

28. Soysal, Ö.M.: Association rule mining with mostly associated sequential patterns. Expert Syst. Appl. **42**(5), 2582–2592 (2015)

29. Strack, B., et al.: Impact of HbA1c measurement on hospital readmission rates: analysis of 70,000 clinical database patient records. BioMed Res. Int. **2014** (2014)

30. Tutun, S., Khanmohammadi, S., He, L., Chou, C.A.: A meta-heuristic LASSO model for diabetic readmission prediction. In: Proceedings of the 2016 Industrial and Systems Engineering Research Conference (ISERC) (2016)

31. WHO: International classification of diseases, 9th revision (ICD-9) - World Health Organization (1999). https://www.who.int/classifications/icd/en/

32. Yu, S., Farooq, F., Van Esbroeck, A., Fung, G., Anand, V., Krishnapuram, B.: Predicting readmission risk with institution-specific prediction models. Artif. Intell. Med. **65**(2), 89–96 (2015)

A Computational Model for Distance Perception Based on Visual Attention Redeployment in Locomotor Infants

Liz A. Jaramillo–Henao$^{(\boxtimes)}$, Adrián A. Vélez–Aristizábal,
and Jaime E. Arango–Castro

Department of Electrical and Electronics Engineering,
National University of Colombia, Manizales, Caldas, Colombia
{lajaramillohe,aavelezar,jearangoca}@unal.edu.co

Abstract. Self-locomotion experience of infants has been argued to improve perception of distance, as visual attention is drawn to previously undetected or ignored depth specifying information. We present a computational model to evaluate how does self-locomotion experience influences the estimation of distance in infants. The model assigns an estimated distance label to salient objects in the scene, through a *Binocular Neural Network (BNN)* that computes binocular disparities. Emphasizing on key aspects of locomotion experience, two *BNN* are trained, one for non-locomotor infants and one for locomotor infants. The validation and test stages of the process show a significant improvement on the distance estimation task for the *BNN* trained with locomotor experience. This result is added to previous evidence which supports that locomotion in infants is an important step in cognitive development.

Keywords: Cognitive Developmental Robotics · Visual attention · Locomotor experience · Binocular Neural Network

1 Introduction

For long time, humans have wished for understanding the mind. What does being a human mean? What is intelligence? How does brain work? How does language emerge? Several contributions to the answer of this questions have been made from different perspectives: Philosophy, psychology, neuroscience, linguistics and, more recently, artificial intelligence. These efforts promoted the appearance of *Cognitive Science* as a new multidisciplinary field. A convergence that have resulted fruitful for each of those disciplines and have inspired the creation of artificial models of cognition, aiming to replicate human intelligence in artificial agents.

L.A. Jaramillo–Henao and A.A. Vélez–Aristizábal—Contributed equally to this work.

A. D. Orjuela-Cañón et al. (Eds.): ColCACI 2019, CCIS 1096, pp. 89–102, 2019.
https://doi.org/10.1007/978-3-030-36211-9_8

For instance, Cognitive Developmental Robotics (CDR) is a paradigm in cognitive science based on both *embodiment*[1] through a robotic synthetic approach and key concepts from developmental psychology [1]. It aims to provide a new understanding about ourselves and a new design theory of humanoids [2]. Researchers in CDR have designed computational models that simulate infants brain functions by robots that interact with an environment [3]. This allows understanding infants acquisition of cognitive abilities and investigating the link between internal organization of infants brain and their behaviors.

Several studies conducted on infants of multiple ages, by means of behavioral experiments, have suggested a relation between motor and visual skills. Thompson *et al.* [4], for example, found a statistically significant relation between stereopsis and fine motor skills in 2 year-old infants. Moreover, some studies strongly suggest that vision may foster self-locomotion, just as locomotion helps in the emergence of some specific visual perception skills [5–9].

Additionally, Campos *et al.* [10] argued that perception of distance shows developmental improvements following the acquisition of locomotion. They provided evidence related to changes in allocation of attention that may occur as a consequence of self-locomotion experience. Hence, they proposed that locomotion can help to calibrate distance perception, since attention is drawn to previously undetected or ignored depth specifying information. This evidence motivates the use of visual attention as a parameter, in order to improve estimation of depth with artificial intelligence techniques.

This paper presents a computational model that improves its ability to estimate distance from binocular disparities, based on visual attention and learning mechanisms. Such model aims to serve as a method to evaluate how does self-locomotion experience influences the estimation of distance by infants. In Sect. 2, we present the hypotheses and experiments that suggest a relation between locomotion and perception of distance. The proposed model for distance perception is described in Sect. 3. In Sects. 4 and 5, we describe the experimental stage and obtained results, respectively. Then, in Sect. 6, we elaborate in the implications of these results, regarding the relation between locomotion experience and distance estimation from binocular disparities. Finally, the conclusions, limitations of the current setting, and future research directions are indicated in Sect. 7.

2   Locomotor Experience and Distance Perception in Infants

Vision, as it is known, is not innate in humans. Infants are born with a very poor vision in many aspects: Newborns have a visual acuity 40 times worse than adults, they can only see some colours, they do not have 3D vision, and they do not recognize direction of motion [11]. These capabilities are developed over time by brain maturation (anatomical and physiological changes) and experience.

---

[1] The idea of a dynamic interaction between brain activity, action through a body, and the environment, as essential for cognition.

Experience is an important factor in the development of some visual capabilities like visual acuity, discrimination of direction of motion, and recognition of human faces. However, by the plasticity of the brain, infants that have a lack of visual experience may obtain it in short time, by practice.

Since locomotor experience has shown to be closely related to visual development, crawling has been considered an important stage in cognitive development of infants by many researchers. Kubicek et al. [7] suggested that 9 month-old infants visual predictive performances of only partly visible objects moving in space, is related to crawling experience. In addition, they propose that crawler infants have developed better visual prediction skills than non-crawler infants. This may be explained by the need of keeping in mind the objective during periods of occlusion of a target object, as crawlers need to anticipate moving objects. Similarly, Gerhard and Schwarzer [9] proposed that, due to the particular visual experience given by learning to move the body through the environment, locomotion could promote the development of mental construction of objects, particularly in mental rotation.

There is also evidence suggesting that locomotor experience have a relevant role in the perception of distance. Campos et al. [10] argued that prelocomotor infants are only interested in objects that they can reach with their hands. Depth specifying information of objects beyond their reach is unattended or can not be perceived. Then, attention of infants is redeployed to farther objects as a function of their locomotor experience. According to this, previously ignored depth information acquired through locomotion experience may help to calibrate distance perception. In a related experimental work, Gustafson [12] compared, for infants between the ages of 6.5 and 10 months, how often did *Locomotor* and *Non-Locomotor* infants look at toys located both near and far from them, with frequencies as event counts. His findings supports this hypothesis.

Depth perception in humans is based on multiple monocular and binocular cues. Our frontally disposed, horizontally separated eyes, provide us of simultaneous images of the real world from different points of view. When the images fall on different parts in its corresponding retina, it occurs a disparity. The computation of depth information from disparities is called *stereopsis*, and it is the main cue for distance perception.

Further evidence supports distance estimation from disparities being improved by visual self-locomotion experiences. For instance, Mann et al. [13] showed that distance estimation from disparities may be improved by means of interaction with the environment. Using a humanoid robot that rotates its neck, they obtained different views of a target attached to the robot's arm, and then, their model estimated the distance to the target from the head of the robot. Knowing that the distance was always the same, they computed the error based on the differences on distance estimation for different angular positions of the neck. Their results suggest that the experience of self-locomotion through different views of the same scene could be applied to improve distance estimation.

3   Computational Model for Distance Estimation

In this work, a computational model aiming to serve as a synthetic approach to the hypothesis of Campos *et al.* [10] is presented. Highlighting key aspects of locomotion experience and its relation with visual attention, we trained a *Binocular Neural Network* under different conditions to represent the non-locomotor and locomotor stages of the infant.

The model consists of two modules (see Fig. 1). An image preprocessing module labels the objects in input stereoscopic images with the real distances, and a disparities estimation module implements a BNN to classify the distances of those objects. The remainder of this section explains in detail such modules.

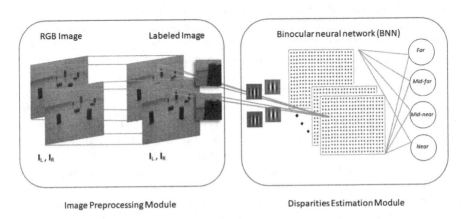

Fig. 1. Computational model for distance estimation.

3.1   Image Preprocessing Module

The inputs to this module are stereoscopic images $I_i^L(r, g, b)$, $I_i^R(r, g, b)$, of scenes containing red objects (the next section provides more details regarding the scenes construction). The module first apply a color transformation, from RGB to YCbCr, to input images, resulting $I_i^L(y, cb, cr), I_i^R(y, cb, cr)$. Since the third component (cr) allows to easily identify red objects, the other two components are discarded and a thresholding process is performed on the former, as shown in (1) and Algorithm 1, respectively:

$$J_i^L = I_i^L(cr) \qquad J_i^R = I_i^R(cr) \tag{1}$$

Then, matrices $M_i^L = J_i^L$ and $M_i^R = J_i^R$ are created, where a value from 1 to 4 (*Near* = 1, *Mid-Near* = 2, *Mid-Far* = 3, *Far* = 4) is assigned to non-zero pixels according to the objects depth distribution in the corresponding scene. Thus, matrices M_i contain the labels for objects in image i. Finally, the initial RGB images I_i are transformed to gray scale, and divided in smaller 30-by-30 pixel images S_i^L and S_i^R. Therefore, the outputs of this module are the image pairs S_i and its corresponding labels.

Algorithm 1. Object Segmentation

if $J_i(x,y) < threshold$ **then**
  $J_i(x,y) = 0$
else
  $J_i(x,y) = 255$
end if

3.2   Disparities Estimation Module

This module learns to classify depth in the input images based on the algorithm proposed and validated by Goncalves and Welchman [14]. Their BNN algorithm makes an emulation of how disparity estimation is achieved by human brain: Mixing disparity detection with *proscription* (exploiting dissimilar features to provide evidence against unlikely interpretations), they account for a type of neurons that respond maximally to images that do not relate to physical features. The current understanding of disparity estimation states that brain needs to identify matching features in the two retinal images for that purpose, i.e., solving the stereoscopic correspondence problem. Goncalves and Welchman argue that it is not optimal, and propose an alternative. Using dissimilar features to acquire information against unlikely interpretations. Therefore, their BNN mix information both for and against the likelihood of a depth structure of a viewed scene.

As shown in Fig. 2, their algorithm consists of a convolutional neural network with 3 layers: An input layer, a convolutional-pooling layer, and a logistic regression layer at the output. It is trained to discriminate near and far distances from 30-by-30 pixel image pairs at the input layer. In the convolutional layer, 28 binocular kernels (19×19 pixels) are applied to the input image pairs resulting into 28 output maps of 12×12 pixels. Each unit a_j of the output map k is the result of applying the corresponding kernel to an specific location s of the input image, plus a bias ($a_j^k = w^k s_j + b_j^k$). Such kernels are initialized as Gabor functions, as shown in (2):

$$w_j^L = w_j^R = \exp \frac{-(x'^2 + y'^2)}{2\sigma^2} \cos\left(2\pi f x' + \phi\right) \tag{2}$$

where $x' = x\cos(\theta) + y\sin(\theta)$ and $y' = -x\sin(\theta) + y\cos(\theta)$. Then, the output maps are down-sampled in the max-pooling layer producing 28 maps of 6×6 pixels. Finally, in the logistic regression layer, the internal activities are mapped to the output nodes by (3):

$$output = softmax(\boldsymbol{W}a + b) \tag{3}$$

where $\boldsymbol{W}$ is the weight matrix, a are the activities and b the bias terms.

The training is conducted through mini batch[2] gradient descent. When all image batches have passed through the network, meaning that one epoch has

---

[2] Number of image samples to be propagated through the network at once.

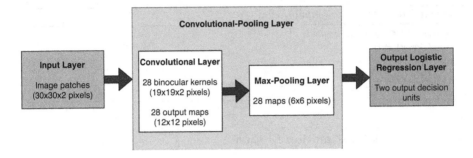

Fig. 2. Binocular Neural Network as proposed in [14].

been completed, a validation is performed with image pairs that were not used for training. A *patience* parameter determines the number of iterations allowed for the algorithm to keep running without obtaining an improvement on validation error of, at least, 0.5%. This parameter increases each time the validation error is improved over that percentage, and then, a test is conducted with image pairs not used for training.

4   Experimental Setting and Assumptions

In a first experimental approach to evaluate the hypothesis proposed in [10], we consider the estimation of binocular disparities as an offline supervised learning process from scenes containing salient objects. This section describes the experimental conditions derived from that consideration, and its underlying conceptions, used in our model. First, we elaborate on the construction of the image database, and then, we establish the relation between the training stage of the model and the hypothesis to evaluate. Figure 3 provides a general view of the complete model.

4.1   Image Database Construction

Contrary to the classical approach of computer vision, humans do not estimate distance quantitatively, but qualitatively. This qualitative measurements have an intrinsic meaning in human cognition, that is, they are grounded.[3] The notion of *embodiment* suggests that computational models can be grounded in interaction with the environment, as several works in CDR have shown [16–21]. In this case, we take the distance estimation as grounded by what is reachable for the infant. Thus, considering a reaching distance of d, objects within d (reachable without displacement) are *Near*, those within $2d$ are *Mid-Near*, those within $3d$ are *Mid-Far*, and those within $4d$ are *Far* (see Fig. 4).

Images were taken with a Webcam of 0.92MP. Scenes were constructed with objects randomly spread throughout a room, with reaching distance $d = 61$ cm.

---

[3] See the *symbol grounding problem* [15].

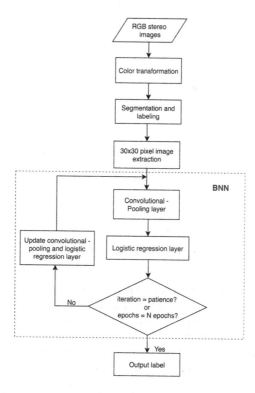

Fig. 3. Flowchart of the model.

Then, stereo pairs were captured with a horizontal separation of 4.5 cm between images, according to findings regarding interpupillary distance in infants [22]. This produced 100 stereo images of 480-by-640 pixels with a minimum shift of 10 pixels and a maximum one of 50 pixels, depending on the depth position of an object in the scene. In the image preprocessing module, the stereo pairs were color transformed and the respective labels for the objects were defined. Then, the original images were divided into smaller 30-by-30 pixel image pairs. Figure 5 summarizes this process. To simplify the classification task, we excluded from the input image pairs those with two or more objects at different depths, as well as those with no objects. Therefore, we obtained 1212 *Near*, 509 *Mid-Near*, 324 *Mid-Far*, and 295 *Far* small image pairs.

4.2 Training Procedure

The training process for the disparities estimation module was conducted under the following considerations:

- An infant without locomotor experience is more likely to pay attention to near than far objects [10,12]. The BNN trained under this consideration is called *Non-Locomotor* BNN.

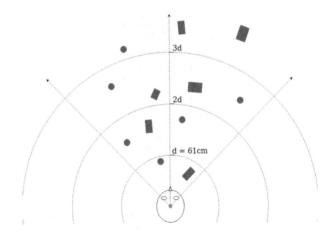

Fig. 4. Scenes construction.

- Visual attention in the infant is redeployed by his locomotor experience [10, 12]. The BNN trained under this consideration is called *Locomotor* BNN.
- We consider experience acquired through time as related to the total number of image pairs used for training.
- We consider visual attention redeployment as a change in the proportion of the image pairs with different depths used for training.
- The proportion of image pairs with different depths used for the two training cases was established according to the findings obtained by Gustafson [12] in his experimental study (see Table 1).

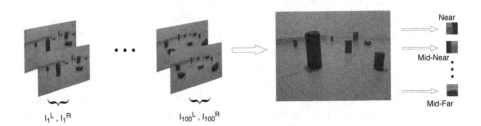

Fig. 5. Image preprocessing.

According to the notion of visual attention redeployment of Campos *et al.* [10], a network "without locomotor experience" should be trained with a greater N_{Near}/N_{Far} relation than a network "with locomotor experience", as shown in (4):

$$\left[\frac{N_{Near}}{N_{Far}}\right]_{Non-Locomotor} > \left[\frac{N_{Near}}{N_{Far}}\right]_{Locomotor} \tag{4}$$

where N is a number of 30-by-30 image pairs.

Table 1. Effects of ability to locomote on measures of looking

	Non-Locomotor	Locomotor
Near Toys	74.45	47.28
Far Toys	1.89	16.24

Based on the results of Gustafson [12], we found the linear relations (5) that defined the number N of images that should be used in training, as comparative percentages. These relations are:

$$\frac{NL - L}{NL} \times 100, \quad \frac{L - NL}{L} \times 100 \tag{5}$$

In Fig. 6, the proportion of images used to train the BNN in the *Non-Locomotor* (Fig. 6a) and *Locomotor* (Fig. 6b) cases is illustrated by comparative visual attention maps. From highest to lowest attention the gradient of color used varies from red to blue respectively.

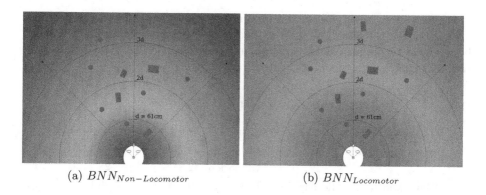

(a) $BNN_{Non-Locomotor}$ (b) $BNN_{Locomotor}$

Fig. 6. Visual attention maps for the two training cases. (Color figure online)

5 Results

The BNN algorithm presented by Goncalves and Welchman [14] enables the implementation of as many output nodes as needed. In our model, we used a maximum of four nodes related to the four distances we aimed to estimate. For comparison purposes, we made three implementations with different number of output nodes: *Near - Mid-Near* estimation, *Near - Mid-Near- Mid-Far* estimation, and *Near - Mid-Near - Mid-Far - Far* estimation. The underlying idea is that models with more output nodes imply greater visual attentional ranges in infants, since their attention have been allocated to farther objects. This section provides the related results.

For the experiments, we essentially set four parameters of the BNN as follows: Epochs were set to 1,000, the batch size was set to 5, the learning rate was set to 0.05, and the patience parameter was set to 20,000. The rest of the parameters of the BNN was set as in [14]. Table 2 shows the number of images of each category used for the *Non-Locomotor* and *Locomotor* training cases. Considering the total amount of *Far* image pairs as reference, we used 15% for validation and test respectively (44 30-by-30 pixel image pairs), for each of the related labels. So, the total amount of *Far* image pairs in the database were used.

Table 2. Number of images used for training

	Non-Locomotor	Locomotor	Validation	Test
Near	316	517	44	44
Mid-Near	257	421	44	44
Mid-Far	27	236	44	44
Far	24	207	44	44

Table 3 summarizes the validation and test errors obtained for each implementation. For the *Near – Mid-Near* model, we observed a significant difference between the errors for *Non-Locomotor* and *Locomotor* BNNs, showing a reduction that can be interpreted as related to experience.

Table 3. Validation and test errors

Model	Error	Non-Locomotor	Locomotor
Near - Mid-Near	Test	44.71%	36.47%
	Validation	42.35%	28.24%
Near - Mid-Near - Mid-Far	Test	49.23%	36.15%
	Validation	50.77%	27.69%
Near - Mid-Near - Mid-Far - Far	Test	63.43%	36.57%
	Validation	64.57%	37.14%

In the *Near – Mid-Near – Mid-Far* case, as can be seen, the error increased for both *Non-Locomotor* and *Locomotor* networks. However, the relation between errors in the previous case was maintained. Results for the *Near – Mid-Near – Mid-Far – Far* model showed a similar behaviour than previous cases. Figure 7 shows the number of epochs reached at the training stage for the three experimental cases. Due to the patience parameter explained before, the number of epochs reached can be interpreted as an indicator of performance for the BNN. For instance, if the BNN is not improving its performance, the patience parameter will stop the training. Thus, a higher number of epochs means the BNN have reached a better classification ability.

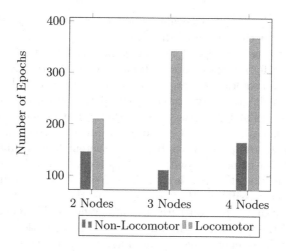

Fig. 7. Number of epochs reached at training.

Table 4 presents the sensitivity (true positive rate) and specificity (true negative rate) measures for test classification results for both *Non-Locomotor* and *Locomotor* BNNs. It can be seen that the networks are specially good at classifying *Near* objects. However, a significant improvement on the classification of *Mid-Near*, *Mid-Far*, and *Far* objects in the *Locomotor* case can also be observed, exhibiting a more balanced performance.

Table 4. Sensitivity and specificity percentages for test classification

Model	Non-Locomotor		Locomotor	
	Sensitivity	Specificity	Sensitivity	Specificity
Near	98	12	77	52
Mid-Near	12	98	52	77
Near	84	56	73	73
Mid-Near	51	74	70	74
Mid-Far	19	98	47	98
Near	75	60	70	84
Mid-Near	55	60	54	79
Mid-Far	9	97	48	94
Far	5	98	72	91

6 Discussion

In this paper we intended to evaluate self-locomotor experience, related with visual attention, as a parameter that improves distance estimation from binocular disparities, as it was proposed by Campos *et al.* [10]. In this way, we conducted three experiments to evaluate how experience could provide a possible improvement for the estimated distance.

The first experiment analyzed the performance related to the ability to classify two distances for infants without self-locomotion experience, compared with those who have locomotion experience. For the second and the third experiments, it was added one and two intermediate distances respectively, increasing their visual attentional field. We assumed that the experience was related to the amount of images the networks used for training, whereas the visual attention was related to the proportions between different labeled images (different distances). Sensitivity and specificity values showed, for the *Locomotor* BNN, a small reduction in the effectiveness classifying *Near* objects, leading to a significant improvement classifying other objects. Thus, the results suggest that both experience and visual attention turn into a significant difference between the performances of the networks with and without self-locomotion, at the distance estimation task. This may suggest that infants with experience had a better performance in distance estimation.

When more nodes are added to the network, an increase in the initial errors was observed. This is related to the proportions of image misclassification. For instance, in the *Near – Mid-Near* model 88 image pairs were used for test (44 for each label); thus, if the model classifies all the image pairs as *Near*, it will be an error of 50%. On the other hand, in the *Near – Mid-Near – Mid-Far – Far* model, that used 176 image pairs for test, if the model classifies all the image pairs as *Near* it will be an error of 75%.

These experiments also showed a high relative error which could be associated to different error sources, among them the amount of images and/or the relations taken from the study of Gustafson [12], as it was a study conducted on a limited number of infants. Then, the relative relations between locomotor and non-locomotor infants, derived from this study, may be improved.

7   Conclusion and Future Work

This paper highlighted the importance of changes in allocation of attention as a consequence of self-locomotion experience in infants, in order to improve the estimation of distance. Based on this knowledge, this work proposed a computational model to estimate distance from binocular disparities by visual attention and a BNN. Experimental results suggested that, in accordance to the hypothesis, learning to compute distance using locomotion experience and its relation with attention, helped to develop and improve this ability.

Regarding the database used for this evaluation, some issues must be considered. First, in relation to the number of 30-by-30 image pairs, it is advisable to have a bigger database in order to improve the estimation of distance, and then, further work is needed to increase the amount of stereoscopic images. Additionally, in [13], Mann *et al.* obtained different views of a same target, which may be considered as visual experience, given by the motion of the body in the environment. It led them to a variety of images that differ from ours. Hence, integrating motor development into the distance estimation learning model, by a mobile robotic platform, will be part of our future work. Adding a dynamic interaction through a robotic synthetic approach would give us a full implementation of CDR. Moreover, different views from a scene in real time would diversify the database, which is another important issue to be addressed.

On the other hand, it would be interesting to extend the model incorporating maturational constraints related to infants. For example, a monocular acuity of 10 cycles/degree (20/60), stereoacuity of 1 or 2 min of arc, and contrast sensitivity. In vision, perceptual immaturity have been used to enhance learning for cognitive functions [18,19,23]. Hence, adding those constraints could elicit the improvement of distance estimation.

Acknowledgment. We would like to express our gratitude to the Soft and Hard Computing (SHAC) research group from the Universidad Nacional de Colombia, Manizales, for their valuable suggestions for this work. We also thank the Electrical and Electronics Engineering Department, and the Faculty of Engineering and Architecture for its support.

References

1. Asada, M., MacDorman, K.F., Ishiguro, H., Kuniyoshi, Y.: Cognitive developmental robotics as a new paradigm for the design of humanoid robots. Rob. Auton. Syst. **37**, 185–193 (2001)
2. Asada, M., et al.: Cognitive developmental robotics: a survey. IEEE Trans. Auton. Ment. Dev. **1**, 12–34 (2009)
3. Fujikado, T., Approaches, S.: Cognitive Neuroscience Robotics A. Springer, Japan (2016). https://doi.org/10.1007/978-4-431-54595-8
4. Thompson, B., et al.: Global motion perception is associated with motor function in 2-year-old children. Neurosci. Lett. **658**, 177–181 (2017)
5. Cicchino, J.B., Rakison, D.H.: Producing and processing self-propelled motion in infancy. Dev. Psychol. **44**, 1232–1241 (2008)
6. Brand, R.J., Escobar, K., Baranés, A., Albu, A.: Crawling predicts infants' understanding of agents' navigation of obstacles. Infancy **20**, 405–415 (2015)
7. Kubicek, C., Jovanovic, B., Schwarzer, G.: The relation between crawling and 9-month-old infants' visual prediction abilities in spatial object processing. J. Exp. Child Psychol. **158**, 64–76 (2017)
8. Forma, V., Anderson, D.I., Goffinet, F., Barbu-Roth, M.: Effect of optic flows on newborn crawling. Dev. Psychobiol. **60**, 497–510 (2018)
9. Gerhard, T.M., Schwarzer, G.: Impact of rotation angle on crawling and non-crawling 9-month-old infants' mental rotation ability. J. Exp. Child Psychol. **170**, 45–56 (2018)
10. Campos, J.J., Anderson, D.I., Barbu-Roth, M.A., Hubbard, E.M., Hertenstein, M.J., Witherington, D.: Travel broadens the mind. Infancy **1**, 149–219 (2000)
11. Daw, N.W.: Visual Development. Springer, Boston (2014). https://doi.org/10.1007/978-1-4614-9059-3
12. Gustafson, G.E.: Effects of the ability to locomote on infants' social and exploratory behaviors: an experimental study. Dev. Psychol. **20**, 397–405 (1984)

13. Mann, T.A., Park, Y., Jeong, S., Lee, M., Choe, Y.: Autonomous and interactive improvement of binocular visual depth estimation through sensorimotor interaction. IEEE Trans. Auton. Ment. Dev. **5**, 74–84 (2013)
14. Goncalves, N.R., Welchman, A.E.: "What Not" detectors help the brain see in depth. Curr. Biol. **27**, 1403–1412.e8 (2017)
15. Harnad, S.: The symbol grounding problem. Phys. D Nonlinear Phenom. **42**, 335–346 (1990)
16. Nagai, Y.: The role of motion information in learning human-robot joint attention. In: Proceedings-IEEE International Conference on Robotics and Automation 2005, pp. 2069–2074 (2005)
17. Nagai, Y., Hosoda, K., Morita, A., Asada, M.: Emergence of joint attention based on visual attention and self learning. In: Learning, pp. 2–7 (2003)
18. Nagai, Y., Kawai, Y., Asada, M.: Emergence of mirror neuron system: immature vision leads to self-other correspondence. In: 2011 IEEE International Conference Development and Learning, ICDL 2011 (2011)
19. Baraglia, J., Nagai, Y., Kawai, Y., Asada, M.: The role of temporal variance in motions for the emergence of mirror neurons systems. In: 2012 IEEE International Conference on Development and Learning and Epigenetic Robotics, ICDL 2012, pp. 1–2 (2012)
20. Kawai, Y., Nagai, Y., Asada, M.: Perceptual development triggered by its self-organization in cognitive learning. In: 2012 IEEE/RSJ International Conference on Intelligent Robots and Systems, pp. 5159–5164. IEEE (2012)
21. Nagai, Y., Asada, M.: Predictive learning of sensorimotor information as a key for cognitive development. In: Proceedings of the IROS 2015 Workshop on Sensorimotor Contingencies for Robotics (2015)
22. Dodgson, N.A.: Variation and extrema of human interpupillary distance. In: Stereoscopic Displays and Virtual Reality Systems XI, pp. 36–46 (2004)
23. Dominguez, M., Jacobs, R.A.: Developmental constraints aid the acquisition of binocular disparity sensitivities. Neural Comput. **15**, 161–182 (2003)

DCGAN Model Used to Generate Body Gestures on a Human-Humanoid Interaction System

Francisco J. González[1(✉)], Andres Perez-Uribe[2], Hector F. Satizábal[2], and Jesús A. López[1]

[1] Universidad Autónoma de Occidente, Cali, Colombia
{francisco_ja.gonzale,jalopez}@uao.edu.co
[2] University of Applied Sciences Western Switzerland,
Yverdon-les-Bains, Switzerland
{andres.perez-uribe,
hector-fabio.satizabal-mejia}@heig-vd.ch

Abstract. The current availability of the humanoid robots opens up a wide range of applications, for instance, in the domain of hospitality the humanoids can be programmed to behave autonomous ways to provide help to people. The aspect of the humanoids and the humanness of interaction are key components of success. We developed a system to endow the humanoid robot Pepper, from SoftBank Robotics, with the capability of both: identify the emotion state of the humans and exhibiting emotional states via gestures and postures generated using a DCGAN model to learn from the human body language and to create originals body expressions to exhibit like-human movements.

Keywords: Artificial neural networks · Generative adversarial model · Humanoid robots · Human-humanoid interaction

1 Introduction

The advances in the robotics have allowed that it be part of many areas of the human develop, even outside of the manufacture and industrial environment [1], constituting new concepts like social and cognitive robotics, which looking for the development of autonomous devices which can be companions to the human beings [2]. For this reason, the development of the humanoid robots destined to be assistance of sick and elderly people, to increase the interest of learning in the education, and serve as hostess in hotels, malls, airports, restaurants etc. [3] have opened the door to new research fields that include form the design until the develop of interaction tools with the humans.

Within the framework of the research project titled *"DESARROLLO DE UN SISTEMA DE INTERACCION HUMANO-HUMANOIDE A TRAVÉS DEL RECONOCIMIENTO Y APRENDIZAJE DEL LENGUAJE CORPORAL"* [4], which objective was to develop a system with solutions to endow the humanoid robot Pepper, of SoftBank Robotics, with capabilities to: first, identify the mood of the human beings decoding

© Springer Nature Switzerland AG 2019
A. D. Orjuela-Cañón et al. (Eds.): ColCACI 2019, CCIS 1096, pp. 103–115, 2019.
https://doi.org/10.1007/978-3-030-36211-9_9

their body language through the implementation of neural network that classify the body posture (expressed with the orientation of the body's joints gotten used the sensor Kinect V2, and saved in a Euler angles format) in six states: Happy, Sad, Angry, Reflexive, Surprised and a Normal state used to classify all different body gestures that could express an human being and don't belong to one of the another five categories.

Second, to perform speech recognition using algorithms based in neural networks; the system generates answers in natural language (verbal answers) coherent with the mood or the speech detected; complementing to the verbal answers is execute a motion sequences on the robot to express non-verbal messages exhibiting emotional states that can be interpreted by the humans beings with a psychological meaning. The Fig. 1 shows the flowchart of the system.

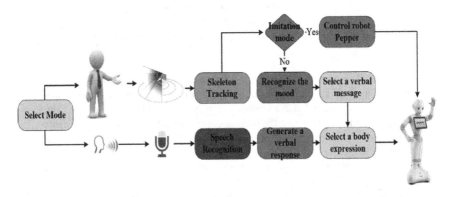

Fig. 1. Flowchart of the system proposed in [4].

This paper is based in the implementation of a **_Deep Convolutional Generative Adversarial Network_** (DCGAN) model generating body gestures through the humanoid Pepper can express emotional states complementing the verbal answers in response to the mood detected or the current speech with the persons. The Sect. 2 explains the theoretical concepts of the GAN model, in the Sect. 3 is showed the methodology used to create the database and the Sect. 5 shows the DC-GAN network designed. The results are showed in the Sect. 5 and finally are described some conclusions of the work proposed in the Sect. 6.

2 Background

The Generative Adversarial Network (GAN) is a relatively new architecture of the neural networks developed by Ian Goodfellow and his coworkers of the University of Montreal in 2014 [5]. The GAN model attends to the non-supervised learning problem, in which the algorithm learns of its mistakes and tries not to reproduce them in the future, implementing two neural networks known as _Generator_ and _Discriminator_; the both compete and collaborate each other to learn how perform their tasks.

The GAN model can be explained how the case of a counterfeiter (Generative Network) and a policeman (Discriminative network). The counterfeiter creates and shows to the policeman "fake money" (the data); the policeman gives to the counterfeiter a feedback saying if the money is real or not. Now, the counterfeiter elaborates new fake data using the information gotten by the policeman, and shows the new fake data to him, the cycle continue until the policeman is cheated by the counterfeiter with a fake data very similar to the real [6].

The train process of the GAN model is performed through a iterative methodology which starts creating fake data using the Generative network, then is trained the Discriminative network using the real data and the fake data created previously; finally is trained the Generative network using the Adversarial model which is the Generative network chained with the Discriminative network, in this step the weights of the Discriminative network don't be modified with the intention that the network can determined if the data is real or not. The Fig. 2 shows the train process described.

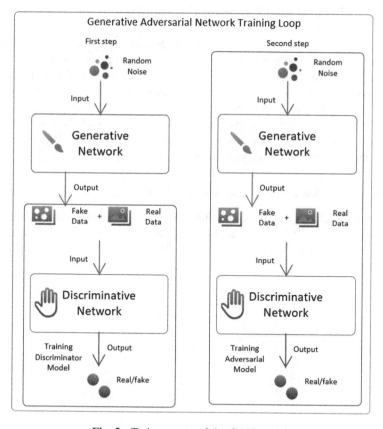

Fig. 2. Train process of the GAN model.

The GAN model can be applied to different neural models, one of them is the DCGAN (see Fig. 3) which takes like input one hundred random numbers with a uniform distribution to draw an image using deconvolutional layers, and then extract features of this images using convolutional and fully connect layers which are components of the *Convolutional Networks* [6].

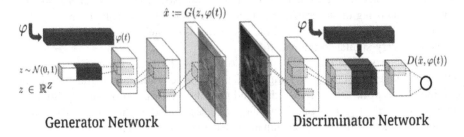

Fig. 3. DCGAN model [6].

3 Data Collection and Creating the Database

Was necessary to create three databases sets to develop the system proposed, one of them used to perform a speech recognition feature with the possible conversations that could take place between the humans and the robot Pepper based in the interaction with personal assistance systems like "Siri" and "Cortana". Also was developed a software tool which, using the sensor Kinect V2 of Microsoft and applying *Skeleton Tracking* allowed to create two databases sets used to train the features of the emotions recognition and to generate body gestures, used to train the DCGAN model, composed by angular values that describe the orientations of the body joints.

3.1 Data Collection Process: Skeleton Tracking

The Skeleton Tracking is an algorithm that can identify gestures and/or body postures [7]. The sensor Kinect V2, can detect the head, neck, elbows, wrists and hands; also, the spin and hips, knees, ankles and feet. See Fig. 4.

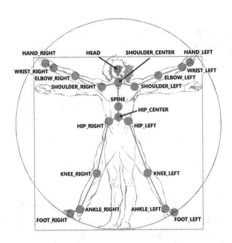

Fig. 4. Body joints detected using skeleton tracking [7].

The process to get the interest data start catching a new color frame in which is looking for one or more bodies, then is selected the nearest body to the sensor to compute the spatial position and the orientation of each body joint saving this information. The process is described with the flowchart of the Fig. 5.

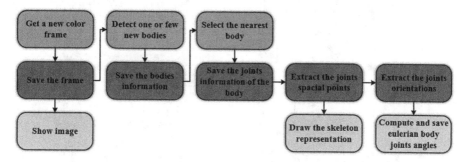

Fig. 5. Skeleton tracking flowchart.

The body detected is represented using the spatial position of each joint, drawing likes (bones) between two contiguous joints. The bones can be green if the joints have been correctly detected or red if one of the haven't been, see Fig. 6.

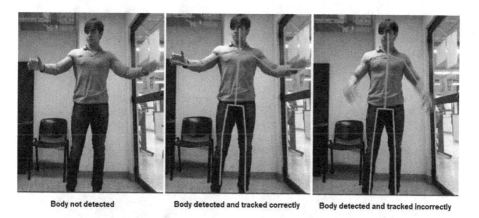

Body not detected   Body detected and tracked correctly   Body detected and tracked incorrectly

Fig. 6. Skeleton tracking representation. (Color figure online)

3.2 Creating Database

Was developed a software tool using python with the wrappers PyQt, pygame and pykinect V2 among others, which were created 32 motion sequences (body gestures) using the Kinect V2 sensor to record and save for a few seconds the Euler angles [Roll, Pitch, Yaw] of the body joints while a human is performing a body gestures, the Fig. 7 shows some of the body gestures expressed by the author and reproduced by the robot

(a)   **(b)**

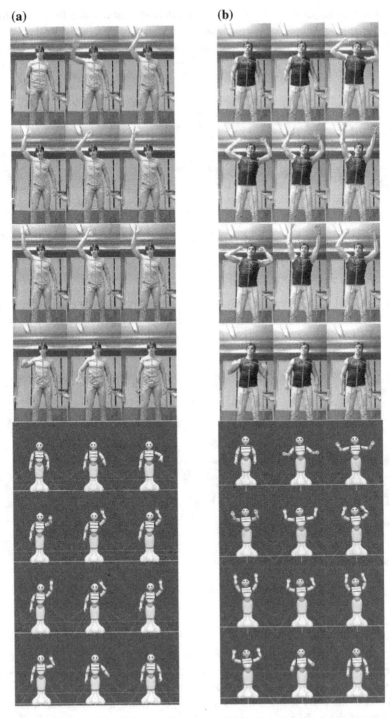

Fig. 7. (a) Body gesture expressing a regard. (b) Body gesture expressing a victory shout

Pepper (in mirror mode reference to the human expressions) using the simulator developed in the software *Choregraphe* designed by SoftBank Robotics to program behaviors on the robot.

The total of angles saved to each motion sequence corresponds to a matrix 40 arrays which get each one has 16 angles, the following Table 1 shows the angles tracked, these angles are corresponding to the Pepper's degrees of freedom. The data saved contains negative and positive values normalized into a distribution between [−1.0, 1.0].

Table 1. Joins angles to control the robot Pepper.

Joint	Roll	Pitch	Yaw
Head		X	= 0
R & L Shoulders	X	X	
R & L Elbow	X		X
R & L Wrist			X
R & L Hand	Close (1.0)/Open (0.0)		
Hip	X	X	

4 Generation of Body Gestures Implementing the DCGAN Model

Was implemented a DCGAN model (see Fig. 8), due to the structure of the data is similar to a gray image, using the advantages of the convolutional layers was easier extract features of the fake and real data to perform the creation of new data similar to the real. The idea to create new motion sequences had as objectives to increase the database of body gestures with the intention to express originality and sensation of spontaneous behavior by the robot performing movements with the same psychological meaning but different in their execution while the interaction with the humans.

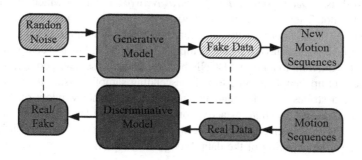

Fig. 8. DCGAN model structure.

4.1 Generative Neural Network

This network synthesizes the fake motion sequences (new body gestures), starting from a 100-dimensional noise with a uniform distribution between [–1.0, 1.0] using the deconvolutional layers. The network designed has four layers and the output, uses a kernel of 4 × 4, the dimension of the data is increased in a factor of two using up-sampling to get better the tuning of the data; with the same factor is decreased the quantity of kernels used, the Fig. 9 shows how is synthesizing the data by the network. Between each layer is used the batch normalization to stabilized the learning, the activation function used is *Hyperbolic Tangent* (tanh) due to the need to have positives and negatives data.

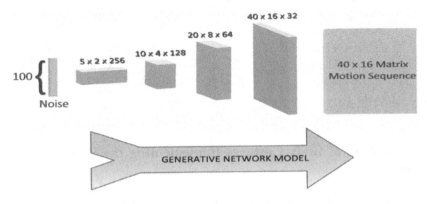

Fig. 9. Generative neural network.

The data created is saved after it has been denormalized multiplying by the maximum value of the real data.

4.2 Discriminative Neural Network

This network is a *Deep Convolutional Neural Network* (DCNN) which decide if the data is real or not. The input is a matrix of 40 × 16 (motion sequence) and the output is determined by the *Sigmoidal* activation function which determine the probability of how real or fake is the data (0.0 means completely fake and 1.0 means completely real). This model is different to a normal DCNN because doesn't use max-pooling, instead of this, implement up-sampling to perform a descending sampling using the same size of the kernel and strides that the Generator network, i.e. kernel window of 4 × 4 and strides of 2. Is used *LeakyRelu* as activation function of the layers (except the output layer) and was implemented dropout between them to prevent the overfitting. The Fig. 10 shows the changing of the data through the network.

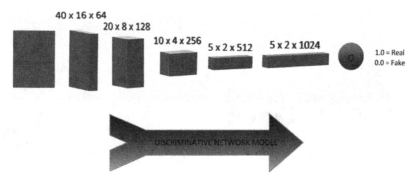

Fig. 10. Discriminative neural network.

4.3   Generative Adversarial Model Training

The both networks, Generative and Discriminative, compose the *Adversarial Model*. To guarantee the correct training of the model is necessary create a second model, the *Discriminative Model* using just the Discriminative Network because is not desired change the weights of this network during the training of the Generative network. The bot models were trained using the *Root Mean Square Backpropagation* (RMSprop) with the parameters showed in the following Table 2.

Table 2. Training parameters of DCGAN model.

Train parameter	Discriminative model	Adversarial model
Learning rate	2e−4	1e−4
Decay	6e−8	3e−8
Loss function: Binary cross entropy	$H(y, \hat{y}) = -\sum_i y_i * log\hat{y}_i - (1 - y_i) * \log(1 - \hat{y}_i)$	

To train the model were copied the 32 original motion sequences to form a 3200 examples dataset. In each iteration were randomly selected 64 examples to try to have different expression to tune the generative network and generate new body expressions similar to the originals.

The Fig. 11 shows the performing of the training which can be conclude that the Discriminative Model starts with a high accuracy classifying the data as real or fake, but at the end of the 1000 epochs it starts to be cheated decreasing its accuracy. On the other hand, the Adversarial Model (in which is trained the Generative Network) goes increasing its accuracy creating data more similar to the real, and also its Loss is decreasing while the develop of the training.

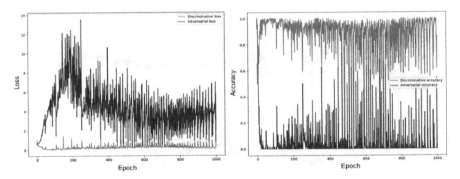

Fig. 11. DCGAN model training – Loss (on the Left) and Accuracy (on the Right).

5   Results

The Fig. 12 shows a comparation of the DCGAN model's performance, gotten in the first epochs sequences of angles values pretty erratic but with the developing of the training were synthesized sequences soft changes. The Fig. 13 shows some examples of the data created by the DCGAN model during the training reproduced by the robot.

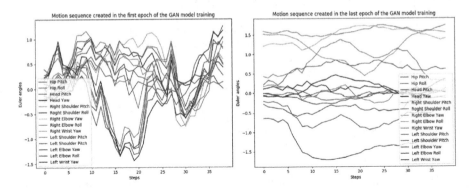

Fig. 12. Data generated in the first epoch (on the left) and in the last epoch (on the right).

The Fig. 14 compares a motion sequences developed by the author and a created by the DCGAN model reproduced by the robot expressing a regard using the right arm (mirror mode) having remarkable differences like the stretching of the arm and inclination of the body.

(a)

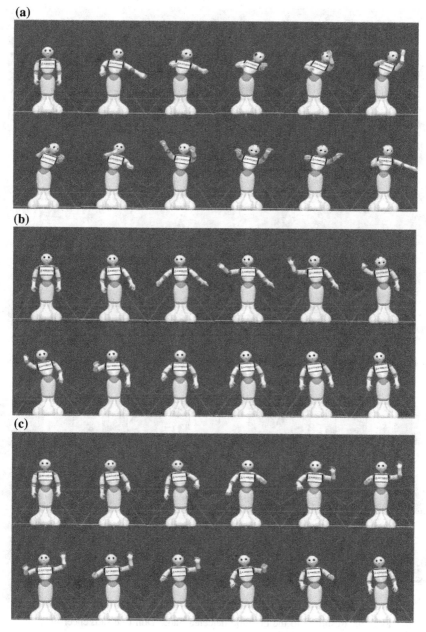

(b)

(c)

Fig. 13. (a) Motion sequences generated in the training epoch 1. (b) Motion sequences generated in the training epoch 700. (c) Motion sequences generated in the training epoch 1000.

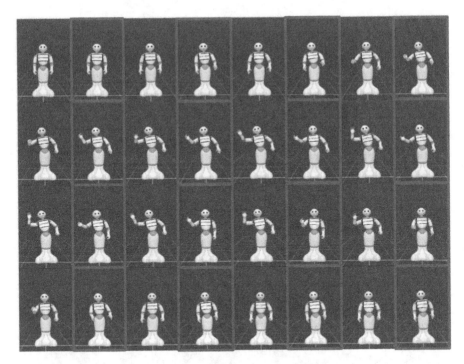

Fig. 14. Real motion sequence vs DCGAN motion sequence (Red frame). (Color figure online)

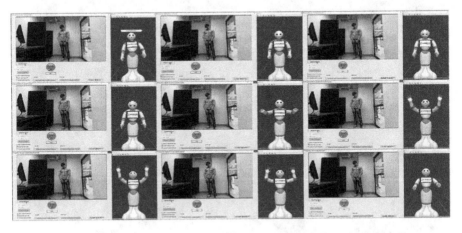

Fig. 15. Response to the emotion detected Sad: "Don't be sad, cheer up".

Finally, the Fig. 15 shows an example of the system using the feature of the emotion recognition generating a response with natural language and body gestures, to be reproduced by the robot, associated with the emotion detected, "Sad" in this case.

6   Conclusions

The motion sequences generated by the GAN model express an equivalent meaning than the motion sequences created by the author, increasing the database with body gestures that have psychological meaning interpreted by the humans beings.

There are differences between the data generated compared to the real data, as was expected and desired, creating motion sequences to give a sensation of spontaneous responses when the robot interact whit the humans beings.

References

1. WordPress.com. Robótica. Aplicación de la robótica. Disponible en: https://nextcomrobotics. wordpress.com/campo-de-aplicacion/aplicacion-de-la-robotica/
2. Raúl, A.M.: Ciencia Cognitiva, IA y Conciencia Artificial. Robótica Cognitiva. Disponible en: http://www.conscious-robots.com/es/2007/08/21/robotica-cognitiva/
3. l'oboticko. Emiex3, robot umanoide che fa l'hostess. Disponible en: https://www.robotiko.it/ emiew3-robot-umanoide-hostess/z
4. González López, F.J.: Desarrollo de un Sistema de Interacción Humano-Humanoide a través del Reconocimiento y Aprendizaje del Lenguaje Corporal. 2018–03-13. Cali, Colombia. Disponible en: http://hdl.handle.net/10614/10162
5. Goodfellow, I.J.: Enerative Adversarial Nets. Université de Montréal. Mibtréal, QC h3C 3J7
6. Karpathy, A.J., et al.: Wojciech Zaremba. Generative Models (2016). Disponible en: https:// blog.openai.com/generative-models/
7. Microsoft Windows. Reto SDK de Kinect: Detectar posturas con skeletal tracking (2011). Disponible en: https://blogs.msdn.microsoft.com/esmsdn/2011/08/09/reto-sdk-de-kinect-detectar-posturas-con-skeletal-tracking/

Social Impact Assessment on a Mining Project in Peru Using the Grey Clustering Method and the Entropy-Weight Method

Alexi Delgado[1](✉), Chiara Carbajal[2], H. Reyes[2], and I. Romero[3]

[1] Pontificia Universidad Católica del Perú – PUCP, Lima, Peru
kdelgadov@pucp.edu.pe
[2] Universidad de Ciencias y Humanidades, Lima, Peru
[3] Universitat Politècnica de València, Valencia, Spain

Abstract. Social impact assessment (SIA) has become a key factor for environmental conflicts prevention. In this study, we conducted SIA using the grey clustering method, which is based on grey systems theory. In addition, the entropy-weight method was applied to determine the most important criterion that could generate a social conflict. A case study was conducted on a mining project located in Cajamarca, Peru. Two stakeholder groups and seven evaluation criteria were identified. The results revealed that for the urban population stakeholder group, the project would have positive social impact; and for the rural population stakeholder group, the project would have negative social impact. In addition, the criterion C7 (Access to drinking water rate per year in the department of Cajamarca) was the most import criterion that could generate a social conflict. Consequently, the method showed quantitative and qualitative results that could help central and local governments to make the best decision on the project. Moreover, the grey clustering method showed interesting results that could be apply to assess other projects or programs from social point of view.

Keywords: Entropy-weight method · Grey clustering · Mining project · Social impact assessment · Social conflict

1 Introduction

On November 29, 2011 there was a clash of interests between the Andean population and the police forces in the department of Cajamarca, Peru, due to the planning of the mining project known as "Conga". From this confrontation dozens of demonstrators were arrested and 15 people were injured, some very seriously as Mr. Elmer Campos, who will remain in a quadriplegic state and wheelchair at 30 years of age [1]. However, the consequences of this mining project did not cease; 4 people died due to this social dispute as a result of the violence in the region [2].

Cajamarca was divided. There was a social group that supported the mining project for various reasons such as the majority economic improvement or increased demand for labor; just as there was an activist group that refused to change, the cry of Conga is not going! However, this division of ideals not only prevailed in Cajamarca, the

A. D. Orjuela-Cañón et al. (Eds.): ColCACI 2019, CCIS 1096, pp. 116–128, 2019.
https://doi.org/10.1007/978-3-030-36211-9_10

Peruvian population adopted two positions, where those who supported the mining project began to treat contemptuously those who rejected it; as well as those who rejected the mining project went against the government and in particular the then president, Ollanta Humala, which caused not only a social but also a political dispute.

Therefore, is needed to indicate that social impact assessment (SIA) is an important factor to prevent environmental conflicts caused by development of projects or programs [3]. In addition, SIA has been mainly conducted by qualitative methods, such as, social impact assessment of earthquakes caused by gas extraction [4] or social impact assessment of land requisition [5]. In this work, we apply the grey clustering method to SIA, which is based on grey systems theory.

The grey clustering method can be applied by incidence matrixes or by whitenization weight functions [6]. In this study, we use the center-point triangular whitenization weight functions (CTWF) method, due to the fact that the CTWF method enables us to classify observed objects into definable classes, called grey classes [6]. Moreover, the CTWF method help us to collect information, as typically people tend to be more certain about the center-points of grey classes in comparison with other points of the grey class. So, the conclusions based on this cognitive certainty could be more scientific and reliable [6].

In addition, SIA is a topic characterized by its high level of uncertainty [7], in this way, SIA should be conducted by a method that considers the uncertainly; in fact, the grey clustering method considers the uncertainty within its analysis, as evidenced by the studies on a water rights allocation system [8], or the classification of innovation strategic alliances [9].

In turn, the stakeholder groups are an important dimension for integrated assessment of projects or programs [10], and environmental conflicts are generated between stakeholder groups within affected population [11, 12]. Therefore, in order to prevent possible environmental conflicts, first SIA should be conducted for each stakeholder group, and then, to analyze total SIA of the project under scrutiny.

Subsequently, in order to apply and test the CTWF method, we conducted the SIA on a mining project in the north of Peru. Therefore, the specific objective of this study is to apply the CTWF method on the SIA of the mining project in Cajamarca, Peru, and to analyze the results. In addition, to determine the most controversial criterion that could generate a possible social conflict the entropy- weight method was applied [13].

Section 2 provides details of the CTWF method to SIA. In Sect. 3 the case study is described, followed by the results and discussion in Sect. 4. Conclusions are provided in Sect. 5.

2   Method

In this section, we described the CTWF method as follows: first, assume that there are a set of m objects, a set of n criteria, and a set of s grey classes, according to the sample value x_{ij} (i = 1, 2,..., m; j = 1, 2, ..., n). Then, the steps of the CTWF method can be described as follows [9, 13]:

Step 1: The intervals of the criteria are divided into s grey classes, and then their center-points λ_1, λ_2... and λ_s are determined.

Step 2: The grey classes are expanded in two directions, adding the grey classes 0 and (s + 1) with their center-points λ_0 and λ_{s+1}, respectively. The new sequence of center-points is $\lambda_0, \lambda_1, \lambda_2$... λs, and λ_{s+1}, see details in Fig. 1. For the kth grey class, k = 1, 2... s, of the jth criterion, j = 1, 2... n, for an observed value x_{ij}, the CTWF is defined by Eq. 1.

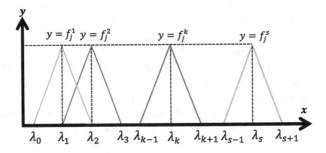

Fig. 1. CTWF functions.

$$f_j^k(x_{ij}) = \begin{cases} 0, & x \notin [\lambda_{k-1}, \lambda_{k+1}] \\ \frac{x - \lambda_{k-1}}{\lambda_k - \lambda_{k-1}}, & x \in [\lambda_{k-1}, \lambda_k] \\ \frac{\lambda_{k+1} - x}{\lambda_{k+1} - \lambda_k}, & x \in [\lambda_k, \lambda_{k+1}] \end{cases} \tag{1}$$

Step 3: The comprehensive clustering coefficient σ_i^k for object i, i = 1, 2... m, in the grey class k, k = 1, 2... s, is calculated by Eq. 2.

$$\sigma_i^k = \sum_{j=1}^n f_j^k(x_{ij}) . \eta_j \tag{2}$$

Where $f_j^k(x_{ij})$ is the CTWF of the kth grey class of the jth criterion, and η_j is the weight of criterion j.

Step 4: If $\max_{1 \le k \le s} \{\sigma_i^k\} = \sigma_i^{k*}$, we decide that object i belongs to grey class k*. When there are several objects in grey class k*, these objects can be ordered according to the magnitudes of their comprehensive clustering coefficients [6].

3 Case Study

As it was mentioned before, SIA was conducted on a mining project located in the department of Cajamarca in Peru, as shown in Fig. 2. The mining company, commonly called Yanacocha [1], planes to conduct a mining process in 19 years, including 2 years of construction and 17 years of operation. The standard annual operation of the mining project entails a very intensive use of water [14]. SIA was conducted on the zone of influence of the project, which is composed of urban areas and rural areas. As an additional information, the mining company has been operating for more than 20 years in the department of Cajamarca, and its relationship with a part of the population has not been good.

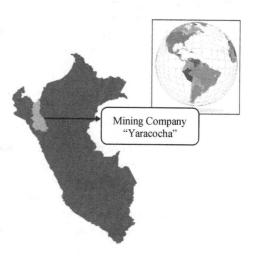

Fig. 2. Mining project location

3.1 Stakeholder Groups

In this study, we identified two different stakeholder groups, the composition of these groups was determined according to similarities found during the overall assessment on the hydrocarbon exploration project. The sample size in each group was determined by means the principle of saturation of discourse, which establish that information gathering should end when respondents do not produce new information relevant to object of study [15]. The stakeholder groups are presented in Table 1:

Table 1. Stakeholder groups in the case study.

Stakeholder group	Description
G1: Urban population	This group was composed by citizens from urban areas into influence area of the project. This group was made up of one hundred and five interviewees
G2: Rural population	This group was composed by citizens from rural areas into influence area of the project. This group was made up of ninety-five interviewees

3.2 Evaluation Criteria

The criteria for the case study were established by taking into account to the economic and social situation of the urban and rural areas of the influence area of the mining project in Cajamarca, Peru. According to situation of the project and the characteristics of the stakeholder groups, we established criteria taking into account the economic primary activities developed in to influence area, such as, trade, agriculture, livestock, and activities that demands to intensive use of water. Therefore, in this study, seven criteria (n = 7) were identified as shown in Table 2.

Table 2. Evaluation criteria in the case study.

Criterion	Description
C1	GDP per capita as soles per month in the department of Cajamarca
C2	Employment rate per year in the department of Cajamarca
C3	Poverty rate per year in the region
C4	Number of inhabitants per doctor (GP) per year in the department of Cajamarca
C5	Enrolment rate in primary education in the region
C6	Number of reported crimes per year in the department of Cajamarca
C7	Access to drinking water rate per year in the department of Cajamarca

In order to know social impact assessment from the mining project, we applied a structured questionnaire, which had five grey classes: S_1 = Decrease noticeably, S_2 = Decrease, S_3 = No effect, S_4 = Increase, and S_5 = Increase noticeably; which $S_1 = [0;2 >$, $S_2 = [2;4 >$, $S_3 = [4;6 >$, $S_4 = [6;8 >$, and $S_5 = [8;10]$. The questionnaire is presented in Table 3.

Table 3. Questions used in the case study.

Questions		Grey classes				
C_1	What effect would the project have on the economic income per person?	S1	S2	S3	S4	S5
C_2	What effect would the project have on the employment rate?	S1	S2	S3	S4	S5
C_3	What effect would the project have on the poverty rate?	S5	S4	S3	S2	S1
C_4	What effect would the project have on the number of inhabitants per doctor (GP)?	S5	S4	S3	S2	S1
C_5	What effect would the project have on the enrolment rate in primary education?	S1	S2	S3	S4	S5
C_6	What effect would the project have on the number of reported crimes?	S5	S4	S3	S2	S1
C_7	What effect would the project have on the access to drinking water?	S1	S2	S3	S4	S5

Then, the information recollected from stakeholder groups was aggregated using the arithmetic mean [16]. The overall results, for each criterion (C_j), are presented in Table 4.

Table 4. Information collected from stakeholder groups.

Group	C_1	C_2	C_3	C_4	C_5	C_6	C_7
G1	8.09	8.31	1.63	3.34	6.54	3.69	8.43
G2	1.97	2.60	8.03	6.26	3.80	6.20	1.57
Total	5.03	5.46	4.83	4.80	5.17	4.94	5.00

3.3 Calculations Using the CTWF Method

The calculations for the case study, based on the CTWF method, are preceded as follows.

Step 1:

The center-points $\lambda 1$, $\lambda 2$, $\lambda 3$, $\lambda 4$, and $\lambda 5$, of five grey classes were determined as shown in Table 5.

Table 5. Center-points of grey classes in the case study.

S_1	S_2	S_3	S_4	S_5
[0;2>	[2;4>	[4;6>	[6;8>	[8;10]
$\lambda_1 = 1$	$\lambda_2 = 3$	$\lambda_3 = 5$	$\lambda_4 = 7$	$\lambda_5 = 9$

Step 2:

The grey classes were extended in two directions by adding the grey classes S_0 and S_6, respectively, with their center-points λ_0 and λ_6; as shown in Table 6 and Fig. 3.

Table 6. Center-points of the extended grey classes.

Center-points of the extended grey classes						
λ_0	λ_1	λ_2	λ_3	λ_4	λ_5	λ_6
0	1	3	5	7	9	10

Now, the values presented in Table 4 were substituted into Eq. 1, to obtain the CTWF of the five grey classes. The results are shown in Eqs. 3–7:

$$f_j^1(x) = \begin{cases} 0, & x \notin [0, 3] \\ \frac{x-0}{1}, & x \in [0, 1] \\ \frac{3-x}{2}, & x \in [1, 3] \end{cases} \tag{3}$$

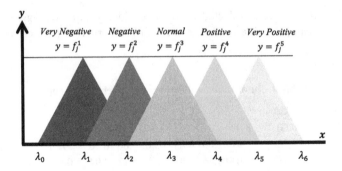

Fig. 3. CTWF for the case study

$$f_j^2(x) = \begin{cases} 0, & x \notin [1,5] \\ \frac{x-1}{2}, & x \in [1,3] \\ \frac{5-x}{2}, & x \in [3,5] \end{cases} \tag{4}$$

$$f_j^3(x) = \begin{cases} 0, & x \notin [3,7] \\ \frac{x-3}{2}, & x \in [3,5] \\ \frac{7-x}{2}, & x \in [5,7] \end{cases} \tag{5}$$

$$f_j^4(x) = \begin{cases} 0, & x \notin [5,9] \\ \frac{x-5}{2}, & x \in [5,7] \\ \frac{9-x}{2}, & x \in [7,9] \end{cases} \tag{6}$$

$$f_j^5(x) = \begin{cases} 0, & x \notin [7,10] \\ \frac{x-7}{2}, & x \in [7,9] \\ \frac{10-x}{1}, & x \in [9,10] \end{cases} \tag{7}$$

Then, the values from Table 4 were replaced into Eqs. 3–7, to calculate the CTWF values of each criterion. The results are shown in Tables 7, 8, and 9.

Table 7. Values of CTWF for each criterion of G1.

C_j	C_1	C_2	C_3	C_4	C_5	C_6	C_7
f_j^1	0.00	0.00	0.00	0.00	0.00	0.00	0.00
f_j^2	0.00	0.00	0.00	0.00	0.00	0.00	0.00
f_j^3	0.00	0.00	0.00	0.17	0.23	0.34	0.00
f_j^4	0.46	0.34	0.31	0.83	0.77	0.66	0.29
f_j^5	0.54	0.66	0.69	0.00	0.00	0.00	0.71

Table 8. Values of CTWF for each criterion of G2.

C_j	C_1	C_2	C_3	C_4	C_5	C_6	C_7
f_j^1	0.51	0.20	0.51	0.00	0.00	0.00	0.71
f_j^2	0.49	0.80	0.49	0.63	0.60	0.60	0.29
f_j^3	0.00	0.00	0.00	0.37	0.40	0.40	0.00
f_j^4	0.00	0.00	0.00	0.00	0.00	0.00	0.00
f_j^5	0.00	0.00	0.00	0.00	0.00	0.00	0.00

Table 9. Values of CTWF for each criterion of total.

C_j	C_1	C_2	C_3	C_4	C_5	C_6	C_7
f_j^1	0.51	0.20	0.51	0.00	0.00	0.00	0.71
f_j^2	0.49	0.80	0.49	0.63	0.60	0.60	0.29
f_j^3	0.00	0.00	0.00	0.37	0.40	0.40	0.00
f_j^4	0.00	0.00	0.00	0.00	0.00	0.00	0.00
f_j^5	0.00	0.00	0.00	0.00	0.00	0.00	0.00

Step 3:

The comprehensive clustering coefficient (σ_i^k) was calculated using Eq. 2. All the criteria had the same weight ($\eta_j = 0.143$), as they are social criteria [15]. The values of σ_i^k obtained are shown in Table 10.

Table 10. Values of σ_i^k in the case study.

	G1	G2	Total
$f_j^1(x)$	0.0000	0.2776	0.0000
$f_j^2(x)$	0.0000	0.5551	0.0000
$f_j^3(x)$	0.1061	0.1673	0.9224
$f_j^4(x)$	0.5224	0.0000	0.0776
$f_j^5(x)$	0.3714	0.0000	0.0000

Step 4:

For G1, $\max\limits_{1 \le k \le s} \{\sigma_i^k\} = 0.5224$ where k = 4. Therefore, G1 belongs to positive grey class.

For G2, $\max\limits_{1 \le k \le s} \{\sigma_i^k\} = 0.5551$ where k = 2. Therefore, G2 belongs to negative grey class.

For Total SIA, $\max_{1 \leq k \leq s} \{\sigma_i^k\} = 0.9224$ where k = 3. Therefore, Total SIA belongs to normal grey class.

4 Results and Discussion

In Table 11, the results are presented, according to the steps of the CTWF method.

Table 11. Results for each stakeholder group.

Stakeholder group	$\max_{1 \leq k \leq s} \{\sigma_i^k\}$	Social impact
G1	0.5224	Positive
G2	0.5551	Negative
Total SIA	0.9224	Normal

Then the discussion, according to specific objective in this study, are presented as follows:

4.1 The Case Study

First, the total SIA of the mining project shown that it would have a normal social impact, which indicate that the project will not generate environmental damages or negative social impacts as the affected population opined. In contrast, there is an antagonism between groups G1 (urban population), which statement that the project would have a positive social impact; and G2 (rural population), which opined that the project would a negative social impact.

Second, the urban population stakeholder group (G1) considered that the criterion C7 (access to drinking water) would have a very positive social impact ($\sigma_i^k = 0.71$), as the mining company established within the environmental impact assessment (EIA) that will construct four water reservoirs to supply all water the population could need [17].

Third, contrarily, the rural population stakeholder group (G2) considered that the criterion C7 (access to drinking water) would have a very negative social impact ($\sigma_i^k = 0.71$), as the rural population strongly believe that the mining company generate environmental pollution on water, and this fact will make that the population will not have drinking water in the future [18].

4.2 The CTWF Method

Social impact assessment is a topic that has high level of uncertainty, and it should be analysed by methods that consider the uncertainty within its analysis. In addition, the CTWF method considers the uncertainty, this fact is an advantage with respect to some classical approaches of multi-criteria analysis, such as Delphi [19, 20] or analytic hierarchy process (AHP) [21, 22], as they do not consider the uncertainty within their analysis, due to the fact that the importance degree of criteria and performance scores of alternatives are assumed to be known precisely [23].

In turn, from statistical approaches the concept of large sample represents the degree of tolerance to incompleteness [6, 24], and considering that one of the criteria to evaluate methods can be the cost [7, 11]; then, an approach based in grey systems would have a lower cost with respect to statistical approach, as sample size influences on the cost during the field work.

Consequently, it could be argued that the CTWF method, based on grey systems theory, would benefit to SIA, as it considers the uncertainty within its analysis, and would have a lower cost than other statistical approaches during its application.

In addition, the entropy-weight method was applied to determine the most controversial criterion that could generate a possible social conflict. The steps of the entropy-weight method are described as follows [13]:

Definition 1: Assume that there are 'm' objects for evaluation and 'n' evaluation criteria, which form the decision matrix $Z = \{z_{ij}; i = 1, 2, \ldots, m; j = 1, 2, \ldots, n\}$. Then, the steps of the entropy-weight method can be expressed as follows:

Step 1: The matrix $X = \{x_{ij}; i = 1, 2, \ldots, m; j = 1, 2, \ldots, n\}$ is normalized for each criterion C_j. The normalized values P_{ij} are calculated by Eq. 2.

$$P_{ij} = \frac{x_{ij}}{\sum_{i=1}^{m} x_{ij}} \tag{8}$$

Step 2: The entropy H_j of each criterion C_j is calculated by Eq. 3 which was constructed from Eq. 1.

$$H_j = -k \sum_{i=1}^{m} P_{ij} \ln(P_{ij}) \tag{9}$$

Step 3: The degree of divergence div_j of the intrinsic information in each criterion C_j is calculated by Eq. 4.

$$div_j = 1 - e_j \tag{10}$$

Step 4: The entropy weight w_j of each criterion C_j is calculated by Eq. 5.

$$w_{ij} = \frac{div_j}{\sum_{i=1}^{m} div_j} \tag{11}$$

Now, from Table 4, the decision matrix was obtained for G1 and G2, then Eqs. 8–11 were applied. The results are presented in Table 12.

Table 12. Results of the entropy-weight method.

	C1	C2	C3	C4	C5	C6	C7
H_j	0.7135	0.7922	0.6548	0.9322	0.9487	0.9530	0.6271
div_j	0.2865	0.2078	0.3452	0.0678	0.0513	0.0470	0.3729
w_{ij}	0.21	0.15	0.25	0.05	0.04	0.03	0.27

From Table 12, we can see that the most important criterion that could generate a possible social conflict was C7 (Access to drinking water rate per year in the department of Cajamarca). Therefore, the local and national authorities from Peru, and the company should make decisions on this criterion, in order to prevent a possible social conflict.

5   Conclusions

The CTWF method showed to be useful during its application on social impact assessment of mining company in Peru. The results obtained in this study could help to central government or local authorities to make the best decision about the project.

The CTWF method would have as main advantage to be more effective than other classical multi-criteria methods, as it considers uncertainty within its analysis; in addition, the CTWF method would have a lower cost than other statistical approaches during its application, as it needs small sample size. Moreover, the main limitation of the CTWF method could be that the approaches based on grey systems are not widely diffused compared to approaches based on multi-criteria analysis or statistics models; in addition, the calculations from the CTWF are still tedious, this fact could be improved by implementing of an information system. In addition, according to the results, the project, in Cajamarca, Peru, would have a normal social impact, that conclusion is made with the total SIA obtained with the applied method (grey clustering). However, there is a difference between the groups G1 and G2, take into account the unbalance between rural (G2) and urban (G1) population. In addition, the most controversial criterion that could generate a possible social conflict would be C7 (Access to drinking water rate per year in the department of Cajamarca).

Finally, the CTWF method could be tested and applied to assess social impact of others project or programs, such as infrastructure projects, protected areas projects, governmental political programs, etc.

References

1. Grufides.org. Conflicto conga: tercera etapa del juicio contra mando policiales y minera Yanacocha por herir gravemente a campesinos/as durante manifestación del 29 de noviembre 2011 (2018). https://www.ocmal.org/conflicto-conga-tercera-etapa-del-juicio-contra-mando-policiales-y-minera-yanacocha-por-herir-gravemente-a-campesinos-as-durante-manifestacion-del-29-de-noviembre-2011/. Accedido 12 Jun 2019. Prenzel, P.V., Vanclay, F.: How social impact assessment can contribute to conflict management. Environ. Impact Assess. Rev. **45**, 30–37 (2014)

2. Fowks, J.: Oro contra agua en Perú. El País, 28 July 2012
3. Prenzel, P.V., Vanclay, F.: How social impact assessment can contribute to conflict management. Environ. Impact Assess. Rev. **45**, 30–37 (2014)
4. Van der Voort, N., Vanclay, F.: Social impacts of earthquakes caused by gas extraction in the Province of Groningen, The Netherlands. Environ. Impact Assess. Rev. **50**, 1–15 (2015). https://doi.org/10.1016/j.eiar.2014.08.008
5. Tang, B., Wong, S., Lau, M.C.: Social impact assessment and public participation in China: a case study of land requisition in Guangzhou. Environ. Impact Assess. Rev. **28**, 57–72 (2008). https://doi.org/10.1016/j.eiar.2007.03.004
6. Liu, S., Lin, Y.: Grey Systems: Theory and Applications. Springer, Heidelberg (2010). https://doi.org/10.1007/978-3-642-16158-2
7. Wittmer, H., Rauschmayer, F., Klauer, B.: How to select instruments for the resolution of environmental conflicts? Land Policy **23**, 1–9 (2006). https://doi.org/10.1016/j.landusepol.2004.09.003
8. Zhang, L.N., Wu, F.P., Jia, P.: Grey evaluation model based on reformative triangular whitenization weight function and its application in water rights allocation system. Open Cybern. Syst. J. **7**, 1–10 (2013)
9. Zhang, Y., Ni, J., Liu, J., Jian, L.: Grey evaluation empirical study based on center-point triangular whitenization weight function of Jiangsu Province industrial technology innovation strategy alliance. Grey Syst. Theory Appl. **4**, 124–136 (2014)
10. Hamilton, S.H., ElSawah, S., Guillaume, J.H.A., Jakeman, A.J., Pierce, S.A.: Integrated assessment and modelling: overview and synthesis of salient dimensions. Environ. Model Softw. **64**, 215–229 (2015). https://doi.org/10.1016/j.envsoft.2014.12.005
11. Arun, E.: Towards a shared systems model of stakeholders in environmental conflict. Int. Trans. Oper. Res. **15**, 239–253 (2008)
12. Luyet, V., Schlaepfer, R., Parlange, M.B., Buttler, A.: A framework to implement stakeholder participation in environmental projects. J. Environ. Manag. **111**, 213–219 (2012)
13. Delgado, A., Romero, I.: Applying grey systems and shannon entropy to social impact assessment and environmental conflict analysis. Int. J. Appl. Eng. Res. **12**, 973–4562 (2017)
14. Delgado, A.: Social conflict analysis on a mining project using shannon entropy. In: 2017 IEEE XXIV International Conference on Electronics, Electrical Engineering and Computing (INTERCON), pp. 1–4. IEEE (2017)
15. Corbetta, P.: Metodología y técnicas de investigación social. McGRAW-HILL, Madrid (2007)
16. Aznar, J., Guijarro, F.: Nuevos métodos de valoración, modelos multicriterio, vol. 2a. Universitat Politèctica de València, Valencia (2012)
17. Piésold, K.: Estudio de Impacto Ambiental del Proyecto Conga. Minera Yanacocha S.R.L., Perú (2010)
18. Sánchez, W.: Por qué el proyecto conga es inviable? Universidad Nacional de Cajamarca, Cajamarca (2011)
19. Landeta, J.: El método Delphi, Una técnica de previsión del futuro. Editorial Ariel, Barcelona (2002)
20. Campos-Climent, V., Apetrei, A., Chaves-Ávila, R.: Delphi method applied to horticultural cooperatives. Manag. Decis. **50**, 1266–1284 (2012). https://doi.org/10.1108/00251741211247003
21. Saaty, T.L.: The Analytic Hierarchy Process. McGraw-Hill, New York (1980)
22. Sadeghi, M., Ameli, A.: An AHP decision making model for optimal allocation of energy subsidy among socio-economic subsectors in Iran. Energy Policy **45**, 24–32 (2012)

23. Baykasoğlu, A., Gölcük, İ.: Development of a novel multiple-attribute decision making model via fuzzy cognitive maps and hierarchical fuzzy TOPSIS. Inf. Sci. **301**, 75–98 (2015). https://doi.org/10.1016/j.ins.2014.12.048
24. Delgado, A.: Why do any secondary students prefer the mathematics? A response using grey systems. In: Proceedings of the 2017 International Symposium on Engineering Accreditation, ICACIT 2017 (2018)
25. Delgado, A., Vriclizar, D., Medina, E.: Artificial intelligence model based on grey systems to assess water quality from Santa river watershed. In: Proceedings of the 2017 Electronic Congress, E-CON UNI 2017, vol. 2018-Janua (2018)

Image Processing

Classification of Satellite Images Using Rp Fuzzy C Means

Luis Mantilla[✉] [ID]

Universidad Católica de Trujillo Benedicto XVI, Trujillo, Peru
l.mantillas@uct.edu.pe

Abstract. The computational capacities increase, the decrease of equipment costs, the growing need for information, among other reasons; It makes possible the increasingly common access to satellite data. In this context. The investigation of techniques related to remote sensing becomes very important because it provide important information about the earth's surface. Currently, segmentation is an essential step in applications that make use of satellite images. However, the main problem is: "the data in a multispectral image shows a low statistical separation and a long quantity of data". In this article we propose to improve the balancing of elements for the clusters. We use a new term to estimate the influence that each element must have for the each cluster. This new term can be understood as a repulsion factor and aims to increase the differences between groups. This modification is inspired by new term that was integrated into the NFCC algorithm (New Fuzzy Centroid Cluster).

For the tests, we use the internal validity of the cluster to compare the algorithms. Using the index we measure the characteristics of the segmentation and corroborate them with the final visual results. Therefore, we conclude that the addition of this new term allows balancing the elements for each group. As a result we conclude that the new term organizes the elements better because it avoids a fast convergence of the algorithm. Finally, the results show that this new factor generates clusters with lower entropy and greater similarity between the elements.

Keywords: Segmentation · Fuzzy clustering · Unsupervised classification · Multispectral images

1 Introduction

Remote sensing is defined as the use of different sensors to take measurements of an object or phenomenon without physical contact, usually remote sensing is understood as taking measurements of the earth using satellites or air crafts [15]. The data captured by satellites and air crafts is stored in form of a matrix called band, it contains measurements of light spectrum on an exact range and coordinates. A set of bands to the same square area is called multispectral image. The operations between bands are called *index* it help us to know a specific material in the land [16]. This is normally applied with another techniques to

© Springer Nature Switzerland AG 2019
A. D. Orjuela-Cañón et al. (Eds.): ColCACI 2019, CCIS 1096, pp. 131–142, 2019.
https://doi.org/10.1007/978-3-030-36211-9_11

make a methodology to remote sensing [26]. Currently remote sensing is applied on different areas such as cartography, remote sensing [13], target detection [4], hydrology, farming [16], natural disasters [10], etc.

The segmentation is principal step in any application that make use of remote sensing data [17], it separates the data in groups with similar characteristics. The segmentation methods can be either supervised or unsupervised. Supervised methods require previously classified data (training data set) to generate data separation making use of mathematical structures. Unsupervised methods not require classified data, it use mathematical mechanisms to divide the data into a groups taking account similarity measures like as l_1, l_2 norm.

Unsupervised algorithms are a good option to segmenting data because those do not need previously classified information. This is the main advantage however these algorithms only will organize the data in clusters using a similarity measure between each sample of the data. These methods only organize the data without spatial, inhomogeneity, corrupt and another information that help the segmentation work [25].

The most studied algorithm is the Fuzzy C-Means (FCM). It was created on 1973 by J.C. Dunn and improve by J.C. Bezdek in 1981 [6]. This algorithm present the principal steps to fuzzy clustering and high accuracy [5,7,9] or similar accuracy in relation with another algorithms specifically such as Support Vector Machine (SVM) [20]. Many improvements were made to this algorithm [2,3, 12,18,19,24], propose the transformation of RGB to Hue Saturation and Value (HSV) [1]. Transform the data to a mathematical signal [10,23], integrate spatial information and variants that integrate Markov Random Fields (MRF) to the FCM model [26], and also there are new proposed models that integrate another measures such as New Fuzzy Centroid Cluster (NFCC) [11].

In this article, we propose the integration of a new term in the FCM algorithm. This term is based on the NFCC [11] algorithm. The main reason is that the NFCC algorithm integrates a new measure that aims to improve segmentation. The FCM algorithm lacks this characteristic and it is crucial in the segmentation of data that present little statistical separation and many elements.

The rest of this paper is organizer as follow: In the Sect. 2, we briefly review the fundamentals for unsupervised fuzzy clustering the FCM and NFCC algorithm. In Sect. 3, we describe the integration of repulsion term in FCM algorithm. In Sect. 4, the experiments are applied to each fuzzy clustering algorithm and the results be compared to measure. Finally In Sect. 5, conclusions are drawn.

2   Fuzzy Clustering

Fuzzy techniques grouping the class of grouping algorithms that use the fuzzy partition concept. A diffuse partition is characterized by the presence of a degree of membership of each element to all the existing groups. This is schematized in Fig. 1. In addition we present the terminology necessary for the next sections.

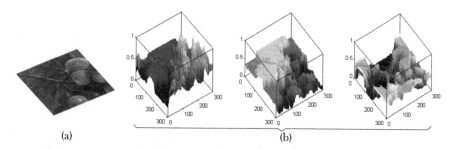

Fig. 1. This image graphically represents the concept of fuzzy membership. (a) The test image contained in x and z axes. (b) The membership degree $u_{ji} \in [0,1]$ of each pixel with respect to each of the three groups is represented on the vertical axis.

- m is the exponent.
- c is the cluster number.
- $\|x_j - v_i\|_2$ is the Euclidean distance between the centroid of the cluster $v_i = (v_{i1}, v_{i2}, ..., v_{ik}) \in R^k$ and the sample of the data $x_j = (x_{j1}, x_{j2}, ..., x_{jk}) \in R^k$.
- X_{nk} is the multispectral image, $k = |$ bands $|$ and $n = |$ samples $|$.
- $u_{ji} \in [0,1], 1 \le j \le n, 1 \le i \le c$ is the membership relation between each sample and cluster, $\sum_{i=1}^{c} u_{ji} = 1, j = 1, 2, 3, ..., n,$ and $0 < \sum_{j=1}^{n} u_{ji} < n, i = 1, 2, 3, ..., c$.
- $\varepsilon_j, j = 1, 2, 3, ..., n$ is a value related to x_j and v_i.

2.1   New Fuzzy Cluster Centroid (NFCC)

This algorithm was proposed by Genitha in [11]. This model add a new term to improve the membership calculation. The objective function to minimize is shown in Eq. (1).

$$J_{NFCC} = \sum_{i=1}^{c} \sum_{j=1}^{n} u_{ij}^m \|x_j - v_i\|^2 + \sum_{j=1}^{n} \varepsilon_j \sum_{i=1}^{c} (u_{ij} - 1), \tag{1}$$

2.2   Fuzzy C-Means (FCM)

FCM is called the generalization of crisp c-means algorithm and the main characteristic is the use of membership degree like a mechanism for clustering. The objective function to be minimized with the FCM algorithm is shown in Eq. (2).

$$J_{fcm}(U, V) = \sum_{i=1}^{c} \sum_{j=1}^{n} (u_{ji})^m \|x_j - v_i\|^2, (m > 1) \tag{2}$$

The usual minimization of the objectives function consist of two parts: the calculation of centroids Eq. (3) and the membership calculation Eq. (4). The answers are successive in order to achieve the convergence of the solutions [6].

$$v_i = \frac{\sum_{j=1}^{n} (u_{ji})^m x_j}{\sum_{j=1}^{n}} \tag{3}$$

$$u_{ij} = \frac{1}{\sum_{k=1}^{c} \left(\frac{||x_j - u_i||}{||x_j - u_k||}\right)^{\frac{2}{m-1}}}. \tag{4}$$

Analysis. The analysis of the degree of membership Eq. (4) for the FCM algorithm is considered an essential part of the study carried out. For this, we denote the Gaussian distance between x_j and v_i as $d_{ji} = ||x_j - v_i||$ and c is an undetermined number of clusters. i.e.

$$u_{ij} = \frac{1}{\sum_{k=1}^{c} \left(\frac{||x_j - u_i||}{||x_j - u_k||}\right)^{\frac{2}{m-1}}},$$

$$u_{ij} = \frac{1}{\left(\frac{d_{ji}}{d_{j1}}\right)^{\frac{2}{m-1}} + \left(\frac{d_{ji}}{d_{j2}}\right)^{\frac{2}{m-1}} + \cdots + \left(\frac{d_{ji}}{d_{jc}}\right)^{\frac{2}{m-1}}},$$

$$u_{ij} = \frac{1}{d_{ji}^{\frac{2}{m-1}} * \left(\frac{1}{d_{j1}^{\frac{2}{m-1}}}\right) + \left(\frac{1}{d_{j2}^{\frac{2}{m-1}}}\right) + \cdots + \left(\frac{1}{d_{jc}^{\frac{2}{m-1}}}\right)}. \tag{5}$$

Part of the previous analysis we can establish that the determining factor in the calculation of the degree of belonging is the distance d_{ji}. This is evidenced in the Eq. (5) and it results in the high influence of the distance between the elements.

3   Our Proposal (Rp Fuzzy C-Means)

3.1   Repulsion Factor Integration

As result of previous study of fuzzy clustering algorithms arise the need to study the possibility of integrating a factor that balancing the membership function. This new factor is conceived as a repulsion factor of the samples furthest away from its centroid. The idea is discriminating the influence of elements much further away of a centroid due those must have a lower ability to change groups compared to the closest elements. This idea is schematized in the Fig. 2. For the calculation of this new factor we propose the Eq. (6).

$$T_{ij} = \left(\frac{1}{1 + ||x_j - c_i||_2}\right) \tag{6}$$

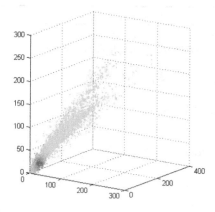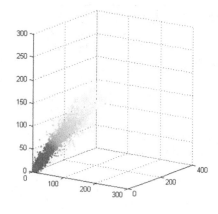

(a) Schematization of the influence of the elements calculated according to the calculation of the usual degree of membership Eq. (4).

(b) Schematization of the influence of the elements calculated according to the proposed repulsion factor Eq. (6).

Fig. 2. With these images we outline the influence of each element in the calculation of the degree of membership. To do this we take a usual scattering of the data contained in an image and the color is added in order to show the influence.

3.2 Repulsion Factor Integration

To mix the results of both terms we propose the use of the Eq. (7). Which performs the multiplication of the term and the membership function of FCM, followed by normalization.

$$u_{ij} = \frac{\frac{1}{\left(\sum_{k=1}^{c} \|x_j - c_i\|_2^2\right)} * T_{ij}}{\sum_{l=1}^{c} \left(\frac{1}{\left(\sum_{k=1}^{c} \|x_j - c_l\|_2^2\right)} * T_{lj}\right)} \tag{7}$$

As a result of the previous steps we present the Algorithm 1. This presents the sequence of steps conceived for the minimization of Eq. (2).

4 Experimental Result and Analysis

4.1 Experimental Data

The set of images used in the experiments consists of 20 multispectral images RapidEye of size 837×837 pixels. Each image contains 5 bands, each pixel represents an area of $5\,m \times 5\,m$, and the gray values present in each band have values between 0 and 2^{16}.

Algorithm 1. Rp Fuzzy C-Means

Require: $c > 1$ cluster number, $x_j = (x_{j1}, x_{j2}, ..., x_{jk}) \in R^k$, $X_{nk} \in R^{nk}$ is a matrix to multidimensional image with $k = |\text{bands}|$ and $n = |\text{samples}|$, $error > 0$.

Ensure:

$$U = [u_{ij}] \quad 1 \le i \le c, 1 \le j \le n$$

$$\sum_{i=1}^{c} u_{ij} = 1, \quad j = 1, 2, 3, ..., n.$$

1: **procedure** RPFCM
2:    **while** $max_{ji}|U_{ji}^{last} - U_{ji}^{new}| > error$ **do**;

$$c_i = \sum_{j=1}^{c} \frac{u_{ij}}{\sum_{k=1}^{n} u_{ik}^m} x_j, \quad j = 1, 2, 3, ..., n.$$

$$T_{ij} = \left(\frac{1}{1 + \|x_j - c_i\|_2} \right)$$

$$u_{ij} = \frac{\frac{1}{\left(\sum_{k=1}^{c} \|x_j - c_i\|_2^2\right)} * T_{ij}}{\sum_{l=1}^{c} \left(\frac{1}{\left(\sum_{k=1}^{c} \|x_j - c_l\|_2^2\right)} * T_{lj} \right)}$$

4.2   Experimental Design

To evaluate the structure generated by the algorithms we use the internal validity of the cluster. The indices are usually used to choose the best number of groupings. However, the indexes reveal important information of the groups.

Internal Cluster Validity. We tested the performance of NFCC and RpFCM. To this propose we use the same methodology and structures for clustering. The first step we loading the image. Second step, we prepare the necessary structures that store and save the results in order to make comparisons. Third step, we executed the algorithms with the same conditions for initial fuzzy membership and cluster number [2, 9]. In the fourth step we compare the results obtained with internal cluster validity. For this we use the following internal validation indexes of clusters.

Partition Coefficient. Measures the amount of overlap between groups [20].

$$F(U; c) = \frac{1}{N} \sum_{i=1}^{c} \sum_{k=1}^{N} (u_{ki})^2$$

Partition Coefficient Modified. It measure the degree of overlap between groups modified [8].

$$MPC(c) = 1 - \frac{c}{c - 1}(1 - PC(c))$$

Entropy. It measures the lack of diffusivity of the groups only, it is similar to the partition coefficient [20].

$$E(U;c) = -\frac{1}{N}\sum_{i=1}^{c}\sum_{k=1}^{N} u_{ki}log u_{ki}$$

Fukuyama and Sugeno. $J_m(u,a)$ measure the compactness and $K_m(u,a)$ the separation to the clustering [22].

$$FS(c) = \sum_{i=1}^{c}\sum_{j=1}^{n} u_{ij}\|x_{j,1,\dots,k} - a_i\|^2 - \sum_{i=1}^{c}\sum_{j=1}^{n} u_{ij}\|a_i - \bar{a}\|^2$$
$$= J_m(u,a) + K_m(u,a)$$
$$\bar{a} = \sum_{i=1}^{c} a_i/c$$

Fuzzy Hypervolume. The covariance is denoted by F_i to the group i, we spected a low value for FHV(c) [22].

$$FHV(c) = \sum_{i=1}^{c}[det(F_i)]^{\frac{1}{2}}$$

$$F_i = \frac{\sum_{j=1}^{n}(u_{ji})^m (x_j - a_i)(x_j - a_i)^T}{\sum_{j=1}^{n}(u_{ji})^m}$$

Xie-Beni. It is defined as the quotient between the total variance, and the minimum separation of the clusters [14, 21, 22].

$$XB = \frac{\sum_{i=1}^{c}\sum_{k=1}^{N}(u_{ki})^m D(x_x, v_i)}{N min_{1<i,j<c}\|v_i v_j\|^2} \tag{8}$$

All the algorithms are implemented using Julia language v1.0 and Intel Core(TM) i5-4200H CPU @ 2.80 GHz 2.80 GHz central processing unit, 8-GB memory and Windows 64-bit operative system.

4.3   Results

The results for the tests are the summaries in the Tables 1 and 2. The images show the NFCC algorithm presents a fast convergence and without properly organizing the elements. The RpFCM algorithm presents a more measured convergence and performs an adequate balancing of the elements. The indexs calculated for the algorithms shows: NFCC algorithm presents low level of overlap for the clusters, a high level of entropy, as well as a higher xie-Beni index. In contrast the proposed algorithm presents a high degree of overlap, small entropy values

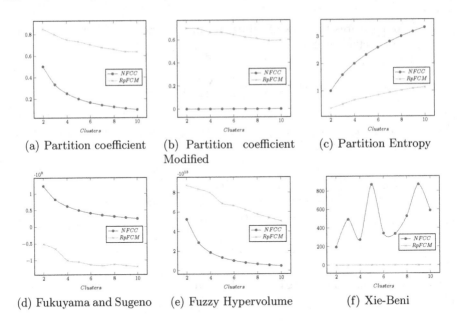

(a) Partition coefficient   (b) Partition coefficient   (c) Partition Entropy
                             Modified

(d) Fukuyama and Sugeno   (e) Fuzzy Hypervolume   (f) Xie-Beni

Fig. 3. Graphs obtained by calculating indices for both algorithms using a range of number of clusters between [2, 10].

Table 1. Results of the indices applied to the internal structure of the clustering produced with the NFCC algorithm in relation to each iteration that belongs to the interval [2, 10].

c	PC	PCM	PE	FS	FHV	XieBeni
2	0.50	2.79E−06	0.99	1.23E+09	5.25E+13	194.80
3	0.33	3.12E−06	1.58	8.22E+08	2.86E+13	492.76
4	0.25	1.31E−06	1.99	6.17E+08	1.85E+13	273.19
5	0.20	6.69E−07	2.32	4.94E+08	1.33E+13	868.71
6	0.17	9.10E−07	2.58	4.11E+08	1.01E+13	341.56
7	0.14	1.45E−06	2.81	3.52E+08	8.01E+12	336.95
8	0.13	9.04E−07	2.99	3.08E+08	6.56E+12	526.46
9	0.11	1.81E−07	3.17	2.74E+08	5.50E+12	870.64
10	0.10	1.62E−07	3.32	2.47E+08	4.69E+12	587.03

and small values respective to the Xie-Beni index. These results are evidenced in the graphs belonging to the Fig. 3.

Visual Results. The visual results for the NFCC algorithm are shown in the Fig. 4. In addition, the visual results obtained for the RpFCM algorithm are shown in the Fig. 5. Finally the Fig. 6 shows results for both algorithms.

Table 2. Results of the indices applied to the internal structure of the clustering produced with the RpFCM algorithm relative to each iteration belonging to the interval [2, 10].

c	PC	PCM	PE	FS	FHV	XieBeni
2	0.85	0.69	0.36	−5.10E+08	8.74E+13	0.31
3	0.79	0.69	0.52	−6.57E+08	8.36E+13	0.32
4	0.75	0.66	0.67	−1.00E+09	7.96E+13	0.33
5	0.73	0.66	0.75	−1.05E+09	6.88E+13	0.29
6	0.70	0.64	0.84	−1.13E+09	6.64E+13	0.33
7	0.68	0.62	0.93	−1.16E+09	6.23E+13	0.34
8	0.66	0.61	1.01	−1.12E+09	5.76E+13	0.32
9	0.64	0.59	1.09	−1.16E+09	5.39E+13	0.34
10	0.64	0.59	1.13	−1.19E+09	5.06E+13	0.30

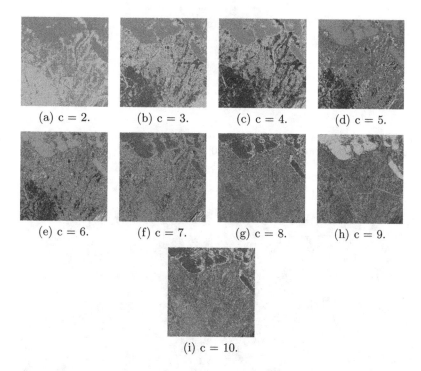

(a) c = 2.   (b) c = 3.   (c) c = 4.   (d) c = 5.

(e) c = 6.   (f) c = 7.   (g) c = 8.   (h) c = 9.

(i) c = 10.

Fig. 4. Obtained images as result of successive segmentation of test images using NFCC algorithm and range between [2, 10] clusters.

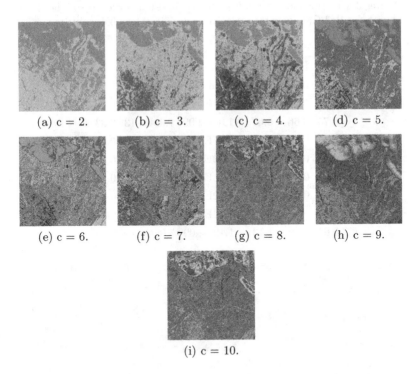

(a) c = 2.   (b) c = 3.   (c) c = 4.   (d) c = 5.

(e) c = 6.   (f) c = 7.   (g) c = 8.   (h) c = 9.

(i) c = 10.

Fig. 5. Obtained images as result of successive segmentation of test images using RpFCM algorithm and range between [2, 10] clusters.

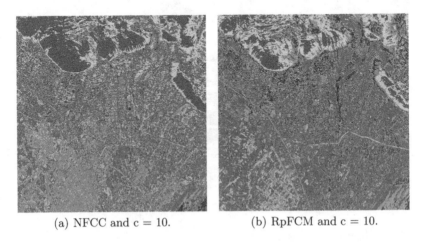

(a) NFCC and c = 10.   (b) RpFCM and c = 10.

Fig. 6. For a better evaluation of the tested algorithms, the results obtained for a number of clusters equal to 10 are shown.

5   Conclusions

The main advantage offered by the algorithm is the integration of a new term allows balancing the elements in the groups formed. This new term influences the results of the algorithm by decreasing or increasing the overlap as necessary. Taking into account the spatial dispersion of the data helps to find a better separation the elements of the cluster. This way we will ensure that the groups formed are adequate.

Due it integrates a term to balance the data. This makes the Rp-FCM algorithm a good option to segment data with low statistical separation and long quantity of elements.

References

1. Agarwal, P., Kumar, S., Singh, R., Agarwal, P., Bhattacharya, M.: A combination of bias-field corrected fuzzy c-means and level set approach for brain MRI image segmentation. In: 2015 Second International Conference on Soft Computing and Machine Intelligence (ISCMI), pp. 84–87. IEEE (2015)
2. Askari, S., Montazerin, N., Zarandi, M.F.: Generalized possibilistic fuzzy c-means with novel cluster validity indices for clustering noisy data. Appl. Soft Comput. **53**, 262–283 (2017)
3. Bai, L., Liang, J., Guo, Y.: An ensemble clusterer of multiple fuzzy k-means clusterings to recognize arbitrarily shaped clusters. IEEE Trans. Fuzzy Syst. **26**(6), 3524–3533 (2018)
4. Bai, X., Wang, Y., Liu, H., Guo, S.: Symmetry information based fuzzy clustering for infrared pedestrian segmentation. IEEE Trans. Fuzzy Syst. **26**(4), 1946–1959 (2018)
5. Banerjee, B., Bovolo, F., Bhattacharya, A., Bruzzone, L., Chaudhuri, S., Mohan, B.K.: A new self-training-based unsupervised satellite image classification technique using cluster ensemble strategy. IEEE Geosci. Remote Sens. Lett. **12**(4), 741–745 (2015)
6. Bezdek, J.C., Ehrlich, R., Full, W.: FCM: the fuzzy c-means clustering algorithm. Comput. Geosci. **10**(2–3), 191–203 (1984)
7. Celebi, M.E.: Partitional Clustering Algorithms. Springer, Cham (2014). https:// doi.org/10.1007/978-3-319-09259-1
8. Dave, R.N.: Validating fuzzy partitions obtained through c-shells clustering. Pattern Recogn. Lett. **17**(6), 613–623 (1996)
9. Ganesan, P., Palanivel, K., Sathish, B., Kalist, V., Shaik, K.B.: Performance of fuzzy based clustering algorithms for the segmentation of satellite images–a comparative study. In: 2015 IEEE Seventh National Conference on Computing, Communication and Information Systems (NCCCIS), pp. 23–27. IEEE (2015)
10. Ganesan, P., Sathish, B., Sajiv, G.: A comparative approach of identification and segmentation of forest fire region in high resolution satellite images. In: World Conference on Futuristic Trends in Research and Innovation for Social Welfare (Startup Conclave), pp. 1–6. IEEE (2016)
11. Genitha, C.H., Vani, K.: Classification of satellite images using new fuzzy cluster centroid for unsupervised classification algorithm. In: 2013 IEEE Conference on Information & Communication Technologies (ICT), pp. 203–207. IEEE (2013)

12. Gu, J., Jiao, L., Yang, S., Liu, F.: Fuzzy double c-means clustering based on sparse self-representation. IEEE Trans. Fuzzy Syst. **26**(2), 612–626 (2017)
13. Guo, Y., Jiao, L., Wang, S., Wang, S., Liu, F., Hua, W.: Fuzzy-superpixels for polarimetric SAR images classification. IEEE Trans. Fuzzy Syst. **26**(5), 2846–2860 (2018)
14. Haouas, F., Dhiaf, Z.B., Hammouda, A., Solaiman, B.: A new efficient fuzzy cluster validity index: application to images clustering. In: 2017 IEEE International Conference on Fuzzy Systems (FUZZ-IEEE), pp. 1–6. IEEE (2017)
15. Kar, S.A., Kelkar, V.V.: Classification of multispectral satellite images. In: 2013 International Conference on Advances in Technology and Engineering (ICATE), pp. 1–6. IEEE (2013)
16. Kawarkhe, M., Musande, V.: Performance analysis of possisblistic fuzzy clustering and support vector machine in cotton crop classification. In: 2014 International Conference on Advances in Computing, Communications and Informatics (ICACCI), pp. 961–967. IEEE (2014)
17. Poojary, N., D'Souza, H., Puttaswamy, M., Kumar, G.H.: Automatic target detection in hyperspectral image processing: a review of algorithms. In: 2015 12th International Conference on Fuzzy Systems and Knowledge Discovery (FSKD), pp. 1991–1996. IEEE (2015)
18. Saxena, A., et al.: A review of clustering techniques and developments. Neurocomputing **267**, 664–681 (2017)
19. Shang, R., et al.: A spatial fuzzy clustering algorithm with kernel metric based on immune clone for SAR image segmentation. IEEE J. Sel. Top. Appl. Earth Obs. Remote Sens. **9**(4), 1640–1652 (2016)
20. Villazana, S., Arteaga, F., Seijas, C., Rodriguez, O.: Estudio comparativo entre algoritmos de agrupamiento basado en SVM y c-medios difuso aplicados a señales electrocardiográficas arrítmicas. Rev. INGENIERÍA UC **19**(1), 16–24 (2012)
21. Wang, W., Zhang, Y.: On fuzzy cluster validity indices. Fuzzy Sets Syst. **158**(19), 2095–2117 (2007)
22. Wu, K.L., Yang, M.S.: A cluster validity index for fuzzy clustering. Pattern Recogn. Lett. **26**(9), 1275–1291 (2005)
23. Xiang, D., Tang, T., Hu, C., Li, Y., Su, Y.: A kernel clustering algorithm with fuzzy factor: application to SAR image segmentation. IEEE Geosci. Remote Sens. Lett. **11**(7), 1290–1294 (2014)
24. Yang, M.S., Nataliani, Y.: Robust-learning fuzzy c-means clustering algorithm with unknown number of clusters. Pattern Recogn. **71**, 45–59 (2017)
25. Zhao, Z., Chang, W., Jiang, Y.: Fuzzy local means clustering segmentation algorithm for intensity inhomogeneity image. In: 2015 8th International Congress on Image and Signal Processing (CISP), pp. 453–457. IEEE (2015)
26. Zou, Y., Liu, B.: Survey on clustering-based image segmentation techniques. In: 2016 IEEE 20th International Conference on Computer Supported Cooperative Work in Design (CSCWD), pp. 106–110. IEEE (2016)

A Feature Extraction Method Based on Convolutional Autoencoder for Plant Leaves Classification

Mery M. Paco Ramos$^{(\boxtimes)}$ ⓘ, Vanessa M. Paco Ramos ⓘ,
Arnold Loaiza Fabian ⓘ, and Erbert F. Osco Mamani ⓘ

Universidad Nacional Jorge Basadre Grohmann, Tacna, Peru
{mpacor,vpacor,aloaizaf,eosco}@unjbg.edu.pe

Abstract. In this research, we present an approach based on Convolutional Autoencoder (CAE) and Support Vector Machine (SVM) for leaves classification of different trees. While previous approaches relied on image processing and manual feature extraction, the proposed approach operates directly on the image pixels, without any preprocessing. Firstly, we use multiple layers of CAE to learn the features of leaf image dataset. Secondly, the extracted features were used to train a linear classifier based on SVM. Experimental results show that the classifiers using these features can improve their predictive value, reaching an accuracy rate of 94.74%.

Keywords: Feature extraction · Image processing · Plant classification · Convolutional Autoencoder · Deep learning · Computer vision

1 Introduction

In recent decades, the dimensionality of data has increased, such as images, videos, genetic information, among others. The data of high dimensionality can contain a high degree of irrelevant and redundant information, which leads to harmful consequences in terms of performance and/or computational cost. One way to deal with this problem is by extracting features from the data set, which reduces the dimensionality of the data, obtaining essential and meaningful information that is used in pattern recognition, computer vision and other tasks.

In pattern recognition and in image processing, feature extraction is a special form of dimensionality reduction [10] and among the main feature extraction methods commonly used are the Principal Component Analysis (PCA) and the Linear Discriminant Analysis (LDA) [15], which project data from a higher dimension to a lower dimension using linear transformation.

However, significant abstract representations of image data are obtained through non-linear transformations [19]. Therefore, one of the architectures of deep learning that have reported promising results for dimensionality reduction

© Springer Nature Switzerland AG 2019
A. D. Orjuela-Cañón et al. (Eds.): ColCACI 2019, CCIS 1096, pp. 143–154, 2019.
https://doi.org/10.1007/978-3-030-36211-9_12

is the autoencoder, especially in image processing and natural language processing [10,15,19,21,22].

On the other hand, the classification of plant species is essential to conserve biodiversity and its cataloging is a rather tedious task [18,23]. Therefore, image processing techniques based on the recognition of leaves can help to find essential features for the representation and classification of plants [4].

This article proposes a new approach for the leaf images classification efficiently and effectively. In this approach, the features are extracted by CAE, therefore, the features extracted were used to train a linear classifier based on SVM.

This paper is organized as follows. Section 2 describes the related research works; in Sect. 3, the theoretical foundation on feature extraction, autoencoders and SVM classifier is introduced; Sect. 4 describes the proposed method; Sect. 5 presents the experiments and results obtained; and finally, Sect. 6 presents the main conclusions and future work.

2   Related Works

A wide variety of approaches have been proposed for the pre-processing, segmentation, extraction of visual descriptors and finally the recognition and classification of plant species through its leaf. This section presents the contributions that obtained outstanding results.

In [25] basic geometric and morphological descriptors are calculated, they are the input vector of the Probabilistic Neural Network (PNN). The PNN is trained by 1800 leaves to classify 32 kinds of plants with an accuracy greater than 90%. Another similar research [17] proposes a foliar image recognition approach using SVM as a classifier. The feature extraction phase is carried out in the same way as in [25]; and the results are compared with the k-Nearest Neighbor (k-NN) approach.

In [3] used the features of shape, color and texture to propose a plant recovery method based on foliar images. The Scale Invariant Feature Transform (SIFT) method is used to extract the main features. In [24] proposes the combination of shape descriptors based on the contour and define a new texture descriptor based on the cortical intersection model. The extraction also requires a pre-processing of the image that includes segmentation, smoothing and enhancement of contrast and texture. For the classification they use SVM.

In [8] identified that the foliage plants have several colors and unique patterns in the leaves, and they used the Fourier transform, the moments of color and veins features to identify the plant species. Reaching an accuracy of 93.13% in the Flavia dataset. In [9] Fourier descriptors are used to extract features of texture, color and shape of the leaves of plants. Although, the processing time of the images is greater, useful features are obtained for the classification stage. In this case, a PNN was used as a classifier.

Finally, in [7] performs an evaluation of the effectiveness of hand-crafted features (HCF) and proposes the use of Convolutional Neural Network (ConvNet) features for image classification. Additionally, a range of variations is introduced to explore the robustness of the features, which include: translation, scaling, rotation, shading and occlusion. The results show that the combined approach: ConvNet and HCF, exceeds the set of traditional features.

3   Background

3.1   Feature Extraction

Feature extraction transforms the high-dimensionality data m to low-dimensional space n, such that $n < m$, minimizing the loss of information. This transformation can be linear or non-linear. In addition, it is expected that the features obtained contain relevant information in order to perform the desired task using this reduced representation instead of the original data [10, 15].

3.2   Autoencoder

An autoencoder (AE) is an unsupervised learning algorithm that applies back-propagation to a set of unlabeled data $\{x^{(1)}, x^{(2)}, x^{(3)}, ..., x^{(n)}\}$ where $x^{(i)} \in \mathbb{R}^d$, setting that the target values must be equal to the inputs. I.e., it uses $\hat{x}^{(i)} = x^{(i)}$.

An AE consists of two clearly identifiable parts [22]:

Encoder maps an input vector $\mathbf{x}$ into hidden representation $\mathbf{z}$ using a function f_θ.

$$\mathbf{z} = f_\theta(\mathbf{x}) = s_f(\mathbf{Wx} + \mathbf{b}) \tag{1}$$

Where f_θ is a function parameterized by $\theta = \{\mathbf{W}, \mathbf{b}\}$, $\mathbf{W}$ is a weight matrix and $\mathbf{b}$ is a bias vector.

Decoder use the latent space representation $\mathbf{z}$ as input to a function $g_{\theta'}$ to reconstruct the input $\hat{\mathbf{x}}$.

$$\hat{\mathbf{x}} = g_{\theta'}(\mathbf{z}) = s_g(\mathbf{W'z} + \mathbf{b'}) \tag{2}$$

In Fig. 1, the AE tries to learn a function $h_{W,b}(\mathbf{x}) \approx \mathbf{x}$. Training an AE involves finding parameters $\theta, \theta' = (\mathbf{W}, \mathbf{W'}, \mathbf{b}, \mathbf{b'})$ that minimize the reconstruction loss:

$$\Theta = \min_{\theta, \theta'} \frac{1}{n} \sum_{i=1}^{n} L\left(\mathbf{x}^{(i)}, g_{\theta'}\left(f_\theta\left(\mathbf{x}^{(i)}\right)\right)\right) \tag{3}$$

Where L is a loss function such as the traditional squared error $L(\mathbf{x}, \hat{\mathbf{x}}) = \|\mathbf{x} - \hat{\mathbf{x}}\|^2$. An alternative loss, suggested by the interpretation of $\mathbf{x}$ y $\hat{\mathbf{x}}$ as either bit vectors is the reconstruction cross-entropy [21]:

$$L(\mathbf{x}, \hat{\mathbf{x}}) = -\sum_{k=1}^{d} \mathbf{x}_k \log \hat{\mathbf{x}}_k + (1 - \mathbf{x}_k) \log(1 - \hat{\mathbf{x}}_k) \tag{4}$$

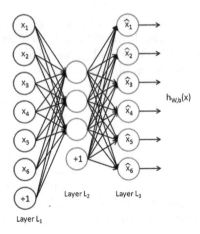

Fig. 1. Basic autoencoder architecture [16].

3.3 Convolutional Autoencoder

The fully connected AEs (see Fig. 1) may ignore the 2-D image structure, transforming it into a 1-D input vector that is connected to each element of the following layer, causing the features found to be global or redundant [13,14]. On the other hand, the Convolutional Autoencoders (CAE) through convolution layers make connections in reduced and localized areas of the image, conserving their spatial structure and discovering local features throughout the entire image [6].

Therefore, CAEs are more suitable for image processing, and they are a cutting-edge tool for learning convolution filters in an unsupervised way. The learned filters are capable of extracting features that can be used for any task that requires a compact representation of the image, for example, classification. Then the main layers of CAE are presented.

Convolution Layer. Given an image $S^l \in \mathbb{R}^{W \times H \times C}$, where W and H denote image dimensions and C the number of channels, the latent representation of the feature map in the layer $l + 1$ when applying n convolution filters $k \in \mathbb{R}^{k \times k \times C}$, is given by:

$$\mathbf{S}_j^{l+1} = \sigma \left(\sum_{i=1}^{l} S_i^l \otimes k_{ij} + b_j \right) \quad j = 1, ..., n \tag{5}$$

Where S_i^l is the i-th features map in the layer l, k_{ij} denotes the i-th channel in the j-th convolution filter (or kernel), $\otimes$ denotes the operator convolution and σ is a nonlinear function activation, for example a rectified linear function (ReLU).

The convolution process consists of sliding the $k \times k$ kernel, through the entire $W \times H$ image using a different size of step (or stride) s, to obtain a new representation of the image of $(\lfloor (W - k + 2p)/s \rfloor + 1) \times (\lfloor (H - k + 2p)/s \rfloor + 1)$. Where p is the padding around the image. Figure 2 shows the sliding process.

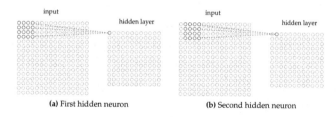

(a) First hidden neuron   (b) Second hidden neuron

Fig. 2. Sliding a local receptive field of 4×4 over an input of 16×16 elements. A feature map of 12×12 elements is produced by using a stride of 1×1 elements [6].

Pooling Layer. These layers are used to simplify the feature maps produced by the previous convolution layers. This simplification has many advantages: by reducing the representation size the amount of parameters to be learned is also reduced, therefore decreasing the computational cost of the whole network [6].

In detail, the pooling layer generates a condensed feature map by summarizing regions with a predefined operation (maximum, average, among others). In Eq. 6 o_j^i represents the i-th output neuron of the features map j using the maximum value in region i (also known as max-pooling).

$$o_j^i = \max \left(\mathbf{x}_j^i \right) \tag{6}$$

Fig. 3 show pooling examples.

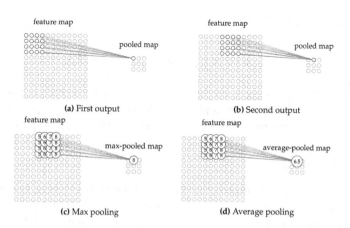

(a) First output   (b) Second output

(c) Max pooling   (d) Average pooling

Fig. 3. Pooling operation over a 12×12 feature map using a filter size of 4×4 and a stride of 4×4 [6].

Unpooling Layer. The resulting feature maps will be used as decoder input, to reconstruct the input image. Therefore, unpooling operations will be applied to counteract pooling (See Fig. 4).

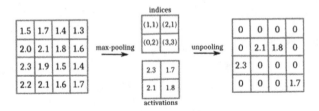

Fig. 4. Illustration of the effects of the max-pooling and unpooling operations on a 4×4 feature map [2].

In addition, convolution or deconvolution layers will also be applied to restore the original image.

3.4   Support Vector Machine (SVM)

Given a separable set of $\{(x_1, y_1), ..., (x_n, y_n)\}$ examples where $x_i \in R^d$ and $y_i \in \{-1, +1\}$ a separation hyperplane can be defined as a linear function that is capable of separating said set. In general, SVM transforms the original data $\mathbf{X}$ to a higher dimensional feature space $\mathbf{F}$ via a kernel function $\mathbf{K}$. In other words, we consider the set of classifiers of the form [1, 5, 20]:

$$f(x) = \left(\sum_{i=1}^{n} \alpha_i K\left(x_i, x\right) \right) \tag{7}$$

We can then rewrite f as:

$$f(x) = \mathbf{w} \cdot \Theta(\mathbf{x}), \text{ where } \mathbf{w} = \sum_{i=1}^{n} \alpha_i \Theta(x_i) \tag{8}$$

Where Θ is the mapping from $\mathbf{X}$ to the feature space $\mathbf{F}$ and "$\cdot$" denotes an inner product. By choosing different kernel functions $\mathbf{K}$, the hyperplanes in $\mathbf{F}$ correspond to more complex decision boundaries in the original space $\mathbf{X}$.

4   Methodology

This section describes the proposed methodology for feature extraction and classification of foliar images. The methodology consists of 4 main parts, as shown in Fig. 5: (1) obtaining samples for training, validation, and model testing; (2) unsupervised feature learning; (3) obtaining the feature vectors and (4) image classification.

The purpose is to use CAE to learn a reduced representation from images and use the encoded layer as input data for SVM classifier.

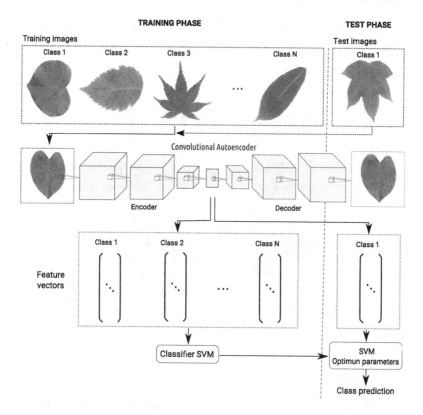

Fig. 5. Proposed methodology

(a) Obtaining samples for training, validation, and model testing: for the training, validation and testing phase of the CAE and SVM models, the data set has been divided into 64% for training, 16% for validation and 20% for testing.

(b) Unsupervised feature learning: In this stage the CAE model is trained and to find the optimal hyperparameters of the model, we will use cross-validation for K iterations. Finally, the generalization error of the model is determined with the test set.

(c) Obtaining the feature vectors: the encoded layers of the trained CAE model are used to extract the feature vectors from the images.

(d) Image classification: in this last stage, the SVM model is trained and tested to classify the feature vectors.

5 Experiments and Results

5.1 Dataset

A publicly available dataset, namely Flavia, has been used. This data set consists of 32 tree leaf species, with a total of 1907 images on three channels (R, G and B) with a resolution of 1600×1200 pixels. The number of images per species varies between 50 to 60 approximately. Some examples of the dataset are shown in Fig. 6.

Fig. 6. Samples from the Flavia dataset [12].

5.2   CAE Architecture

Our CAE network contains seven convolution layers, three max-pooling layers and three unpooling layers with a total of $333, 955$ parameters to extract features hierarchically, addition it receives as input an image of $224 \times 224 \times 3$ pixels. The specific network structure is shown in Fig. 7, the encode and decode layers are highlighted green and blue respectively. Additionally, each convolution layer is followed by a ReLU activation function:

$$ReLU\,(x) = \begin{cases} x \; x \geq 0 \\ 0 \; x < 0 \end{cases} \tag{9}$$

5.3   Unsupervised Feature Learning

Unsupervised feature learning is the key for classification. Unlike other conventional methods which do need to manually extract features, the CAE can learning feature automatically. Prior to training the CAE model, all images are resized to 224×224 pixels. Then the values of pixels are mapped from $[0, 255]$ to $[0, 1]$.

Therefore, the optimum hyperparameters of the model were determined by the cross-validation strategy 10-fold, which consists of randomly dividing the data set into 10 subsets, one for test and the rest for training the model. The final model was trained with the following hyperparameters found: epochs: 103,

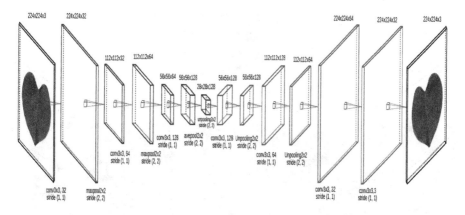

Fig. 7. CAE architecture for feature extraction.

mini-batch size: 60, activation function: ReLU and optimizer: RMSprop with a learning rate of 0.001.

To evaluate the performance for the model, we randomly selected 5 images from test dataset. Therefore, the results of the original and reconstructed images are shown in Figure 8.

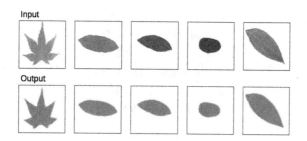

Fig. 8. CAE results on the test set.

Figure 9 shows the outputs of the convolution layers for the CAE model. Specifically, the first and the twelfth convolution layer, both with a filter of $3 \times 3 \times 32$. Each of these layers belongs to the CAE encoder and decoder respectively.

5.4   Classification and Comparison with Other Methods

After to train the CAE model, we proceed to remove the decoder layers (layers 8 to 13), and with the remaining model (encoder) we generate the feature vectors, which will be used as inputs to train the SVM classifier with a linear kernel. We compare the accuracy of our model with other previous works, according to Table 1 the accuracy of our model outperforms the results. Compared to other schemes, our model is able to automatically extract highly abstract features of raw data.

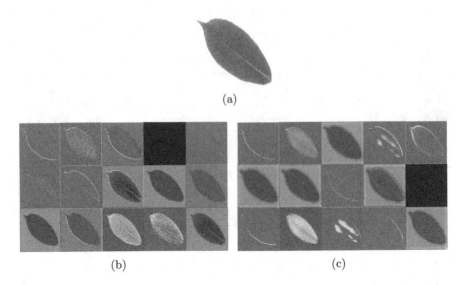

(a)

(b)   (c)

Fig. 9. (a) Original image (b) Output of the convolution layer # 1 (c) Output of the convolution layer # 12.

Table 1. Comparison with other methods

Method	Accuracy
Wu et al. [25]	90.31%
Kadir et al. [8]	93.13%
Wu y Tsai [26]	92.13%
Kumar et al. [11]	94.37 %
Proposed	**94.74%**

6   Conclusions and Future Work

In this paper, we use unsupervised learning for the hierarchical feature extraction and a classifier based on Support Vector Machine to predict leaf types. The experimental results show that the convolutional autoencoder is able to extract significant information from the leaf images, being more robust and abstract. Consequently, they contribute to improving the results of the classification, reaching an accuracy of 94.74%.

The proposed work can be extended to other main models of autoencoders, such as Sparse Autoencoders, Denoising Autoencoders, Contractive Autoencoders, among others. In addition, Autoencoders can be trained through parallel processing by GPUs. On the other hand, the vectors of features obtained can be used for other tasks than the classification and other models of Machine Learning.

Acknowledgments. The authors would like to express their sincere gratitude to Vicerectorate of Research (VIIN) of the National University Jorge Basadre Grohmann (Tacna) for promoting the development of scientific research projects and to Dr. Cristian López Del Alamo, Director of Research at the University La Salle (Arequipa) for motivation and support with computational resources.

References

1. Ahmed, N., Khan, U.G., Asif, S.: An automatic leaf based plant identification system. Sci. Int. **28**(1), 427–430 (2016)
2. Audebert, N., Saux, B.L., Lefèvre, S.: Beyond RGB: very high resolution urban remote sensing with multimodal deep networks. ISPRS J. Photogrammetry Remote Sens. **140**, 20–32 (2018). https://doi.org/10.1016/j.isprsjprs.2017.11.011
3. Bama, B.S., Valli, S.M., Raju, S., Kumar, V.A.: Content based leaf image retrieval (CBLIR) using shape, color and texture features. Indian J. Comput. Sci. Eng. **2**(2), 202–211 (2011)
4. Di Ruberto, C., Putzu, L.: A fast leaf recognition algorithm based on SVM classifier and high dimensional feature vector. In: 2014 International Conference on Computer Vision Theory and Applications (VISAPP), vol. 1, pp. 601–609 (2014)
5. Gala García, Y.: Algoritmos SVM para problemas sobre big data. Master's thesis (2013)
6. Garcia-Garcia, A.: 3D object recognition with convolutional neural network (2016)
7. Hall, D., McCool, C., Dayoub, F., Sunderhauf, N., Upcroft, B.: Evaluation of features for leaf classification in challenging conditions. In: 2015 IEEE Winter Conference on Applications of Computer Vision, pp. 797–804. IEEE (2015)
8. Kadir, A., Nugroho, L.E., Susanto, A., Santosa, P.I.: Foliage plant retrieval using polar fourier transform, color moments and vein features. arXiv preprint arXiv:1110.1513 (2011)
9. Kadir, A., Nugroho, L.E., Susanto, A., Santosa, P.I.: Leaf classification using shape, color, and texture features. arXiv preprint arXiv:1401.4447 (2013)
10. Kumar, G., Bhatia, P.K.: A detailed review of feature extraction in image processing systems. In: 2014 Fourth International Conference on Advanced Computing Communication Technologies, pp. 5–12, February 2014. https://doi.org/10.1109/ACCT.2014.74
11. Kumar, P.S.V.V.S.R., Rao, K.N.V., Raju, A.S.N., Kumar, D.J.N.: Leaf classification based on shape and edge feature with k-nn classifier. In: 2016 2nd International Conference on Contemporary Computing and Informatics (IC3I), pp. 548–552, December 2016. https://doi.org/10.1109/IC3I.2016.7918024
12. Laga, H., Kurtek, S., Srivastava, A., Golzarian, M., Miklavcic, S.J.: A Riemannian elastic metric for shape-based plant leaf classification. In: 2012 International Conference on Digital Image Computing Techniques and Applications (DICTA), pp. 1–7, December 2012. https://doi.org/10.1109/DICTA.2012.6411702
13. Masci, J., Meier, U., Cireşan, D., Schmidhuber, J.: Stacked convolutional autoencoders for hierarchical feature extraction. In: Honkela, T., Duch, W., Girolami, M., Kaski, S. (eds.) ICANN 2011. LNCS, vol. 6791, pp. 52–59. Springer, Heidelberg (2011). https://doi.org/10.1007/978-3-642-21735-7_7
14. Mei, X., Dong, X., Deyer, T., Zeng, J., Trafalis, T., Fang, Y.: Thyroid nodule benignty prediction by deep feature extraction. In: 2017 IEEE 17th International Conference on Bioinformatics and Bioengineering (BIBE), pp. 241–245, October 2017. https://doi.org/10.1109/BIBE.2017.00-48

15. Meng, Q., Catchpoole, D., Skillicom, D., Kennedy, P.J.: Relational autoencoder for feature extraction. In: 2017 International Joint Conference on Neural Networks (IJCNN), pp. 364–371, May 2017. https://doi.org/10.1109/IJCNN.2017.7965877

16. Ng, A.: Sparse autoencoder. CS294A Lect. Notes **72**, 1–19 (2011)

17. Priya, C.A., Balasaravanan, T., Thanamani, A.S.: An efficient leaf recognition algorithm for plant classification using support vector machine. In: International Conference on Pattern Recognition, Informatics and Medical Engineering (PRIME-2012), pp. 428–432. IEEE (2012)

18. Redolfi, J.A., Sánchez, J.A., Pucheta, J.A.: Identificación de hojas de plantas usando vectores de fisher. In: Argentine Symposium on Artificial Intelligence (ASAI 2015)-JAIIO 44, Rosario 2015 (2015)

19. Schmid, U., Günther, J., Diepold, K.: Stacked denoising and stacked convolutional autoencoders (2017)

20. Tong, S., Koller, D.: Support vector machine active learning with applications to text classification. J. Mach. Learn. Res. **2**, 45–66 (2002). https://doi.org/10.1162/153244302760185243

21. Vincent, P., Larochelle, H., Bengio, Y., Manzagol, P.A.: Extracting and composing robust features with denoising autoencoders. In: Proceedings of the 25th International Conference on Machine Learning ICML 2008, pp. 1096–1103. ACM, New York (2008). https://doi.org/10.1145/1390156.1390294

22. Vincent, P., Larochelle, H., Lajoie, I., Bengio, Y., Manzagol, P.A.: Stacked denoising autoencoders: Learning useful representations in a deep network with a local denoising criterion. J. Mach. Learn. Res. **11**, 3371–3408 (2010)

23. Wäldchen, J., Mäder, P.: Plant species identification using computer vision techniques: a systematic literature review. Arch. Comput. Methods Eng. **25**(2), 507–543 (2018). https://doi.org/10.1007/s11831-016-9206-z

24. Wang, Z., et al.: Plant recognition based on intersecting cortical model. In: 2014 International Joint Conference on Neural Networks (IJCNN), pp. 975–980, July 2014. https://doi.org/10.1109/IJCNN.2014.6889656

25. Wu, S.G., Bao, F.S., Xu, E.Y., Wang, Y.X., Chang, Y.F., Xiang, Q.L.: A leaf recognition algorithm for plant classification using probabilistic neural network. In: 2007 IEEE International Symposium on Signal Processing and Information Technology, pp. 11–16. IEEE (2007)

26. Wu, Y.J., Tsai, C.M., Shih, F.: Improving leaf classification rate via background removal and ROI extraction. J. Image Graph. **4**(2), 93–98 (2016)

Acquisition System Based in a Low-Cost Optical Architecture with Single Pixel Measurements and RGB Side Information for UAV Imagery

Arnold Guarin$^{(\boxtimes)}$ ⓘ, Homero Ortega ⓘ, and Hans Garcia ⓘ

Department of Electrical Engineering, Universidad Industrial de Santander,
Bucaramanga, Colombia
aguarin@radiogis.uis.edu.co

Abstract. Spectral imaging has a wide range of applications, like remote sensing or biomedical imaging. In recent years, with the increasing use of unmanned aerial vehicles (UAVs), it is common to attach a spectral camera to an UAV to acquire information. Unfortunately, the spectral cameras used with UAV are expensive. Therefore this work proposes a low-cost optical architecture to acquire spectral images. The proposed architecture takes advantage of the UAV movement to spectral imaging. The proposed optical architecture is composed of two arms, one has an RGB camera, and the other a single-pixel spectrometer. The results show that depending on the sensing conditions selected, it is possible to retrieve high-quality spectral images. Simulation results show that the proposed architecture improves image quality in terms of PSNR compared with an RGB camera and the single-pixel camera (SPC), up to 1.31 dB and 20.44 dB respectively, also obtained a performance similar to an architecture that combine the SPC and RGB, and even besting it improving the quality of the image in terms of PSNR up to 0.49 dB. Moreover, the optical architecture proposed has the advantage of reducing the amount of sensed information in comparison to SPC and SPC + RGB; also, the implementation costs are reduced drastically because the proposed architecture does not use a digital micromirror device (DMD) to codify the incoming scene, which is the case of the SPC and SPC + RGB architectures.

Keywords: Imaging · UAV · Low-cost · Optical architecture

1 Introduction

Spectral images (SI) sets of information that varies over the spatial coordinates (x, y) and the spectral wavelength (λ) [14]. The SI are used in different fields because of the information that can be collected at all the spectral wavelengths, the main applications are on remote sensing for land-cover classification [3], mineral exploration, agricultural assessment [15] and biomedical imaging [11].

© Springer Nature Switzerland AG 2019
A. D. Orjuela-Cañón et al. (Eds.): ColCACI 2019, CCIS 1096, pp. 155–167, 2019.
https://doi.org/10.1007/978-3-030-36211-9_13

Unfortunately, the use of SI comes with a set of problems, like high processing and storage costs, the costs of the acquisition systems, high prices that grow proportional to the spatio-spectral resolution. For this reason, compressed sensing (CS) principles have been applied to spectral imaging. Where, assuming that the SI has a sparse representation in some basis $\boldsymbol{\Psi}$, an SI can be retrieved with a lower set of samples compared with the traditional scanning methods such as push broom, whisk broom or filtered camera [4].

Let $\mathbf{f}$ be a vectorized SI, with $\mathbf{f} \in \mathbb{R}^{MNL}$, where M and N are the spatial dimensions and L is the number of spectral bands. If $\mathbf{f}$ has an sparsity S, $\mathbf{f}$ can be represented as a linear combination of S vectors in any basis $\boldsymbol{\Psi}$, such as $\mathbf{f} = \boldsymbol{\Psi\theta}$, with $||\boldsymbol{\theta}||_0 = S \ll MNL$. This allows to retrieve $\mathbf{f}$ from $K \ll MNL$ samples of the scene, having into account that K is not necessarily equal to S. In other words, if $\mathbf{f}$ have a sparse representation, it can be reconstructed from a minimal number of samples, reducing the load of information needed. The sensing process can be represented in matrix form as $\mathbf{g} = \mathbf{Hf}$, where $\mathbf{g}$ is the sensed information, $\mathbf{H}$ is the transfer matrix of the acquisition system, and $\mathbf{f}$ is the spectral scene [2]. The inverse problem given by $\mathbf{f} = \mathbf{H}^{-1}\mathbf{g}$ could reconstruct the signal $\mathbf{f}$ using the transfer matrix and the sensed information, but, this problem is ill-conditioned and can not be used to recontruct $\mathbf{f}$, because the number of measurements are less than the number of voxels, and $\mathbf{H}^{-1}$ does not exist. Therefore, $\mathbf{f}$ is obtained by optimization algorithms that take advantage of the sparse representation of $\mathbf{f}$ in a basis $\boldsymbol{\Psi}$.

One example of the application of CS in spectral imaging is the single-pixel camera (SPC) architecture, where an SI can be retrieved using a single-pixel detector and a coded aperture to codify the scene [6]. However, the SPC architecture presents low frame rates because of the number of measurements needed to sample a scene [13]; on the other hand, even though the SPC architecture is cheaper than some of the commercially available spectral sensors, the construction of this architecture is still expensive because some of its components are expensive like the digital micromirror device (DMD) used to generate the aperture code.

Sometimes high spatio-spectral resolution SI are needed to discriminate between different materials on a scene. Like in remote sensing, where the spatial resolution given by the satellite images do not give the information desired over a specific area. To solve this problem, the use of SI acquired from unmanned aerial vehicles (UAVs) is a possible solution. The acquisition of SI with UAVs have become a trend in some fields, like precision agriculture [8], forestry [12], disaster evaluations [1], etc. However, spectral sensors are expensive, and with the risk of accident present during an UAV flight, it is common not to use spectral sensors with high resolution. With this problem in mind, in this paper, we propose an optical architecture using an RGB camera, a single spatial pixel sensor, an optical slit, and the movement of the UAV, to spectral imaging with low-cost components. The main advantages of the proposed architecture are the low-cost and capture speed in comparison with the commercial sensors and the SPC, mainly, because this architecture takes the samples from the scene using a cheap optical slit.

2   Sensing Architecture

The sensing architecture is shown in Fig. 1. There, the light through over a beam splitter that split the light and redirects it to an RGB sensor and to an optical slit. To obtain information with a high spatial resolution we use the RGB sensor to capture data, referred now on as side information; and to obtain information with a high spectral resolution we use the single spatial pixel sensor, that captures the information of the scene after the optical slit condensed in a single point by a condenser lens.

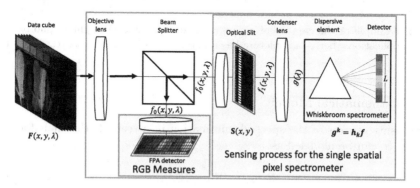

Fig. 1. Optical scheme constructed for the acquisition of information using a single pixel spatial sensor with RGB side information.

2.1   UAV Effect over the Sensing

The single pixel camera is an architecture that uses the CS principles to retrieve SI from a scene [6]. The architecture of the SPC is very similar to the architecture proposed in this work, the main difference is that the information captured from the scene is codified by an aperture code in the SPC architecture, this with the intention of obtaining different information of the scene with each shot. The architecture proposed in this work also takes different information about the scene with each shot using an optical slit. The reason of why use just a slit, it is because we take advantage of the UAV movement during the flight, and knowing that the architecture will be moving along with the UAV, each shot taken will have different information of the scene. Normally, the use of UAVs in remote sensing applications involves the construction of orthomosaics by a series of pictures taken successively with a certain overlap percentage, as shown in Fig. 2, this process is called photogrammetry [7]. With the application of photogrammetry, each shot taken during the flight will have different parts of the scene, with the number of shots of the same scene depending on the overlap percentage of the pictures, and the size of the picture captured with the sensor.

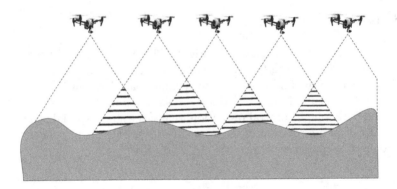

Fig. 2. Example of the capture of photographs during an UAV flight in photogrammetry applications, here, each picture has a percentage of overlap with respect to the others.

2.2   Mathematical Model

The sensing process of the spectral information in a scene $\mathbf{F}$ that it is focused to a slit $\mathbf{S}$, can be modeled as

$$\hat{\mathbf{F}}^k_{(i,j,l)} = \mathbf{F}_{(i,j,l)}\mathbf{S}^k_{(i,j)}, \tag{1}$$

where i, j index the spatial coordinates, l is the spectral band and k is the snapshot taken. Then a condenser lens integrates all the information in a single spatial point, which is captured by a single pixel detector that acquires the information of each spectral band l as

$$\mathbf{g}^k_l = \sum_i \sum_j \mathbf{F}_{(i,j,l)}\mathbf{S}^k_{(i,j)}, \tag{2}$$

for $i = 1, 2, \ldots, M$, $j = 1, 2, \ldots, N$ and $l = 1, 2, \ldots, L$, where M and N are the height a width of the scene in pixels respectively, and L the total number of bands of the scene. This process can be modeled in vector form as

$$\mathbf{g}^k_l = \mathbf{h}^T_k\mathbf{f}_l, \tag{3}$$

where $\mathbf{h}_k$ is the vectorization of the slit effect over the scene for each snapshot, and $\mathbf{f}_l$ is the vectorization of the l band in $\mathbf{F}$. The parameter $\mathbf{h}_k$ is the vector form of a matrix of zeros with some columns of ones which represent the part of the scene that passes over the optical slit, these columns will be referred as window. The number of columns in the window depends on the slit thickness, and the window moves over the scene with each shot taken, which relates the movement of the window with the overlap percentage. In general, the sensing model for all snapshots can be written as

$$\mathbf{g}_l = \mathbf{H}\mathbf{f}_l, \tag{4}$$

where $\mathbf{g}_l = \left[\mathbf{g}_l^1, \ldots, \mathbf{g}_l^K\right]^T$, $\mathbf{H}$ is a $K \times MN$ matrix given by $\mathbf{H} = \left[\mathbf{h}_1^T, \ldots, \mathbf{h}_K^T\right]$, and K is the number of shots. It is important to highlight that $\mathbf{h}_1 \neq \mathbf{h}_k$, because the architecture will be capturing information over the UAV during the flight course, then the optical architecture will move along with the UAV capturing different information of the scene in each shot. The model can be generalized for all the spectral bands and all shots as

$$\mathbf{g} = \hat{\mathbf{H}}\mathbf{f}, \tag{5}$$

where $\mathbf{g} = \left[(\mathbf{g}_0)^T, \ldots, (\mathbf{g}_{L-1})^T\right]^T$, and $\hat{\mathbf{H}}$ is the sensing matrix that can be obtained with $\hat{\mathbf{H}} = \mathbf{I}_L \otimes \mathbf{H}$, where $\otimes$ is the Kronecker product, $\mathbf{I}_L$ is an $L \times L$ identity matrix, so that the number of columns and rows of $\hat{\mathbf{H}}$ is MNL and γMNL respectively, where $\gamma = \frac{K}{MN}$ is the compression ratio, taking values between 0 and 1. The matrix $\hat{\mathbf{H}}$ is presented in Fig. 3, where the number of shots depends on the overlap percentage. It is important to highlight that in each row of $\hat{\mathbf{H}}$ is represented the position of the architecture in the scene when the shot was taken, which is represented as ones over a row of zeros.

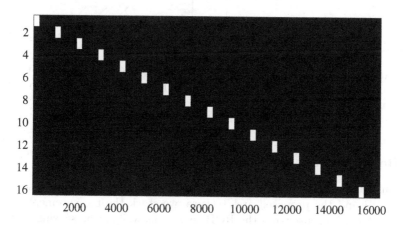

Fig. 3. The matrix $\hat{\mathbf{H}}$ that represents the effect of the slit over the scene, where the black values are zeros and the white values are ones. Each white block represents a shot and the position where the shot was taken in the scene. In this example a $128 \times 128 \times 30$ scene was captured with an overlap of 75%, giving a total of 16 shots.

On the other hand, to model the acquisition of the side information, the architecture use an RGB sensor that will be moving along with the UAV, therefore, capturing different parts of the scene in each shot with a certain percentage of overlap. If $\mathbf{F}$ is a scene of $M \times N$, in this model the picture captured by the RGB sensor is of $M \times \hat{n}$, with $N > \hat{n}$. Therefore, the number of shots taken in a scene can be obtained by

$$K = \left\lceil \frac{N}{\lceil \hat{n}(1-o) \rceil} \right\rceil, \tag{6}$$

where o is the overlap percentage with $0 \leq o \leq 1$. Then, for each shot taken, the sensor captures a segment of the scene where it assumes that all the spectral bands inside the R, G o B band have the same response. Each shot captured can be modeled as

$$\mathbf{R}^k = \mathbf{I}_3 \otimes \left(\mathbf{1}_{1 \times L/3} \otimes \mathbf{A}\right), \qquad (7)$$

where $\mathbf{R}^k$ is a $3MN \times MNL$ matrix, and $\mathbf{A}$ is a $MN \times MN$ matrix with a $\mathbf{I}_{M\hat{n}}$ matrix over the diagonal and the rest of the matrix have values of zero. The $\mathbf{I}_{M\hat{n}}$ matrix will be moving over the diagonal of $\mathbf{A}$ depending on where the picture of the RGB sensor is acquired in the scene. Then the sensing matrix $\bar{\mathbf{H}}$ can be constructed by $\bar{\mathbf{H}} = \sum_L \mathbf{R}^k$. In Fig. 4 the matrices $\mathbf{R}^k$ and $\bar{\mathbf{H}}$ are presented. Finally, the process of acquisition of the side information can be modeled as

$$\bar{\mathbf{g}} = \bar{\mathbf{H}}\mathbf{f}. \qquad (8)$$

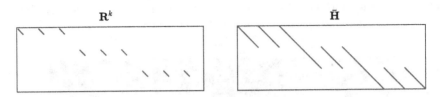

Fig. 4. At the left side is the matrix $\mathbf{R}^k$ for a determined shot, and in the right side is the matrix $\bar{\mathbf{H}}$ for all the shots and spectral bands. In this figure an scene of 9 spectral bands is modeled.

2.3 Reconstruction of Spectral Images

To reconstruct spectral images with side information, which is the case of the SPC + RGB and the proposed architecture, we stack the measurements of the single-pixel spatial sensor and the RGB sensor, as well as the sensing matrices of each measurement as

$$\tilde{\mathbf{H}} = \begin{bmatrix} \hat{\mathbf{H}} \\ \bar{\mathbf{H}} \end{bmatrix}, \tilde{\mathbf{g}} = \begin{bmatrix} \mathbf{g} \\ \bar{\mathbf{g}} \end{bmatrix}. \qquad (9)$$

Finally, the spectral image can be obtained by solving the optimization problem given by

$$\tilde{\mathbf{f}} = \mathbf{\Psi}\{\mathrm{argmin}_{\tilde{\theta}} \|\tilde{\mathbf{H}}\mathbf{\Psi}\tilde{\theta} - \tilde{\mathbf{g}}\|_2^2 + \tau\|\tilde{\theta}\|_1\}, \qquad (10)$$

where τ is a regularization parameter, and $\tilde{\theta}$ is the representation of $\tilde{\mathbf{f}}$ in the basis $\mathbf{\Psi}$. With this new reconstruction, the compression factor changes, this factor is given by $\bar{\gamma} = \frac{3MN+LK}{MNL}$, where $\bar{\gamma} \approx \gamma$ as L increase.

3   Simulations and Results

As mentioned before, the photogrammetry process implies the successive capture of snapshots to construct an orthomosaic, which requires a processing that we assume it is already done. The goal of the proposed architecture, it is that during the process of capture for the orthomosaic construction, at the same time, it captures the information of a single pixel spatial spectrometer. With this in mind, to do the performance analysis of the proposed architecture, we utilized two spectral scenes with a spatial resolution of 128×128 pixels, varying the number of spectral bands from 6 to 30. These scenes are equivalent to the orthomosaic obtained during the photogrammetry process with the UAV. With these scenes, we apply our proposed method varying the optical slit thickness and the percentage of overlap between each shot. For the slit thickness, we used two values, 2 and 5 pixels. For the percentage of overlap between each shoot, we made a comparison with two cases: an ideal case where all the information of the scene is captured by different shots, with an overlap of 99%; and one case with an overlap of 75%, which is commonly utilized in photogrammetry applications with UAVs [7]. Finally, we use $\hat{n} = N/4$ for the size of the acquired information in the UAV, to satisfy the restriction of $N > \hat{n}$.

The results were compared to three different approaches. In the first approach, we use only the RGB information obtained with (8). The second approach uses the classical SPC, using a traditional coded aperture design based on randomly permuted rows of the Hadamard transform [16], with a compression ratio of $\gamma = 0.06$ (approximately 1024 shots). Finally, the third approach uses the classical SPC with stacked RGB side information (SPC + RGB) as in (9), with $\bar{\mathbf{H}} = \mathbf{I}_3 \otimes (\mathbf{1}_{1 \times L/3} \otimes \mathbf{I}_{MN})$, and using traditional Hadamard patterns [5, 9, 10].

For each simulation, the measures are obtained by (5) and (8). The SI is recovered by solving the minimization problem (10). The basis representation utilized, it is given by $\boldsymbol{\Psi} = \boldsymbol{\Psi}_1 \otimes \boldsymbol{\Psi}_2$, where $\boldsymbol{\Psi}_1$ is a 2D wavelet Symmlet 8 basis, and $\boldsymbol{\Psi}_2$ is a 1D discrete cosine transform (DCT). The comparisons are made in terms on the peak signal-to-noise ratio (PSNR) and with the spectral signature in two random points inside the scenes. To analyze the PSNR response, first, we made a comparison to see which configuration have better results using the scene free of noise, then, a further analysis was made adding white noise to the scene at different levels of SNR (5, 10 and 20 dB). The noise simulation was made modifying (10), particularly, the parameter $\tilde{\mathbf{g}}$ will be replaced to $\tilde{\mathbf{g}}_n$, where $\tilde{\mathbf{g}}_n = \tilde{\mathbf{g}} + \boldsymbol{\eta}$, and $\boldsymbol{\eta}$ is standard white Gaussian noise.

The Fig. 5 shows the quality of the reconstruction for the two scenes at different bands, where we can see that the proposed approach have different behaviors depending on the percentage of overlap, also, varying the slit thickness, the changes obtained are subtle; from the results of the Fig. 5 is noticeable that the configuration with an overlap of 99% and a slit thickness of 5 pixels presented the best results for the proposed architecture, but an overlap of 99% is not something practical in the real life, it is common to use overlap percentages of 75% whose results are comparable to the ones at 99%.

For the data cube 1, the results in Fig. 5 show that our proposed architecture has better results that SPC and the RGB architecture in almost all the configurations, being the major difference in PSNR of 1.31 dB for the RGB, and 20.44 dB with the SPC; although the SPC + RGB architecture has better estimations, with the major difference in PSNR of 3.47 dB with the configuration of *ov*99%-5. On the other hand, for the data cube 2, our proposed architecture outperformed the other architectures with a configuration of *ov*99%-5, with the major difference of PSNR of 1.08 dB with RGB, 12.18 dB with SPC and 0.49 dB wit SPC + RGB; only losing to the SPC + RGB architecture for the reconstruction of a scene with 9 and 24 spectral bands. From this analysis, we can conclude that we achieve good results, first because the results showed that our proposed architecture outperformed the RGB and the SPC architectures, and even if the SPC + RGB architecture outperforms us in some cases, the difference was not remarkable. Second, the difference in the number of shots taken in each methodology, where in SPC + RGB the number of shots is approximately 1024, with our architecture, the maximum number of shots is 128 with an overlap of 99%, which can be interpreted as lower sensing times. Finally, our proposed architecture is made up of low-cost elements, because it takes advantage of the UAV movement during the flight, which made possible to use a cheap optical slit instead of an expensive DMD.

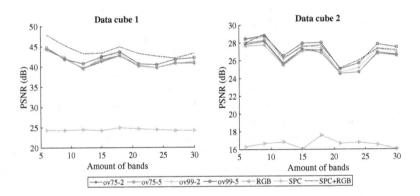

Fig. 5. Reconstruction quality using the architectures RGB, SPC, SPC + RGB, and using the proposed approach with two values of overlap percentage (99 and 75), and two values of slit thickness (2 and 5).

Complementing the analysis in Fig. 5, the results of the PSNR analysis from both data cubes at different levels of white Gaussian noise are shown in Figs. 6 and 7. To make this analysis, the architectures RGB, SPC and SPC + RGB were compared with the proposed architecture with a configuration ov99-5 (which showed the best results). It is shown in the plots that in both data cubes the RGB architecture presents one of the best results, contrary to the SPC who shows the worst results in almost all cases; on the other hand, our proposed architecture shows good results to low levels of SNR in both data cubes, losing only to the RGB architecture at 5 and 10SNR, and at high levels of SNR, the SPC + RGB architecture shows the best results in both data cubes. It is important to highlight that even if the RGB architecture showed good results compared to the other architectures, further we will show that this architecture has a bad spectral response.

On the other hand, Fig. 8 show a comparison of the RGB mappings for the data cubes reconstructed with different architectures, in each sub-figure, there are two marked points where a spectral signature was extracted. Moreover, the Figs. 9 and 10 show the spectral signatures of the points selected from the data cubes. From these spectral signatures, the spectral angle error was computed and shown in Table 1. It is noticeable that the proposed architecture outperformed the RGB and the SPC architectures in both data cubes. On the other hand, the architecture was capable achieve results similar to the SPC + RGB architecture, and even outperform it in the point 2 of the data cube 1 and the point 1 of the data cube 2.

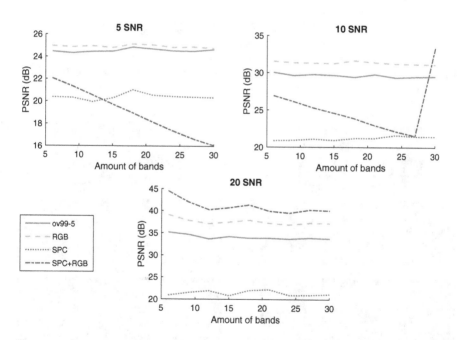

Fig. 6. PSNR results of the data cube 1, using three different levels of SNR and four architectures.

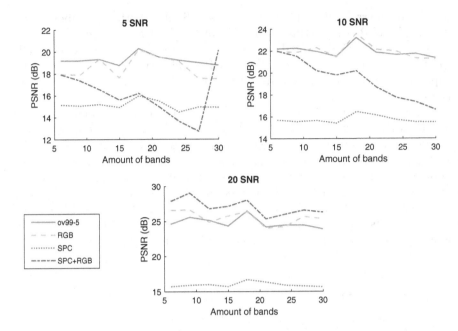

Fig. 7. PSNR results of the data cube 2, using three different levels of SNR and four architectures.

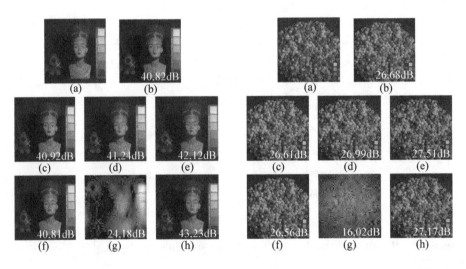

Fig. 8. Comparison between the original scene with the reconstruction from different the approaches used, for the data cube 1 (left) and data cube 2 (right) with spatial dimensions 128×128, $L = 30$ and $\gamma = 0.06$. Each image shows in the lower right corner the PSNR of the reconstruction. (a) Original scene; and the reconstruction using (b) overlap 75% - slit 2, (c) overlap 75% - slit 5, (d) overlap 99% - slit 2, (e) overlap 99% - slit 5, (f) RGB, (g) SPC, (h) SPC + RGB.

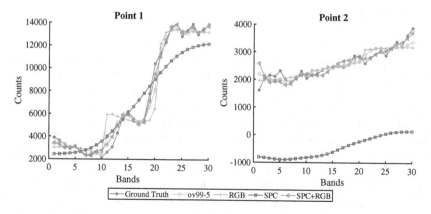

Fig. 9. Comparison of the spectral signatures of the recovered data cube 1 with $L = 30$, using the proposed approach with an overlap of 95% and a slit thickness of 5px, also using the architectures of RGB, SPC, and SPC + RGB.

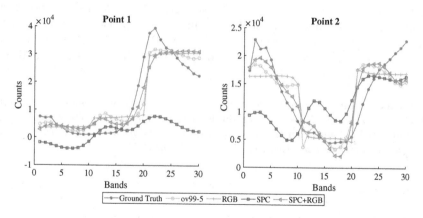

Fig. 10. Comparison of the spectral signatures of the recovered data cube 2 with $L = 30$, using the proposed approach with an overlap of 95% and a slit thickness of 5px, also using the architectures of RGB, SPC, and SPC + RGB.

Table 1. Spectral angle error in radians.

	SAE			
	Data cube 1		Data cube 2	
Architecture	P1	P2	P1	P2
Proposed ov99-5	0.0767	**0.0807**	**0.2762**	0.2729
RGB	0.1484	0.0909	0.3311	0.2660
SPC	0.1479	2.2405	0.6587	0.4660
SPC + RGB	**0.0447**	0.0875	0.2783	**0.2202**

4   Conclusion

A low-cost architecture to retrieve spectral images from an UAV was proposed in this paper. The architecture uses an RGB camera and a single-pixel spatial sensor, taking advantage of the UAV movement during the flight time. The simulations show that the proposed architecture was capable of retrieving spectral images with considerable quality in comparison to other architectures. Our proposed architecture outperformed the RGB architecture by 1.31 dB, the SPC architecture by 20.44 dB, and managed to outperform the SPC + RGB architecture by 0.49 dB. It is important to highlight that our proposed architecture had results similar to the SPC + RGB in all the tests, with the max difference in PSNR of 3.47 dB. On the other hand, we showed that our proposed architecture presents one of the best results at low levels of SNR in comparison to the other architectures, also, present two of the best performances retrieving the spectral information at the points in the scenes. Even though our architecture lost in some cases to the SPC + RGB architecture, we can conclude that our architecture showed good results for various reasons, one of them is that the proposed architecture needed 128 shots (with an overlap of 99%, which is the case that presents the major quantity of shots) to fully sense a scene, which is lower in comparison to other architectures like SPC or SPC + RGB (1024); also, it is important to remark the difference in costs between the SPC + RGB and our proposed architecture.

Acknowledgment. This work was supported by the investigation center Centro TIC with financial support of the vicerrectoria de investigación y extención of the Universidad Industrial de Santander through the project *"Plataforma IoT para el Desarrollo de Servicios Inteligentes de Apoyo al Monitoreo Ambiental"*.

References

1. Adams, S.M., Friedland, C.J.: A survey of unmanned aerial vehicle (UAV) usage for imagery collection in disaster research and management. In: 9th International Workshop on Remote Sensing for Disaster Response, vol. 8 (2011)
2. Arguello, H., Rueda, H., Wu, Y., Prather, D.W., Arce, G.R.: Higher-order computational model for coded aperture spectral imaging. Appl. Opt. **52**(10), D12–D21 (2013)
3. Colomina, I., Molina, P.: Unmanned aerial systems for photogrammetry and remote sensing: a review. ISPRS J. Photogram. Remote Sens. **92**, 79–97 (2014)
4. Donoho, D.L., et al.: Compressed sensing. IEEE Trans. Inf. Theory **52**(4), 1289–1306 (2006)
5. Garcia, H., Correa, C.V., Arguello, H.: Multi-resolution compressive spectral imaging reconstruction from single pixel measurements. IEEE Trans. Image Process. **27**(12), 6174–6184 (2018)
6. Garcia, H., Correa, C.V., Sánchez, K., Vargas, E., Arguello, H.: Multi-resolution coded apertures based on side information for single pixel spectral reconstruction. In: 26th European Signal Processing Conference (EUSIPCO), pp. 2215–2219. IEEE (2018)

7. Gonçalves, J., Henriques, R.: UAV photogrammetry for topographic monitoring of coastal areas. ISPRS J. Photogram. Remote Sens. **104**, 101–111 (2015)
8. Honkavaara, E., et al.: Processing and assessment of spectrometric, stereoscopic imagery collected using a lightweight UAV spectral camera for precision agriculture. Remote Sens. **5**(10), 5006–5039 (2013)
9. Jerez, A., Garcia, H., Arguello, H.: Single pixel spectral image fusion with side information from a grayscale sensor. In: 1st Colombian Conference on Applications in Computational Intelligence (ColCACI), pp. 1–6. IEEE (2018)
10. Jerez, A., Garcia, H., Arguello, H.: Spectral image fusion for increasing the spatio-spectral resolution through side information. In: Orjuela-Cañón, A.D., Figueroa-García, J.C., Arias-Londoño, J.D. (eds.) ColCACI 2018. CCIS, vol. 833, pp. 165–176. Springer, Cham (2018). https://doi.org/10.1007/978-3-030-03023-0_14
11. Lu, G., Fei, B.: Medical hyperspectral imaging: a review. J. Biomed. Opt. **19**(1), 010901 (2014)
12. Näsi, R., et al.: Using UAV-based photogrammetry and hyperspectral imaging for mapping bark beetle damage at tree-level. Remote Sens. **7**(11), 15467–15493 (2015)
13. Phillips, D.B., et al.: Adaptive foveated single-pixel imaging with dynamic super-sampling. Sci. Adv. **3**(4), e1601782 (2017)
14. Schowengerdt, R.A.: Remote Sensing: Models and Methods for Image Processing. Elsevier, Saint Louis (2012)
15. Shaw, G.A., Burke, H.K.: Spectral imaging for remote sensing. Lincoln Lab. J. **14**(1), 3–28 (2003)
16. Warnell, G., Bhattacharya, S., Chellappa, R., Başar, T.: Adaptive-rate compressive sensing using side information. IEEE Trans. Image Process. **24**(11), 3846–3857 (2015)

Integration of an Adaptive Cellular Automaton and a Cellular Neural Network for the Impulsive Noise Suppression and Edge Detection in Digital Images

Karen Angulo[1]([✉]) [ID], Danilo Gil[1] [ID], and Helbert Espitia[2] [ID]

[1] Systems Engineering, Universidad Distrital Francisco José de Caldas, Bogotá, Colombia
{kvangulos, dggils}@correo.udistrital.edu.co
[2] Faculty of Engineering, Universidad Distrital Francisco José de Caldas, Bogotá, Colombia
heespitiac@udistrital.edu.co

Abstract. This article proposes the combination of two bio-inspired computational models that are sequentially implemented to eliminate impulsive noise and edge detection in grayscale images. In general, this procedure consists of: (1) implementing a cellular automaton (CA) with an adaptive behavior that expands the Moore neighborhood when it considers that the information obtained from its first level neighbors is insufficient. Based on the above, the image affected by noise is processed, in order to eliminate the corrupted pixels and perform reprocessing that will lead to the improvement of the quality of the image, (2) the resulting image is defined as an input of the cellular neural network (CNN) together with the training images, so that by defining three templates (feedback (A), cloning (B) and threshold or bias (I)), contour detection of objects within the image thrown by the initial method can be performed. The results for the noise elimination present a restoration of the image that oscillates between 70.63% and 99.65%, indicating that the image does not lose its quality despite being exposed to high noise levels, similarly it occurs for the edge detection, which presents an approximate efficiency of 65% with respect to the algorithms established within the framework of comparison.

Keywords: Image processing · Cellular Neural Networks · Adaptive algorithm · Noise elimination · Edge detection

1 Introduction

Image processing goes back hundreds of years when philosophers and scientists like Alhazen, Aristotle, Roger Bacon and Leonardo Da Vinci, among others, focused their efforts on the study of imaging in the human eye (optics) [1]. This being the first step for years later, researchers and experts in the field made use of these concepts as a fundamental basis to trigger a research trend focused on the treatment of optical phenomena that were subsequently useful for the creation of images [1]. Years later,

© Springer Nature Switzerland AG 2019
A. D. Orjuela-Cañón et al. (Eds.): ColCACI 2019, CCIS 1096, pp. 168–181, 2019.
https://doi.org/10.1007/978-3-030-36211-9_14

thanks to the theory developed by the mathematician Jean-Baptiste-Joseph Fourier (1768–1830), it was verified that the basis of image processing for both optical media and digital media is based on the Fourier theorem, since the representation of the variation of the irradiance or brightness of an image can be seen as a sum of sine-wave distributions of several frequencies [2].

Currently, images play an important role in the perception of reality, because the movement can be interpreted as a sequence of images (frames) that are displayed in a second and from these frames it is possible to identify relevant characteristics of an object in particular or its environment in general. Therefore, this subject is of utmost importance in various scientific fields such as: medical analysis and diagnostics, space exploration, computational vision, image recognition, etc. [3], since with the use of images significant contributions have been generated in these fields and at the same time, the development of techniques that aim to improve the appearance of the image and highlight the details that are desired to make it more visible has been unleashed [1, 2].

Among the techniques most frequently used in image processing, those include noise elimination and edge detection, which have been used in a number of applications that encompass methodology developments that start with simple and efficient, and end in complex and robust [3].

The main objective of the techniques of noise elimination is to reduce the pixels that take a level of intensity different from their neighbors, either by the process of capture, digitalization and/or image transmission [4]. To cover this problem, there are different types of algorithms that are aligned with this object. The most common noise filters are linear filters that are divided into: media filter and Gaussian filter, which perform a convolution operation between the image to be filtered and a mask, without offering satisfactory results, due to the fact that the resulting image is blurred and in many cases, the edges are lost [4], also, it is important to emphasize that for images that present low densities of noise these methods are quite efficient [5].

On the other hand, there are non-linear filters, such as the median filter, which in general terms, runs through each pixel of the image and replaces it with the median of the neighboring pixels, thus reducing image defects [4, 6]; however, this process significantly increases the computational complexity, because in order to calculate the median, the different values that appear inside the mask must be ordered and then determine which is the central value [5]. In addition, it should be noted that this method has drawbacks with images that have high densities of noise [7], since it operates on all the pixels of the image.

Regarding the detection of edges, the objective of this technique involves the identification of intensity changes in an image (luminance variation), that is, through a series of mathematical operations it is sought to detect the discontinuities between the pixels [8].

Among the methods that focus on solving this issue, we can highlight the work done by Lawrence Roberts in 1963 and John Canny in 1986, who made use of gradient-based methods to estimate the magnitude and direction of the gradient, this in order to identify the pixels that are considered as edges [9], which means that the edges are detected by the spatial derivatives of the image that are calculated using convolution operators. It should be noted that in addition to those presented above, there are Sobel and Prewitt operators that also use the first order derivative.

On the other hand, the Laplacian of Gaussian (or LoG) uses the second derivative of the image and given this quality, the filter is sensitive to noise [10]. When evaluating the results offered by each of these operators, it can be seen that although the results obtained are remarkable (visually), all of these have flaws in images that contain a certain amount of noise and, consequently, the quality of the detection is affected by the location of false edges [11].

In synthesis, a system is proposed that consists of the integration of an adaptive cellular automaton and a cellular neural network to eliminate salt and pepper type noise, and at the same time to detect the contours of the objects present in the images, which would lead to generating a robust and bio-inspired method able to adapt to the conditions of their environment to make decisions and thus generate effective results.

2   Algorithm of Integration Between Cellular Automata and Cellular Neural Network

The presented proposal seeks to develop a two-phase algorithm that encompasses the characteristics of both a CA and those of a CNN. In the first phase, we try to create an adaptive algorithm based on CA's that efficiently eliminates salt and pepper noise in digital images; and in the second phase, that the resulting image is an entrance to the CNN together with a series of training images which, through pre-established parameters, manage to detect the edges of the image.

2.1   Adaptive Algorithm for Noise Elimination

In this section, it is presented method based on CA's that seeks to remove impulsive noise in gray-scale digital images as shown in [7], therefore, it is essential to define the neighborhood to be used, since by means of this, it is possible to obtain information about the environment. Moore neighborhood (see Fig. 1B) offers a more effective solution because its configuration is set in a 3×3 matrix and it can cover a larger number of pixels than Von Neumann neighborhood (see Fig. 1A).

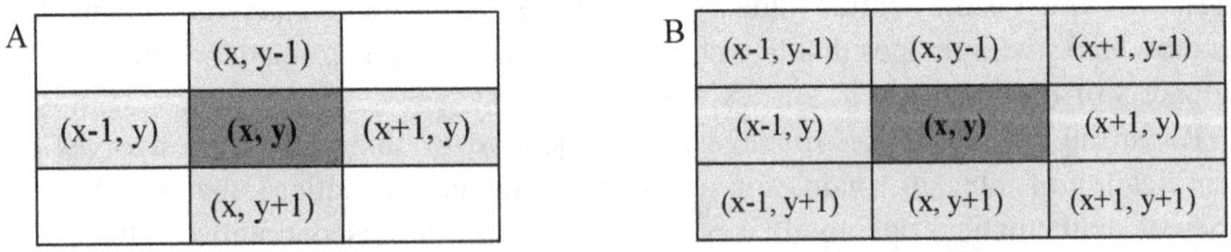

A				B			
	(x, y-1)				(x-1, y-1)	(x, y-1)	(x+1, y-1)
(x-1, y)	(x, y)	(x+1, y)			(x-1, y)	(x, y)	(x+1, y)
	(x, y+1)				(x-1, y+1)	(x, y+1)	(x+1, y+1)

Fig. 1. 2D Neighborhood. (a) Von Neumann. (b) Moore.

From the point of view of digital image processing, a two-dimensional image (2D) is represented as a matrix of size $m \times n$, which has two main characteristics: (1) Each position of the matrix corresponds to a pixel inside the image. (2) The value assigned to a particular position of the CA refers to an intensity value of the image at that point [20].

Considering the above, it is possible to establish a correlation between each cell of the CA and one pixel of the image, and thus, the utility of a two-dimensional CA ($D = 2$) with a Moore neighborhood begin to prevail. In addition, it is necessary to specify the boundary conditions $C(i_0, j_0)$ and for this, both the first and the last row and column of the image were extended, in such a way that when the CA (N) is positioned in the limits of the image does not affect the processing. When defining these initial parameters and taking into account that the Moore neighborhood (M) is described by (1), we proceeded to segment the universe into groups to facilitate the processing of information.

$$N(i_0, j_0)^M = \{(i, j) : |i - i_0| \leq r, |j - j_0| \leq r\} \tag{1}$$

In Eq. (1) r is the range, which for this case is equal to one because the initial neighborhood has 8 neighbors (see Fig. 1). Among the aspects to be taken into account, it is important to note that in a grayscale image, discrete values can be assigned between 0 and 255 to each pixel and that these in turn act as the state values of the CA. Based on this definition, and starting from the generality of Moore neighborhood, a local 2D rule was established for the proposed cellular automaton, as shown below:

$$C^{t+1}(i,j) = \begin{cases} C^t(i,j), & \text{if } v_{min} < C^t(i,j) < v_{max} \\ Cn^t(i,j), & \text{if } C^t(i,j) = v_{min} \text{ or } C^t(i,j) = v_{max} \end{cases} \tag{2}$$

In Eq. (2), v_{min} and v_{max} are the minimum and maximum values that a grayscale image can take, which, for this case, can be seen as noisy pixels (according to the definition of salt and pepper noise). Also, $C^{t+1}(i,j)$ is the value that the pixel will take in the next iteration ($t + 1$) and this will be directly related to the conditions presented in (2) to obtain the final result. In both cases, the decision is affected by $C^t(i,j)$, which corresponds to the current value of the cell under evaluation. For the case where the result is equal to $C^t(i,j)$, if the value of the pixel under evaluation is greater than 0 and less than 255, the algorithm will ignore this position and continue with the next position, until finding a value that complies with case number two of (2), which defines that if the value of the pixel under evaluation is equal to 0 or to 255, it will be executed (3).

$$Cn^t(i,j) = \begin{cases} C(2n+1)2-1, & \text{if } \forall C^t(i,j) \in N, C^t(i,j) \neq v_{min} \text{ or } C^t(i,j) \neq v_{max} \text{ and } N = \emptyset \\ avg(C^t(i,j)), & \text{if } \forall C^t(i,j) \in N, \exists C^t(i,j) \neq v_{min} \text{ or } \exists C^t(i,j) \neq v_{max} \end{cases} \tag{3}$$

When considered a pixel as noisy, the sub-rule described in (3) is applied, in the case where Moore neighborhood only has maximum or minimum values, it will be adapted and extended in one level (5×5 matrix), in order to obtain the value of the pixel in evaluation by calculating the average from the new information (that is, 24 neighbors) excluding the maximum and minimum values. Otherwise, all the values that take intensities of 0 and 255 will be eliminated, and then apply an average over the remaining values of the neighborhood.

2.2   Design of a Cellular Neural Network for the Detection of Edges

The concept of Cellular Neural Network was introduced by Leon Chua and Lin Yang in 1988 through the articles "Cellular Neural Networks: Theory" and "Cellular Neural Networks: Applications". Its objective was to demonstrate that by means of the implementation of a mathematical model of a CNN with static inputs it is possible to achieve the convergence of the processing units so that they are used in calculations. Later [21, 22], that is, by using a wide variety of dynamically coupled circuits in a non-linear way it is possible to process large volumes of information in real time.

Based on the above, a CNN can be defined as an array of locally interconnected non-linear processors operating in parallel. A cellular neural network has a two-dimensional grid structure of analog processing units called cells, where each cell is locally connected only to its neighboring cells through a ruleset called "cloning templates", which are responsible for determining the dynamic behavior of the CNN (see Fig. 2) [22]. According to [23], a CNN is very similar to a neural network, in terms of the processing unit and the structure, however, the big difference is that in a CNN the connections are limited to a predefined local neighborhood, whereas in neural network connections they can be global.

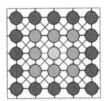

Fig. 2. Structure of a two-dimensional cellular neural network with neighborhood radius $r = 1$.

According to [23], the dynamic behavior of a cell in a CNN can be defined in terms of its state and output equations, as shown below:

$$\begin{cases} \frac{d x_{ij}(t)}{dt} = -x_{ij}(t) + \sum_{m,n \in N(i,j)} a_{mn} y_{mn}(t) + \sum_{m,n \in N(i,j)} b_{mn} u_{mn}(t) + I_{ij} \\ y_{ij}(t) = f(x_{ij}(t)) = \frac{1}{2}(|x_{ij} + 1| - |x_{ij} - 1|) \end{cases} \quad (4)$$

Where a_{mn}, b_{mn} and I_{ij} are the elements of the feedback template (A), the cloning template (B) and the threshold or bias (I), respectively. Also in (4), x_{ij} and y_{ij} are the states of input and output. As mentioned above, each cell is defined by $C(i,j)$ where $(i,j) \in \{1 \leq i \leq M, 1 \leq j \leq N\}$ which has identical connections with each cell present in the previously defined neighborhood. This is defined mathematically by (5).

$$N_r(i,j) = \{C(k,l) | max\{|k - i|, |l - j|\} \leq r, 1 \leq k \leq M, 1 \leq l \leq N\} \quad (5)$$

Where r, is a positive integer that determines the size of the neighborhood and ordered pair (i,j) and (k,l) are the indices that determine the position of the cell.

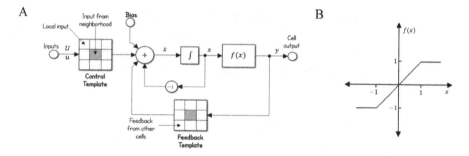

Fig. 3. Structure system Eq. (4). (a) The block diagram of a CNN cell. (b) Output function.

By defining the proposed structure for a CNN (see Fig. 3) with a neighborhood of 3×3, there is a string of 19 real numbers called the CNN gene, which includes: (1) A, which is composed of nine feedback values, (2) B, which consists of nine control values and I that has a value which acts as a bias.

$$A = \begin{pmatrix} a_{-1,-1} & a_{-1,0} & a_{-1,1} \\ a_{0,-1} & a_{0,0} & a_{0,1} \\ a_{1,-1} & a_{1,0} & a_{1,1} \end{pmatrix}, B = \begin{pmatrix} b_{-1,-1} & b_{-1,0} & b_{-1,1} \\ b_{0,-1} & b_{0,0} & b_{0,1} \\ b_{1,-1} & b_{1,0} & b_{1,1} \end{pmatrix}, I = I_{ij} \quad (6)$$

Then, $A = \{\bar{a}_{ij}\} \in R^{n \times n}$ and $B = \{\bar{b}_{ij}\} \in R^{n \times n}$ are feedback and control matrices respectively, describing the interaction between each cell and its neighbors in terms of their input and output variables [23].

Assume $n = M \times N$ and by means of re-numbering the cells from 1 to n, (4) can be define in compact vector form as shown in (7).

$$\begin{cases} \dot{x}(t) = -x(t) + \bar{A}y(x(t)) + \bar{B}u + \bar{I}, \\ y(x(t)) = f(x(t)) = \frac{1}{2}(|x(t) + 1| - |x(t) - 1|) \end{cases} \quad (7)$$

Where $x(t)$ is the state vector, $y(x(t))$ is the output vector then $f(x(t))$ is the output function vector, u is a static input vector which is independent of time, $\bar{A}$ is the feedback matrix, $\bar{B}$ is control matrix and $\bar{I}$ is the vector containing the bias of each cell. It can be note that despite that $\bar{A}$ (control matrix) and $\bar{B}$ (feedback matrix) are different from A (control template) and B (feedback template), respectively, but their relation is quite close [23].

Considering the information presented in [23] and taking into account that in the matrix A of (6), all the values are 0 except in the position $a_{0,0} = a$, and assuming, that $a < 1$, y and the initial condition $x_{ij}(0) = 0$, it can be said that the final state is $|x_{ij}(\infty)| > 1$, this implies that the CNN will enter a state of stabilization, that is, it has found all the edges of the image. According to the following rules:

$$\begin{cases} x_{ij} = edge, & if\ x_{ij}(1) > 0,\ then\ y_{ij}(1) = 1 \\ x_{ij} = no\ edge, & if\ x_{ij}(1) < 0,\ then\ y_{ij}(1) = 1 \end{cases} \tag{8}$$

As a summary, the proposed model in graphic form is shown in Fig. 4.

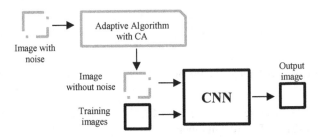

Fig. 4. Flow chart for edge detection and noise removal.

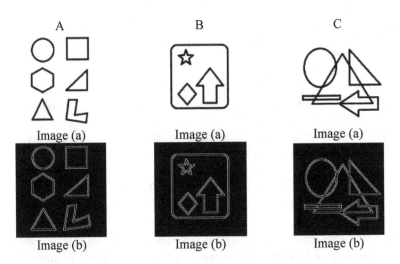

Fig. 5. Training images. (a) Input image. (b) Image with ideal edges.

3 Simulation

In this section, a number of cases is presented showing the effectiveness of the proposed method. Firstly, for the elimination of noise, a series of grayscale images exposed to different levels of salt and pepper noise were used. Secondly, for the edge detection process, the images resulting from the noise elimination algorithm were used, the three training images (see Fig. 5), and the templates shown below to detect the contours present in an image.

$$A = \begin{pmatrix} 0 & 0 & 0 \\ 0 & a & 0 \\ 0 & 0 & 0 \end{pmatrix}, B = \begin{pmatrix} -0.9804 & -0.9804 & -0.9804 \\ -0.9804 & 8.0025 & -0.9804 \\ -0.9804 & -0.9804 & -0.9804 \end{pmatrix}, I = -0.5387 \quad (9)$$

To evaluate the performance of the exposed model, the use of different performance indices was proposed. In the first part, the results are focused on measuring the effectiveness of the method developed to eliminate noise by means of the Peak Signal-to-Noise Ratio or PSNR, the Structural Similarity Index or SSIM and the Mean Squared Error or MSE.

$$MSE = \frac{1}{MN} \sum_{i=1}^{M} \sum_{j=1}^{N} (\bar{y}_{ij} - \hat{y}_{ij})^2 \quad (10)$$

$$PSNR = 10 \log_{10} \frac{(2^B - 1)}{MSE} \text{dB} \quad (11)$$

Where, $\bar{y}_{ij}$ is the pixel of the original image y $\hat{y}_{ij}$ is the pixel of the image reconstructed from the Adaptive Algorithm based on Cellular Automata (hereinafter, Method of Integration of a CA and a CNN or MECNN).

The SSIM, as shown in (12), is an indicator that measures the quality of digital images and is used to establish the similarity between two images. Its objective is to determine how different the original image is from the distorted image, for this three indices are calculated using the values of luminance (l), contrast (c) and structure (s) of a pair of images [7, 15].

$$SSIM(x, y) = [l(x, y)]^\alpha \cdot [c(x, y)]^\beta \cdot [s(x, y)]^\gamma \quad (12)$$

This index establishes a value with a range between 0 and 1, d where zero equals the total loss of similarity and one is the absolute similarity [7, 15].

The results in visual terms are shown in Fig. 6, where in the left box the image with noise is displayed and in the right the result after the application of the MECNN.

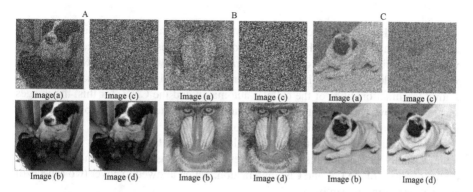

Fig. 6. Images with and without noise (A) Dogs. (B) Baboon. (C) Pug. Columns: (a) Input image with 50%. noise. (b) Resulting image of the MECNN. (c) Input image with 90%. noise. (d) Resulting image of the MECNN.

In the same way, Table 1 and Fig. 7 shows the MECNN data when is applied to the Dogs, Baboon and Pug images, qualitatively observing, the noise was effectively reduced at most of the exposed noise levels. Which means that the restoration of images with the proposed method was successful, as can be seen and according to the definition of the PSNR, the higher the value the closer the image is to the original image and also the SSIM, the closer to 1 more similar are the evaluated images, which corresponds exactly to what is shown in Fig. 6.

Table 1. SSIM, MSE and PSNR for a restored image that was exposed to different noise levels.

Dogs

Noise	5%	10%	20%	30%	40%	50%	60%	70%	80%	90%
SSIM	0,9937	0,9873	0,9734	0,9580	0,9399	0,9190	0,8924	0,8566	0,8078	0,7242
MSE	0,64	1,26	2,59	4,07	5,76	7,59	9,81	12,57	19,55	23,21
PSNR	45,55	42,50	39,19	37,19	35,59	33,96	32,53	31,05	28,96	25,93

Baboon

Noise	5%	10%	20%	30%	40%	50%	60%	70%	80%	90%
SSIM	0,9894	0,9781	0,9536	0,9257	0,8929	0,8513	0,7994	0,7334	0,6381	0,5644
MSE	2,51	5,17	10,36	15,73	17,36	20,94	25,63	31,06	37,78	45,71
PSNR	36,63	33,58	30,39	28,45	26,89	25,49	24,12	22,85	21,31	19,41

Cameraman

Noise	5%	10%	20%	30%	40%	50%	60%	70%	80%	90%
SSIM	0,9754	0,9640	0,9393	0,9121	0,8818	0,8463	0,8037	0,7501	0,6814	0,5864
MSE	3,78	4,98	7,59	10,13	13,21	16,62	20,55	25,07	30,66	39.15
PSNR	40,14	38,27	35,86	34,11	32,52	31,14	29,60	27,92	25,67	22,91

Pug

Noise	5%	10%	20%	30%	40%	50%	60%	70%	80%	90%
SSIM	0,9983	0,9964	0,9924	0,9872	0,9812	0,9714	0,9564	0,9324	0,8886	0,8019
MSE	0,22	0,46	0,96	1,66	2,46	3,68	5,47	8,30	12,55	21,95
PSNR	51,73	48,62	45,25	42,71	40,86	38,66	36,37	34,10	30,97	27,38

The second part focuses on showing two types of results. On one side, the qualitative results and on the other side, the quantitative results of the edge detection process. The first ones are oriented to graphically show the characteristics of the proposed development. In this sense, a scenario is initially proposed that allows presenting the functionalities of the cellular automaton and the CNN, for this, the images illustrated below was subjected to an initial transformation in order to simulate the impulsive salt and pepper noise at a level of 5%.

In Fig. 8, it can be seen that the model proposed in this work, has the ability to obtain visually acceptable results at different noise levels, this is mainly due to the special qualities of the CA and CNN interaction, which allowed to cover two aspects of image processing efficiently.

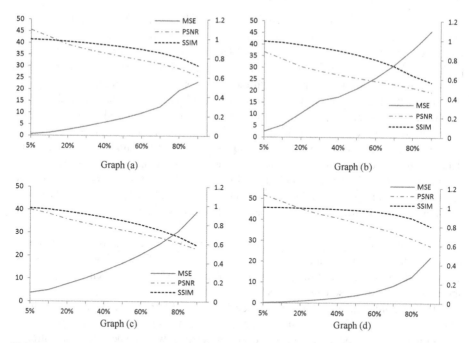

Fig. 7. Comparison of performance indices in images: (a) Dogs. (b) Baboon. (c) Cameraman. (d) Pug.

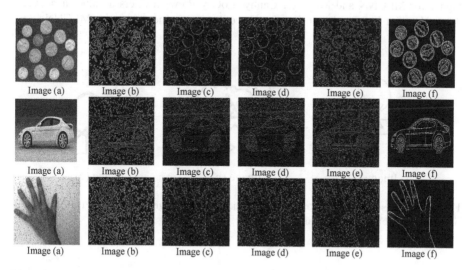

Fig. 8. Edge detection with 5% noise (a) Base image. Resulting image (b) Canny. (c) Prewitt. (d) Sobel. (e) LoG. (f) proposed algorithm.

Regarding the calculation of the quantitative results of the CNN, some test images were used that can be considered as a laboratory case or ideal, since they have horizontal, vertical lines, diagonals and clearly defined curves, which facilitates the comparison of the proposed model against the usual methods of Canny, Prewitt and LoG, and also generates some coherence with the conditions set by each author.

Due to the fact that until now there is no technique that can be established as a fundamental basis for edge detection, the images in Fig. 9, were used as a reference to make an objective comparison. In this work, three performance indices were used: (1) the Mean Square Error (MSE), is the squared norm of the difference between the data and the approximation divided by the number of elements [12, 15], (2) Maximum Error (MAXERR), is the maximum deviation to the absolute square of the data (real value signal), from the approximation (reconstructed image) [24] and (3) the L2RAT, which is the ratio of the squared norm between the reconstructed image and the original image [24].

With a clear objective of each of these indices, we proceeded to make the comparison of the resulting images (see Fig. 10) of the Canny, Prewitt, and LoG methods and the MECNN compared to those with ideal edges. The data presented in Table 2 show the results of these calculations.

The resultant images quality is verified by using different quality measures like, MSE, MAXERR, L2RAT, through these it has been found that the proposed edge detection has had a better performance and efficiency with respect to conventional methods. MSE is minimum for MECNN and maximum for LoG, Prewitt operator and Canny that holds similar values. MAXERR is the same for all the operators. L2RAT is higher for MECNN and lower for Canny, LoG y Prewwit offers a value in between them. Hence it is proved that the edge detection rate is increases with MECNN.

Image (a)   Image (b)   Image (c)

Fig. 9. Ideal cases for the proposed model application. (a) Image A (ideal case 1). (b) Image B (ideal case 2). (c) Image C (ideal case 3).

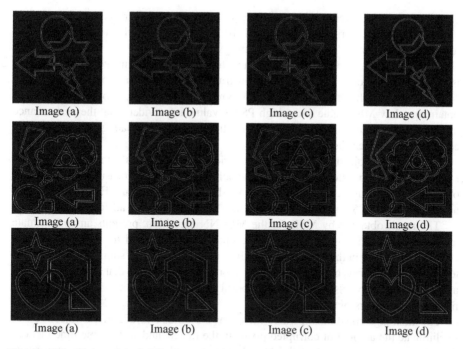

Fig. 10. Edge detection with CNN for the ideal case 1. (a) Canny resulting image. (b) Resulting image Prewitt. (c) Resulting image LOG. (d) MECNN Resulting image.

Table 2. Metrics applied in images A, B, and C.

		Canny	Prewitt	LoG	MECNN
Image A	MSE	8,963E+07	8,964E+07	8,963E+07	5,850E+07
	MAXERR	255	255	255	255
	L2RAT	1,924E+09	2,286E+09	2,212E+09	9,930E−01
Image B	MSE	7,926E+07	7,926E+07	7,927E+07	5,213E+07
	MAXERR	255	255	255	255
	L2RAT	1,701E+09	2,021E+09	1,956E+09	9,924E−01
Image C	MSE	9,818E+07	9,837E+07	9,805E+07	6,519E+07
	MAXERR	255	255	255	255
	L2RAT	2,116E+09	2,514E+09	2,433E+09	9,697E−01

4 Discussions and Results

According to Table 1, the similarity between the original image and the result of MECNN is between a range of 70.63% and 99.65%, indicating that although there is a considerable impact on the image, the cellular automaton can efficiently repair the quality of the affected image. Regarding the Mean Square Error (MSE), these decrease approximately 32 units (from 50.63 to 18.36) as the noise increases, which imply that visually there is no disproportionate difference between the final result and the original. Finally, the PSNR varies between 25.51 dB and 51.78 dB, which in general terms represents good quality in the resulting image.

With the exposed data, it could be established that the performance of the algorithm is efficient, because the error in the reconstructed signal with respect to the original signal is low, which means that the signal to noise ratio is large, in other words, when obtaining a low MSE value and a high PSNR value, it is evident that the performance of the noise elimination method is effective. In addition to indicating a high degree of coincidence between the images.

To make an objective comparison, a series of "ideal cases" (those that use elementary forms) and different estimators capable of numerically measuring the qualities of the image were used, these are shown in Table 2. The Maximum Error (MAXERR), always located at 255, showing that the trace is continuous for all found objects.

The result obtained by MSE for the MECNN algorithm, presents an approximate improvement of 65% with respect to the other algorithms and the L2RAT index is considerably lower in the MECNN algorithm, indicating that the similarity between the test images and those obtained is almost absolute. It is shown that, according to the analysis of the previous indices, the proposal is genuinely efficient when it comes to finding the contours present in an image.

For the image comparison, where there was a 5% noise level and the objective was to eliminate the amount of corrupted pixels in the image, and at the same time identify the edges, it was evident that the MECNN performed these tasks in an appropriate manner without losing the details of the image, and although the image was exposed to high noise levels, it was observed that the restoration of the image was in no case less than 70%, that is, that the details were maintained and the quality of the image was optimized.

References

1. Nieto, A., Díaz, I.: Evolución del procesamiento digital de imágenes [Evolution of digital image processing]. Centro Universitario UAEM Ecatepec (2018)
2. Malacara, D.: Óptica tradicional y moderna [Traditional and modern optics]. 3rd abbreviated edn. Fondo de Cultura Económica, Mexico (2002)
3. Diwakar, M., Patel, P.K., Gupta, K.: Cellular automata based edge-detection for brain tumor. In: 2013 International Conference on Advances in Computing, Communications and Informatics (ICACCI), Mysore, India, pp. 53–59. IEEE (2013)
4. Esqueda, J.J., Palafox, L.E.: Fundamentos de procesamiento de imágenes [Fundamentals of image processing]. Universidad Autónoma de Baja California, Mexicali, Baja California (2005)
5. Pitas, I., Venetsanopoulos, A.N.: Nonlinear Digital Filters: Principles and Applications. Kluwer Academic Publishers, Norwell (1990)
6. Yaroslavsky, L.: Digital Holography and Digital Image Processing: Principles, Methods, Algorithms. Kluwer Academic Publishers, Norwell (2003)
7. Tourtounis, D., Mitianaudis, N., Sirakaulis, G.: Salt-n-pepper noise filtering using cellular automata. J. Cell. Automata 13(1–2), 81–101 (2018)

8. Rosin, P.L., Sun, X.: Edge detection using cellular automata. Cell Automata Image Process. Geom. **10**, 85–103 (2014)
9. Wongthanavasu, S.: Cellular automata for medical image processing. In: Cellular Automata Innovative Modelling for Science and Engineering, pp. 395–410 (2011)
10. Öztürk, Ş., Akdemir, B.: Comparison of edge detection algorithms for texture analysis on glass production. Procedia Soc. Behav. Sci. **195**, 2675–2682 (2015)
11. Xiao, W., Hui, X.: An improved canny edge detection algorithm based on predisposal method for image corrupted by Gaussian noise. In: 2010 World Automation Congress, Kobe, Japan, pp. 113–116. IEEE (2010)
12. Echeverri, A., Rudas, J.E., Toscano, R., Ballesteros, R.: Impulsive noise elimination in color images using interpolation with radial-basis functions. Revista Ingeniería **16**(1), 27–35 (2011)
13. Garnett, R., Huegerich, T., Chui, C., He, W.: A universal noise removal algorithm with an impulse detector. IEEE Trans. Image Process. **14**(11), 1747–1754 (2005)
14. Chan, R.H., Ho, C.W., Nikolova, M.: Salt-and-pepper noise removal by median-type noise detectors and detail-preserving regularization. IEEE Trans. Image Process. **14**(10), 1479–1485 (2005)
15. Sahin, U., Uguz, S., Sahin, F.: Salt and pepper noise filtering with fuzzy-cellular automata. Comput. Electr. Eng. **40**(1), 59–69 (2014)
16. Sahota, P., Daemi, M., Elliman, D.: Training genetically evolving cellular automata for image processing. In: Proceedings of International Conference on Speech, Image Processing and Neural Networks, ICSIPNN 1994, Hong Kong. IEEE (1994)
17. Batouche, M., Meshoul, S., Abbassene, A.: On solving edge detection by emergence. In: Ali, M., Dapoigny, R. (eds.) IEA/AIE 2006. LNCS (LNAI), vol. 4031, pp. 800–808. Springer, Heidelberg (2006). https://doi.org/10.1007/11779568_86
18. Slatnia, S., Batouche, M., Melkemi, Kamal E.: Evolutionary cellular automata based-approach for edge detection. In: Masulli, F., Mitra, S., Pasi, G. (eds.) WILF 2007. LNCS (LNAI), vol. 4578, pp. 404–411. Springer, Heidelberg (2007). https://doi.org/10.1007/978-3-540-73400-0_51
19. Selvapeter, J., Hordijk, W.: Genetically evolved cellular automata for image edge detection. In: Proceedings of the International Conference on Signal, Image Processing and Pattern Recognition, Delhi, India (2013)
20. Wongthanavasu, S., Sadananda, R.: A CA-based edge operator and its performance evaluation. J. Vis. Commun. Image Represent. **14**(2), 83–96 (2003)
21. Chua, L.O., Yang, L.: Cellular neural networks: theory. IEEE Trans. Circ. Syst. **35**(10), 1257–1272 (1988)
22. Adhikari, S.P., Kim, H., Yang, C., Chua, L.O.: Building cellular neural network templates with a hardware friendly learning algorithm. Neurocomputing **312**, 276–284 (2018)
23. Li, H., Liao, X., Li, C., Huang, H., Li, C.: Edge detection of noisy images based on cellular neural networks. Commun. Nonlinear Sci. Numer. Simul. **16**(9), 3746–3759 (2011)
24. El Abbadil, N.K., Al-Bakry, A.M.: New Efficient Technique for Compression of ECG Signal. IJCSI Int. J. Comput. Sci. Issues **10**(4), 139–146 (2013)

Sweet Citrus Fruit Detection in Thermal Images Using Fuzzy Image Processing

Ingrid Lorena Argote Pedraza[1]([✉]), John Faber Archila Diaz[2],
Renan Moreira Pinto[1], Marcelo Becker[1], and Mario Luiz Tronco[1]

[1] São Carlos School of Engineering, University of São Paulo,
Av. Trab. São Carlense 400, São Carlos, Brazil
ingridargote@usp.br
[2] Industrial University of Santander,
Calle 10 26-58, Bucaramanga, Santander, Colombia

Abstract. In agriculture, intelligent systems applications have generated great advances in automating some processes in the production chain. To improve the efficiency of those systems is proposes a vision algorithm to estimate the amount of fruits in sweet orange trees. This study proposes a computer vision system based on the capture of thermal images and fuzzy image processing. A bibliographical review has been done to analyze the state-of-the-art of the different systems used in fruit recognition, and also the different applications of thermography in agricultural systems. The algorithm developed for this project uses the intensification operator to contrast-enhanced and the fuzzy divergence for segmentation and Hough transform for fruit identification. It estimates the numbers of fruits in the tree, a task that is currently manually performed. In order to validate the proposed algorithm a database was created with images of sweet orange acquired in the Maringá Farm. The validation process indicated that the variation of the tree branch and the fruit temperature is not very high, making it difficult to segment the images using a temperature threshold. Errors in the segmentation algorithm could mean the increase of false positives in the fruit-counting algorithm. Recognition of isolated fruits with the proposed algorithm presented an overall accuracy of 93.5% and grouped fruits accuracy was 80%. The experiments show the need of other image hardware to improve the recognition of small temperature changes in the image.

Keywords: Agricultural systems · Citrus · Fuzzy image processing · Thermal images

1 Introduction

The Brazilian citrus industry is one of the most productive national agro-industrial sector. Every year are harvested about 16 million tons of citrus fruits,

Supported by organization CNPq, CAPES, EMBRAPA, CITROSUCO and EESC-USP.

© Springer Nature Switzerland AG 2019
A. D. Orjuela-Cañón et al. (Eds.): ColCACI 2019, CCIS 1096, pp. 182–193, 2019.
https://doi.org/10.1007/978-3-030-36211-9_15

which represents about 25% of world production and currently, approximately 85% of the orange juice that is consumed in the world is produced in Brazil. All these factors favored for Brazil to become the world's largest producer of orange juice, which represents about 5% of the Product Gross Domestic (GDP) agricultural. In this scenario, the improvement of the various tasks involved in the pre-harvest; using for example precision agriculture techniques in the harvest and post-harvest activities; it is important to the Brazil citrus producers because it can reduce costs and optimize the entire industry supply chain. Especially in the state São Paulo, the country's largest citrus producer.

Thus, the need to improve the quality of agricultural products and increase production capacity in agriculture places a huge interest in the research for new technologies that can improve these processes. An example is the harvest of oranges on farms in São Paulo state. This is a task that has a direct impact on industry costs, nearly 30% of citrus production costs are related to harvesting activities [11]. Thus, the focus of this work is the development of a vision system that can be further embedded in a vehicle and perform the identification fruits task. Bulanon et al. [4] developed a survey to assess changes in orange canopy using thermal imaging for the fruit detection. Their results suggest that the largest variation in temperature between the tree and fruit happens between 16:00 and midnight. Such temperature difference facilitated the fruit recognition using method proposed. The following year Bulanon et al. [5] proposed the fusion thermal and visible images to detect fruit (more specifically, oranges).

Another application of thermography in agriculture is the monitoring of water status in the plant. The measurement of leaf temperature is the physiological characteristic used for the development of the proposed method in [10]. The developed method showed good correlation between the temperature of the kaki tree canopy and plant water status. In the case of citrus crop, it failed to show a correlation between tree canopy temperature and plant water status. Several studies focused on water stress citrus trees. Among the most relevant, we can mention: [2,3,7,8,13].

2   Methodology

The methodology shown in Fig. 1 was used to develop the counting fruit algorithm using thermal images. Each step of this methodology is detailed in the following subsections.

2.1   Thermal Emissivity and Reflected Temperature

The first step of the methodology is orange fruit emissivity determination. According to the literature, it is important to know the emissivity value of study object to improve the accuracy of temperature value measured by the thermal cameras. The emissivity and reflected temperature are used to configure the thermal camera parameters. This setup shall be carried out before the images acquisition.

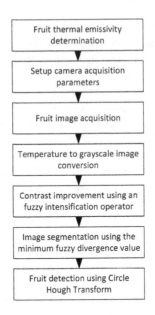

Fig. 1. Fruit identification methodology

The proposed experiment for determining thermal emissivity of sweet orange fruit is based on experiments proposed by [9] and [4]. The method used on this research is based on a adhesive marker in the fruit surface as object emitter of reference. For this initial study images were acquired every two minutes in a closed environment with a controlled temperature of 19 C. Thermal variations of the acquired images were analyzed using dedicated software for processing of thermal images supplied by the manufacturer. Furthermore, a room temperature sensor enabled a finer control of the variables that affect the temperature measurement using thermal cameras. To determine emissivity, the samples were placed on a flat surface approximately 0.35 m from the camera vertically. Over the fruit sample, an isolating tape tab (3M Scotch 33+) was placed, whose emissivity is 0.95 [4]. This experimental setup is based on the emissivity measurement method proposed in [12]. The thermal camera was positioned as shown in Fig. 2. The images were acquired in periods of two minutes for each of the samples, while the ambient temperature was monitored. We conducted a simple experiment for measuring the reflected temperature because were present in the environment and they could in the measurement as the temperature radiated by the walls, the lamps and the electronic equipment. It should be emphasized that the reflected temperature has a considerable influence in the measurement, when the objects to be measured have a very low emissivity. Just as with emissivity, reflected temperature must be measured to have a correct temperature measurement with the camera, In this experiment, the reflected temperature was measured to be set the largest number of parameters that can influence the measurement taken by the camera.

2.2   Image Acquisition

This study uses a thermal camera FLIRA35s with a micro bolometer detector VOX type uncooled. It has a sensitivity 0.05 °C, fixed focus, resolution of 320 × 256 pixels a spectral range from 7.5 to 13 nm, an accuracy ±5 °C or ±5% in reading and a dynamic range of 14 bits. TCP/IP protocol is used of communication between the camera and acquisition software. We used TESTO-175 model to monitor the environment. It is an instrument used to store and perform the reading of a series of measures. To acquire thermal imaging we used the camera's manufacturer software FLIR: FLIR Tools+. This choice was based on the fact that this software allows the user to easily configure various parameters, such as emissivity, reflected temperature, the distance between the camera and the subject, atmospheric temperature and relative humidity. In addition, the software allows selection of areas of interest in the image and calculates the average temperature in the selected area.

The image acquisition system was mounted on Mirã Fig. 2(a). This mobile robot was developed to be a modular platform for test different sensor configurations and to perform basic maneuvers to navigate with ease in the crops. The robot electronic architecture is composed by a computer Raspberry - Pi; that is in charge of the data processing and communication with the Arduino boards tasked with motors control and sensors data acquisition Fig. 2(b). To develop this study the robotic platform was used to make the sequential capture of images in the farm. The tripod was adapted on top of the robot.

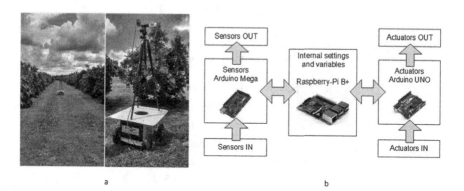

a   b

Fig. 2. Experimental setup for image acquisition. (a) Mirã robot platform [1] and (b) Electric robot diagram

The image database was collected in field 111 of Maringá Farm, located in Gavião Peixoto - SP, the trees were the variety Ruby *(Citrus sinensis (L.) Osbeck)* and they were planted in November 2010 (the date of the last harvest was 17–26 June 2014). Each orange tree produces on average 2.5 boxes of 40.8 kg per year, which is about 600 fruits. 561.600 images were acquired on days 58 and 133 of year, at different times of day (morning, afternoon and evening). From this database, 50 images of trees with completely visible fruits in the frame were selected. The recorded video used for the experiments had 98 trees: some of them had no fruit, and some others had been ripped out because of greening disease. The images were obtained in natural lighting conditions, the relative humidity and temperature parameters were adjusted for each image. During the experiments, the distance from the camera to the tree varied between 1 m and 2 m, to cover a larger area of the tree.

2.3   Image Processing

The image processing methodology has four steps: Temperature to gray-scale image conversion, contrast enhanced with an fuzzy intensification operator, image segmentation using the minimum fuzzy divergence value and fruit detection using Circle Hough Transform. Below, the details of each step are describe.

Temperature to Gray-Scale Image Conversion. The conversion of the temperature values acquired by the thermal camera to gray levels was implemented using MATrix LABoratory (MATLAB). The conversion was carried out using Eq. 1 provided by FLIR, where known measuring ranges are employed; the registers related to gain modes are shown in Table 1. The Temperature value is measured in degrees Kelvin.

$$Temperature = \frac{B}{Ln\frac{R}{(S-O)+F}} \tag{1}$$

Table 1. Camera parameters

Name	Type of variable	Description
R	Integer	Constant R
B	Float	Constant B
		Range: 1300–1600
F	Float	Constant F
		Range: 0.5–2
O	Float	Off-set Constant O
		Only positive values
S	Integer	Digital signal 14bits

The emissivity is another important parameter for correct measurement of temperature. In Eq. 1, emissivity parameter is not displayed as a parameter for the conversion, but the S parameter can be changed in Eq. 1 by the R_{obj} parameter in Eq. 2 when the emissivity ε and the reflected temperature $temp_R$ are known.

$$R_{obj} = \frac{S(1 - \varepsilon)RAW}{\varepsilon} \qquad (2)$$

$$RAW = \frac{R}{\left(\varepsilon^{\frac{B}{temp_R}} + F\right) - O} \qquad (3)$$

ε: Emissivity value of the object
$temp_R$: Reflected temperature

Contrast Enhanced with Fuzzy Intensification Operator. The algorithm used for the segmentation is based on the work proposed by [6]. After acquiring the images, Eq. 4, proposed by [4], is used to convert the temperature values measured in degrees Kelvin to gray levels.

$$I_{(i,j)} = 255 \left(\frac{T_{(i,j)} - min\left(T_{(i,j)}\right)}{max\left(T_{(i,j)}\right) - min\left(T_{(i,j)}\right)} \right) \qquad (4)$$

where:

$T_{(i,j)}$: Temperature value at position i, j
$I_{(i,j)}$: Gray level intensity for the position i, j

After obtaining the gray-scale image is used the contrast improvement method using enhancement operator.

Equation 5 shows the membership function used to construct this operator for a gray-scale image of size *(mxn)*.

$$\mu_{(mn)} = \left[1 + \frac{max\left(g\right) - g_{(mn)}}{F_d}\right]^{-F_e} \qquad (5)$$

where:

g: Gray level in the image
F_d : Denominational fuzzifier
F_e : Exponential fuzzifier

The fuzzifiers controls the amount of grayness ambiguity. The values of the membership function defined by Eq. 5 that are higher than 0.5 are converted to much higher values and values lower that 0.5 to much lower, which improves the contrast in the image. The intensifier operator is shown in Eqs. 6 and 7.

$$\mu'_{mn} = 2\left[\mu_{mn}\right]^2 \quad 0 \leq \mu_{mn} \leq 0.5 \qquad (6)$$

$$\mu'_{mn} = 1 - 2\left[1 - \mu_{mn}\right]^2 \quad 0.5 \leq \mu_{mn} \leq 1 \qquad (7)$$

After applied the intensification operator is used the inverse function shown in Eq. 8 to transformed the gray values to spatial domain.

$$g'_{mn} = max(g) - F_d \left[\left(\mu'_{mn}\right)^{-\frac{1}{F_e}} - 1\right] \qquad (8)$$

Segmentation Using Fuzzy Divergence. For the segmentation, it was used the method proposed by [6], whose membership function is known as Gamma function. This function is used to find the values of the member function for each pixel in the image, and to facilitate the calculation of fuzzy divergence for selection of the appropriate level for threshold.

The first step to use this technique is choose the regions number that must be segmented. For each of these regions the average gray levels is calculated using the Eq. 9.

$$m_x = \frac{\sum_{f=0}^{t_x} f \cdot count(f)}{\sum_{f=0}^{t_x} count(f)} \tag{9}$$

where:

m_x: Mean of gray levels of the region x
t_x: Threshold to the region x
f: Gray level value
$count(f)$: Number of occurrences of the gray level f in the image
b: Maximum gray level in the image.

The gamma function is used to classify the pixels in the image considering the mean values of each region. The general equation for the probability density function of the gamma distribution is shown in Eq. 10.

$$f(x) = \frac{\left(\frac{x-b}{\beta}\right)^{\gamma-1} exp\left(-\frac{x-b}{\beta}\right)}{\Gamma(\gamma)} \quad x \geq b; \gamma, \beta > 0 \tag{10}$$

γ: Shape parameter
b: Location parameter
β: Scale parameter
Γ: Gamma function

For the case of region segmented, the parameters are defined as: $b \neq 0$, $\beta = 1$ and $\gamma = 1$. Then, the Eq. 10 take the form shown in Eq. 11.

$$f(x) = exp(-(x-b)) \quad as \ \Gamma(1) = 1 \tag{11}$$

To perform the region segmentation, a relation between each pixel value and the regions average gray levels is defined. The membership function of each pixel depends on its proximity to a region. The relationship between the pixel and its closest region is determined by the absolute distance between the pixel and the region average gray level.

The fuzzy divergence is used to select the optimum threshold value. Equation 12 shows the total fuzzy divergence between A and B. A is the original image MxM and B is an ideally segmented image MxM.

$$D(A, B) = \sum_{i=0}^{M-1} \sum_{j=0}^{M-1} \left(\begin{matrix} 2 - (2 - \mu_A(a_{ij})) \cdot e^{\mu_A(a_{ij})-1} \\ -\mu_A(a_{ij}) \cdot e^{1-\mu_A(a_{ij})} \end{matrix} \right) \tag{12}$$

$\mu_A(a_{ij})$: Membership function of (i,j)th pixel in the image A

The divergence between the real image and the ideal image is performed for all possible threshold values, the threshold with lowest divergence is chosen as the optimal threshold.

3   Results

3.1   Emissivity Determination

For this experimental stage, orange fruits were harvested to be used as samples. The harvest was carried out in Maringá Farm owned by CITROSUCO company. The harvested oranges belonged to a commercial orchard of Ruby orange grafted on Swingle rootstock. Six samples of orange fruit were collected from each tree: two in the cup, two in the lower part and another two from inside. In total, 240 fruits from 40 orange trees were randomly selected from a 95 ha orchard. The first emissivity measurement was performed on the day of sampling and additional measurements were performed over the following two days. The obtained emissivity was $0.94 \pm 5\%$; with 95% a confidence interval.

3.2   Image Processing

The following are the results for each of the processing steps. For the development of the proposed algorithm a database of 50 was used to validate the proposed algorithm. This group of images was divided into two subgroups: images taken in the afternoon and images taken at night. The separation of the images was performed after observing temperature changes related to the period of the day, between the fruits and the other structures of the tree. Morning images were discarded because it was not possible to differentiate objects.

The enhanced-contrast images are shown in Fig. 4(a), (b) and (c). The image (a) was acquired in the afternoon and images (b) and (c) were acquired in the evening.

Figure 3 shows the result of the contrast-enhanced process, and the histograms before and after this pre-processing step. The image (a) corresponds to the original image and (b) is its histogram; the image (c) is the image after being pre-processed and (d) its histogram. It can be seen that the contrast-enhanced process produced a uniformly distributed histogram in different gray levels, Indeed, a good contrast-enhanced algorithm decreases the difference between the most and least bright pixels.

Figure 4(d), (e) and (f) show fruit segmentation results. It is important to note that some parts of the tree trunk still remain in the processed image even after it was segmented. This is because after an analysis of temperature variation, it was found that these parts were in a similar temperature and due to the camera sensor sensitivity, it was not possible to obtain a significant difference between them.

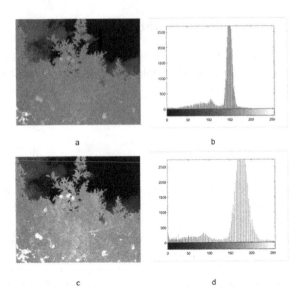

Fig. 3. Enhancement contrast histogram. (a) and (b) show respectively the original image and its histogram. (c) and (d) show enhances contrast image and its histogram.

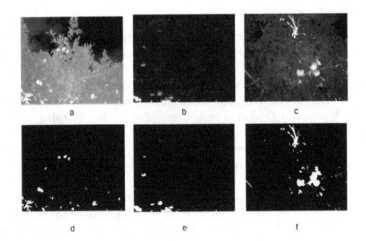

Fig. 4. Results obtained with the segmentation algorithm. (a), (b) and (c) show some examples of the images after the contrast-enhanced algorithm and (d), (e) and (f) shows fruit segmentation results

To detect and count the fruits, the circular Hough transform was applied to the segmented images. The choice of this method of circle detection was based physical orange fruits characteristics. Figure 5 shows the results for the sample images. Manual counting was performed to validate the results. It is important to note that some of the fruits were occluded, thus the camera cannot detect them.

Fruit number count corresponds to the number of centroids of circles recognized by the Hough transform; this value is stored in a vector and is then used as the amount of fruit recognized.

Fig. 5. Results obtained with the fruit recognition algorithm.

Confusion matrices were built for data validation and three metrics were used to validate the result: Accuracy Eq. (13), positive reliability Eq. (14) and sensitivity Eq. (15).

The study was divided into two groups: isolated fruits (those fruits that appear isolated on the images) and the occluded fruits are those where there is a grouping of various fruits.

$$Accuracy = \frac{TP + TN}{TP + TN + FP + FN} \tag{13}$$

$$Positive\ Reliability = \frac{TP}{TP + FP} \tag{14}$$

$$Sensitivity = \frac{TP}{TP + FN} \tag{15}$$

We performed a manual count on the 50 images and the quantities are shown in Table 2.

Table 2. Total fruits on the images

	Real
Isolated fruits	150
Occluded fruits	275
Total fruit	425

Tables 3 and 4 illustrate the confusion matrix of the classification results for each of the groups are presented. Table 3 shows the recognition of isolated fruits. In this case the overall accuracy was 93.5%, positive reliability was 97.9%, and the sensitivity was 95.3%. Table 4 shows the recognition of isolated fruits. In this case, the overall accuracy was 80%, the positive reliability was 87.6%, and sensitivity was 90.2%.

Table 3. Confusion matrix for isolated fruits recognition

	Current class (expectation)	
Predicted class (Observation)	143	3
	True positive	False positive
	7	0
	False negative	True negative

Table 4. Confusion matrix for occluded fruits recognition

	Current class (expectation)	
Predicted class (Observation)	248	35
	True positive	False positive
	27	0
	False negative	True negative result

Some of the lost objects make reference to those fruits that are outside the average radius established for recognition. Because in a tree it is possible to find fruits of different flowering, size uniformity is not guaranteed. Some of unexpected data make reference to those images where tree trunk portion is erroneously recognized as a fruit.

4   Conclusions

The night was the best time of day to make the image acquisition because the temperature difference between the tree of components was higher than at other times of the day, that according to the literature due to the fact that the fruit contain a larger amount of liquid which take longer to reach thermal equilibrium with the rest of the environment. The use of pre-processing image and fuzzy techniques show that it is possible to use simple techniques for fruit recognition and obtain satisfactory results used the type of technology of thermal image used for the study. The segmentation step statistics showed that the algorithm had a 64% satisfactory results, 20% of images had a segmentation error and 16% showed other errors type. This possibly happened due to the temperature difference between the fruit and other parts of the tree not being large enough to be distinguished as gray levels. The images obtained in the evening, due to environmental temperature differences and fruit, are the best to apply the images proposed processing techniques. Finally, the fruit counting algorithm has been divided into two groups; isolated and grouped fruits. For the group of isolates fruits was obtained an accuracy of 93.5% and 80% grouped fruits with a database of 50 pictures.

References

1. Archila Diaz, J.F., Argote Pedraza, I.L., Saavedra Guerra, J.L., Milori, D.M.B.P., Magalhães, D.V., Becker, M.: Mirã rover characterization. In: Proceedings (2015)
2. Ballester, C., Castel, J., Jiménez-Bello, M.A., Castel, J., Intrigliolo, D.: Thermographic measurement of canopy temperature is a useful tool for predicting water deficit effects on fruit weight in citrus trees. Agric. Water Manage. **122**, 1–6 (2013)
3. Ballester, C., Jiménez-Bello, M.A., Castel, J.R., Intrigliolo, D.S.: Usefulness of thermography for plant water stress detection in citrus and persimmon trees. Agric. For. Meteorol. **168**, 120–129 (2013)
4. Bulanon, D., Burks, T., Alchanatis, V.: Study on temporal variation in citrus canopy using thermal imaging for citrus fruit detection. Biosyst. Eng. **101**(2), 161–171 (2008)
5. Bulanon, D., Burks, T., Alchanatis, V.: Image fusion of visible and thermal images for fruit detection. Biosyst. Eng. **103**(1), 12–22 (2009)
6. Chaira, T., Ray, A.K.: Segmentation using fuzzy divergence. Pattern Recogn. Lett. **24**(12), 1837–1844 (2003)
7. García-Tejero, I.F., Durán-Zuazo, V.H., Muriel-Fernández, J.L., Jiménez-Bocanegra, J.A.: Linking canopy temperature and trunk diameter fluctuations with other physiological water status tools for water stress management in citrus orchards. Funct. Plant Biol. **38**(2), 106–117 (2011)
8. Gonzalez-Dugo, V., et al.: Using high resolution uav thermal imagery to assess the variability in the water status of five fruit tree species within a commercial orchard. Precision Agric. **14**(6), 660–678 (2013)
9. Hellebrand, H.J., Beuche, H., Linke, M.: Determination of thermal emissivity and surface temperature distribution of horticultural products. In: Sixth International Symposium on Fruit, Nut and Vegetable Production Engineering, Potsdam, Germany (2001)
10. Jiménez-Bello, M.A., Ballester, C., Castel, J., Intrigliolo, D.: Development and validation of an automatic thermal imaging process for assessing plant water status. Agric. Water Manage. **98**(10), 1497–1504 (2011)
11. Neves, M.F., Trombin, V.G., Milan, P., Lopes, F.F., Cressoni, F., Kalaki, R.: O retrato da citricultura brasileira. Ribeirão Preto: CitrusBR (2010)
12. Vollmer, M., Möllmann, K.P.: Infrared Thermal Imaging: Fundamentals, Research and Applications. Wiley, New York (2017)
13. Zarco-Tejada, P.J., González-Dugo, V., Berni, J.A.: Fluorescence, temperature and narrow-band indices acquired from a uav platform for water stress detection using a micro-hyperspectral imager and a thermal camera. Remote Sens. Environ. **117**, 322–337 (2012)

Miscellaneous

Bayesian Inference for Training of Long Short Term Memory Models in Chaotic Time Series Forecasting

Cristian Rodríguez Rivero[1], Julián Pucheta[1], Daniel Patiño[2],
Jose Luis Puglisi[3], Paula Otaño[4], Leonardo Franco[5], Gustavo Juarez[6],
Efrén Gorrostieta[7], and Alvaro David Orjuela-Cañón[8(✉)]

[1] Universidad Nacional de Córdoba, Córdoba, Argentina
[2] INAUT-UNSJ, San Juan, Argentina
[3] California North State University, Elk Grove, CA, USA
[4] Universidad Tecnológica Nacional – FRC, Córdoba, Argentina
[5] University of Malaga, Malaga, Spain
[6] Universidad Nacional de Tucumán, San Miguel de Tucumán, Argentina
[7] Universidad Autónoma de Querétaro, Querétaro, Mexico
[8] Universidad del Rosario, Bogotá D.C., Colombia
alvaro.orjuela@urosario.edu.co

Abstract. For time series forecasting, obtaining models is based on the use of past observations from the same sequence. In those cases, when the model is learning from data, there is not an extra information that discuss about the quantity of noise inside the data available. In practice, it is necessary to deal with finite noisy datasets, which lead to uncertainty about the propriety of the model. For this problem, the employment of the Bayesian inference tools are preferable. A modified algorithm used for training a long-short term memory recurrent neural network for time series forecasting is presented. This approach was chosen to improve the forecasting of the original series, employing an implementation based on the minimization of the associated Kullback-Leibler Information Criterion. For comparison, a nonlinear autoregressive model implemented with a feedforward neural network was also presented. A simulation study was conducted to evaluate and illustrate results, comparing this approach with Bayesian neural-networks-based algorithms for artificial chaotic time-series and showing an improvement in terms of forecasting errors.

Keywords: Bayesian approximation · Time series forecasting · Nonlinear autoregressive models · Recurrent neural networks

1 Introduction

The importance of the use of Bayesian methods as a natural methodology for implementation in Time Series Forecasting (TSF) has increased rapidly over the last decade. In particular, this technique provides a formal way to incorporate the prior information from the underlying process related with data generation before of its knowing. Then, this is seen as a resource in sequential learning and decision making, where it is

© Springer Nature Switzerland AG 2019
A. D. Orjuela-Cañón et al. (Eds.): ColCACI 2019, CCIS 1096, pp. 197–208, 2019.
https://doi.org/10.1007/978-3-030-36211-9_16

possible to establish a direct relation between the exact results and the small samples. Moreover, the Bayesian paradigm takes into account all parameters and the uncertainty of the model [1], making relevant the relation between the predictive distribution and the sampling information, where the forecasting is allowed when all parameters are integrated based on a posterior distribution.

Commonly, the selection of a particular model is not specified by some theory or experience, and many adopted models can be trained with the purpose of obtaining that information [2]. Models comparison can be implemented based on a Bayesian framework through the so-called posterior odds, computed as the product of the prior odds and the Bayes factor. This Bayes factor measurement is obtained from any two models, estimated by the likelihood ratio of the marginal likelihood of two competing hypotheses represented by the models, quantifying the support of one model over another based on the available data.

Long short-term memory (LSTM) models are widely utilized for TSF because its architecture based on a special sort of recurrent neural network (RNN) [3, 4]. This kind of this artificial neural network (ANN) architecture is known due to the connections between units, which form a directed cycle. In this way, an internal state of the network is built up, which allows it to exhibit dynamic temporal behavior. In spite of the feedforward architecture of this network, their internal memory can process arbitrary sequences of inputs [5]. However, RNN are difficult to train using the stochastic gradient descent, according to the so-called "vanishing" gradient and/or "exploding" gradient phenomenon. This limits the ability of simple RNN to learn sequences with relatively long dependencies [6], making that its employment was reconsidered. For this, proposals like vanilla RNN deal with the vanishing or exploding gradient problem, but remaining the long-term dependence problem, making very difficult the training [7]. Improving the mentioned problems, the LSTM introduces the gate mechanism to prevent back-propagated errors from vanishing or exploding problem, which has been shown to be more effective than conventional RNNs, preventing the overfitting and limitations with long-term sequences [8].

Applications of this kind of ANN can be seen in the work from Zhao et al. [9], which proposed a LSTM network for considering temporal–spatial correlation in traffic system. That ANN was composed of many memory units, comparing this architecture to other representative forecasting models, achieving a better performance. In addition, Kang et al. [10] employed the mentioned RNN to analyze the effect of various inputs settings on its performance. In [11] the authors used a model of ANN combined with a LSTM in a similar way that a Deep Neural Network (DNN), including the autocorrelation coefficients to improve the model accuracy and providing a better precision than traditional ones. Some recent works as in [12], where an adaptation of a LSTM to forecast sea surface temperature (SST) values was employed, including one day and three days information as past inputs. Then the RNN was compared to other models that employed information from weekly mean and monthly mean.

In this paper, a LSTM based on Bayesian Approach (LSTM-BA) method is proposed to predict time series data from well-known chaotic systems. The motivation to use this model is related to the property of this network with one full-connected layer to obtain a regression model for prediction. Also, the LSTM layer has been utilized to model the temporal relationship among time series data, using the Bayes information of the weights updated and a heuristic approach to adjust the number of training iterations. This requires the ability to integrate a sum of terms in the log joint likelihood using the factorized distribution. In some cases, the integral operations are not in closed form, which is typically handled by using a lower bound showed by Wang et al. [13], where a new method called improved Bayesian combined model.

This work is organized as follows: Section two describes LSTM with the proposed approach (RNN-BA) using Bayesian inference-based heuristic. Section three shows details about the architectures employed for forecasting and an experimental design. The fourth section offers results conducted throughout chaotic time series. Section five provides a discussion based on the used implementation. Finally, section six concludes about this work.

2   Recurrent Neural Networks: Long-Short Term Memory

Classical feedforward neural networks, whose connections are directed and without cycles, only maps the current input vector to output vector [14]. This represents a disadvantage because they cannot memorize previous input data, and in addition, a determination of an optimal time lags size cannot be obtained. The mentioned problems are increased due to the input data must be truncated into specific length for developing of the model, producing prediction results not desirable.

Opposite to the classical networks, the RNN allow cyclical or recurrent connections, mapping the complete historical input data to each output. At the same time, these recurrent connections provide a special aspect to memorize information from previous inputs that persists in the network's internal state, influencing the network output. This attribute is useful when noisy signals or sequences with abrupt changes are treated, for example, chaotic series. Different applications have been developed with this architecture, which can change of complexity according to the number of units and connections. Likewise, for standard RNN architecture, the internal influence is given by the number of neurons in the hidden layer, which can decline or blowing up exponentially the value of the synaptic weights. This, according to the cycling behavior established by the recurrent connections. For this, some RNN models are trained with backpropagation through the time and real time recurrent learning for avoiding the vanishing and exploding error problem.

The main advantages of the LSTM are to model long-term dependencies and to determine the optimal time lags for TSF problems. These aspects are desirable for long-term future predictions specially, due to the lack of priori knowledge between samples. In addition, the problem of the sum of error signals increment, a proposal based on the constant error carrousel (CEC) was proposed in a first version. The LSTM architecture is modified, including a pair of gates, which can allow the flow from inputs to outputs. In the enhanced version, it adds a reset gate called forget gate [8], including the notion of memory cells as shown in Fig. 1 by the yellow blocks.

In the present proposal, a LSTM model is trained with focus on the exploration of solutions by employing a Bayesian heuristic method. In this way, an improvement given by the overfitting problem was searched [17]. Therefore, in order to make the topology of LSTM as simple as possible, it is important to delete unnecessary units,

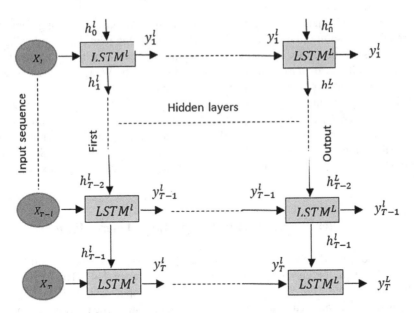

Fig. 1. Flow chart inside the LSTM RNN. (Color figure online)

layers and connections, thus, to optimize the training and topology of RNN, we proposed a heuristic adjustment, as follows:

$$1 \leq i_t \leq 2(H_0 - KL) \tag{1}$$

$$H_0 \leq N_p \leq KL + I_x \tag{2}$$

where I_x is the dimension of the input vector, N_p is the number patterns, and H_0 is the initial value of hidden neurons. Then, a heuristic adjustment for the pair (i_t, N_p), the number of iterations and patterns as function of the hidden units H_o and KL (Kullback-Leibler Information Criterion), according to the membership functions shown in Fig. 2. Finally, an approximation for the network weights and biases was developed, where all the model parameters were modelled as Gaussian distributions with a diagonal covariance. An exception for latent states, which was modelled as a Gaussian distribution with an almost diagonal covariance.

3   Experimental Design

Experiments with data generated from an artificial chaotic systems, which were performed to obtain five common benchmark series with length of 1500 points. This length was chosen intentionally, for determining whether this a limitation in order to compare the model against other much simpler models with probable less overfitting.

For chaotic series, the generation of such aspect belongs to reaching the attractor. To do this, the system was allowed to evolve after one hundred samples, achieving the

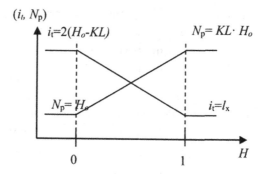

Fig. 2. Heuristic adjustment of (i_t, N_p) in terms of KL after each epoch.

corresponding attractor. According to this, we assumed that the number of iterations guarantees the state of the dynamic system, ending the initial transient on the attractor. In spite of this, there are no reliability that the system will revisit future events similar to those observed during training.

3.1 Employed Datasets

For assessment of built models, seven datasets with artificial chaotic time series were used. Each of these series is describe next:

Mackey-Glass Series: The dataset MG17 and MG30 are by sampling the Mackay-Glass (MG) equations, given by the expression (3), as follows:

$$\dot{x}(t) = \frac{ax(t - \tau)}{1 - x(t - \tau)^c} - bx(t) \tag{3}$$

with a, b, c, τ setting parameters shown as follows in Table 1.

Table 1. Parameters to generate MG time series

Series	N	a	b	c	T
MG17	1500	0.2	0.1	10	17
MG30	1500	0.2	0.1	10	30

Logistic Time Series: The dataset LOG01 and LOG02 series were mapped from logistic system and represent in (4), which is defined by:

$$x(t + 1) = ax(t)[1 - x(t)] \tag{4}$$

where $a = 4$, the iterations in Eq. (4) perform a chaotic time series (see Table 2).

Table 2. Parameters to generate LOG time series

Series	N	a	X_0
LOG01	1500	4	0.1
LOG02	1500	4	0.3

Henon Chaotic Time Series: This time series can be constructed by following Eq. (5), however, it presents many aspects of dynamical behavior of more complicated chaotic systems.

$$x(t+1) = b + 1 - ax^2 \qquad (5)$$

where a and b were fixed as shown in Table 3. These same parameters were used in both cases.

Table 3. Parameters to generate HEN time series

Series	N	a	b	X_0	Y_0
HEN01	1500	1.4	0.3	0	0
HEN02	1500	1.3	0.22	0	0

Lorentz Time Series: The Lorenz model is given by the Eq. (6), the data is derived from the Lorenz system, which is given by three time-delay differential systems. Table 4 specifies the values employed to generate the data samples.

$$\begin{cases} \frac{dx}{dt} = a(y-x) \\ \frac{dx}{dt} = bx - y - xz \\ \frac{dx}{dt} = xy - bz \end{cases} \qquad (6)$$

Table 4. Parameters to generate LOR time series

Series	N	a	b	c	X(0)	Y(0)	Z(0)
LOR01	1500	0.2	0.2	5.7	12	9	2
LOR02	1500	0.42	0.42	0.42	0.1	0.1	2

Rössler Chaotic Time Series: In this example, the data was derived from the Rössler system, which is given by three time-delay differential systems represented in expression (7).

$$\begin{cases} \frac{dx}{dt} = -y(t) - z(t) \\ \frac{dx}{dt} = x(t) + ay(t) \\ \frac{dx}{dt} = b + z(t)(x(t) - c) \end{cases} \qquad (7)$$

The dataset was built by using four-order Runge–Kutta method with the initial value as shown in Table 5, and the step size was chosen as 0.01.

Table 5. Parameters to generate ROS time series

Series	N	a	b	c	X(0)	Y(0)	Z(0)
ROS01	1500	0.2	0.2	5.7	12	9	2
ROS02	1500	0.42	0.42	0.42	0.1	0.1	2

Ikeda Time Series: The Ikeda map was given in expression (8) as follows:

$$\dot{x} = 1 - \mu[xcos(t) - ysin(t)]$$
$$\dot{y} = \mu[xcos(t) - ysin(t)] \qquad (8)$$

where $t = 1/(1 + x^2 + y^2)$. This system displays chaotic behavior over a range of values for the parameter, including the values chosen in Table 6.

Table 6. Parameters to generate IK time series

Series	N	μ	X(0)	Y(0)
IK01	1500	0.9	0.5	0.5
IK02	1500	0.8	0.9	0.6

In the experiments, the datasets were splitted into two parts: the training set and the test set. In the training phase, each of the individual models was trained with optimized parameters given by each filter. This means that every model was constructed with a sequence of data different to the test set samples. Figure 3 shows examples from each generated dataset for the five cases.

3.2 Neural Networks Models

The architecture of the LSTM model was composed by an input with length (i_x) of 25 samples. The nonlinear gate was given by the sigmoid function and the nonlinearity from input to output was established by a hyperbolic tangent function. The number of epochs for training was adjusted to 50 as maximum. Learning rate was 2e-3 with a training percent of 0.80 and 512 units in just one hidden layer, dropout rate of 1.0 and weight decay of 1e-8.

As a way to compare the results in terms of ANN models, a nonlinear autoregressive model (NAR) was employed. This is an architecture that is based on feed-forward connections as classical proposals of neural networks but with considerable results for forecasting tasks [15–17]. The main difference is determined by the recurrence that is missing in this model as previously mentioned. For developing the forecasting the expression (7) describes this model, in the way:

$$y_i = tanh\left(\sum_{k=1}^{p} a_i y_{i-k} + b\right) \tag{9}$$

where y_i is the time series to be modeled, a_i are the coefficients of the model, which are called synaptic weights (w_{ij}) in other applications models. Parameter b is a bias value used to fix the function to be found. It is possible to see nonlinearity in the hyperbolic tangent (tanh) in (3) known as transfer function of the units or neurons in the neural model.

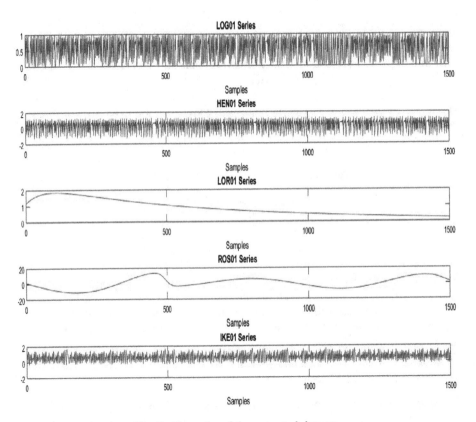

Fig. 3. Examples of the generated datasets.

For NAR model, some equivalent parameters were fixed as LSTM model. For example, an input vector with 25 samples was used and 50 epochs for training. One hidden layer was also employed, modifying the number of neurons from two to ten and computing the results in an experimental mode. The resilient backpropagation algorithm was employed for adjusting the synaptic weights due to its fast convergence and low computational cost.

3.3   Prediction Error Metrics

To assess the performance of the forecasting, the symmetric mean absolute error (sMAPE) was employed as suggested in [18], and as shown in expression (10):

$$sMAPE = \frac{1}{n} \sum_{i=1}^{n} \frac{|X_t - F_t|}{(|X_t| + |F_t|)/2} * 100 \tag{10}$$

where t is the observation time, n is the size of the test set, X_t is the original series and F_t is the forecasted series.

Finally, the Root Mean Square Error (RMSE) was employed to obtain the error as in [19], given by the computation in (11) as follows:

$$RMSE = \sqrt{\frac{1}{n} \sum_{i=1}^{n} (X_t - F_t)^2} \tag{11}$$

where t, n, X_t and F_t are the same as in (10).

4   Results

Table 7 shows the results computed for sMAPE and RMSE average across all datasets when the LSTM model and its modification with the Bayesian Approach (LSTM-BA) were trained. Two horizons for this forecasting were highlighted because the best results. As a complement, Table 8 shows the results for NAR implemented models, where information about the neurons in the hidden layer and average for sMAPE and RMSE from computation in all datasets are shown.

Table 7. Mean forecast-error metrics computed by LSTM approaches employing all datasets.

Method	Horizon Forecast of 3 out-of-sample		Horizon Forecast of 18 out-of-sample	
	sMAPE	RMSE	sMAPE	RMSE
LSTM-BA	**0.056**	**0.132**	**0.033**	**0.120**
LSTM	0.057	0.138	0.039	0.135

The BA approach shows a level improvement, indicating the necessity of information from prior distribution for an adequate model with better results in terms of prediction error. The evaluation of the results across the 10 series analyzed through its mean value evinced, with the use of sMAPE and RMSE indices, that there was an increment when the horizon is deeper for each series. Note that there is a little improvement of the forecasting given by LSTM-BA approach compared with the traditional LSTM one, which resulted from the use of a stochastic characteristic to generate a deterministic result for long-short-term prediction.

Table 8. Forecast-error metrics computed by NAR approaches employing all datasets.

Neurons	Measures	
	RMSE	sMAPE
2	0.465	0.099
3	0.301	0.081
4	0.336	0.085
5	**0.269**	**0.072**
6	0.299	0.077
7	0.301	0.074
8	0.311	0.076
9	0.415	0.103
10	0.329	0.078

For the NAR model, the results remained under the results of the LSTM, showing the advantages of RNN compared with feedforward networks. In spite of the comparison was not equitable due to the number of units and optimization parameters to train the models, the results exhibit advantages of the recurrent strategies.

5 Discussion

The assessment of the obtained results, comparing the performance of the proposed algorithm, shows a significance improvement measured either by sMAPE and RMSE index for the LSTM-BA and LSTM ones contrasted to NAR models. According to the literature, it is not properly justified or experimentally proven that LSTM networks are appropriate for modeling chaotic series. However, as consequence of using the present proposal, there was an increment of the network in terms of learning of long sequences. This approach came from the idea that only the most recent data are important, and the sliding time window methods are very useful for pattern recognition, for datasets with highly dependence on the past bulk of observations.

LSTM models are powerful enough to learn the most important past behaviors and understand whether those past samples are important features in the making prediction process. This could not exposed by the NAR models, which, in spite of its utility in TSF, did not have better results than the RNN proposals. As mentioned, recurrent connections present capacity to memorize nonlinear relations between the samples, which allow to performance the forecasting in a better way. Other aspect for the NAR model is related with the number of neurons in the hidden layer. For both error measures, it was exhibited that with five neurons the models presented the best performance. After this number, the networks showed an overfitting incrementing the error in the test set.

In the specific case of chaotic time series, alternative models have been worked based on other Bayesian proposals. Examples of this, can be seen in [20], where a Bayesian enhanced ensemble approach, or in [21] with a Bayesian enhanced modified proposal, and in [22, 23] with BA extended and BA basic proposals, respectively. In all these models, the results were comparable and lightly under the present ones.

The limited amount of available input and a flexible prior over a large space of possible nonlinear models produces significant posterior uncertainty on the dynamics and the global prediction, converging to the long-term mean with large variance. This is due to the poor estimation of the mean error values using so little amount of data. In order to improve the value of the results, more prior information such as the apparent periodicity and trend of the signal must be considered.

6 Conclusions

In this paper, a proposal that includes a Bayesian heuristic approach to optimize the training and architecture of LSTM, allowing modifying its parameters in a better way. For this, the addition of information as the number of feedback layers, past input layers and incorporation of self-adaptive heuristic, adjusts the training process. Furthermore, we have shown that our model yields neural networks with higher prediction capability for time-series data, comparing the performances of the proposed algorithm and the existing one through the numerical experiments, using well-known benchmark series. An alternative proposal based on NAR models was presented with low performance compared to the LSTM ones.

References

1. MacKay, D.J.C., Mac Kay, D.J.C.: Information Theory, Inference and Learning Algorithms. Cambridge University Press, Cambridge (2003)
2. Hippert, H.S., Taylor, J.W.: An evaluation of Bayesian techniques for controlling model complexity and selecting inputs in a neural network for short-term load forecasting. Neural Networks 23, 386–395 (2010)
3. Greff, K., Srivastava, R.K., Koutník, J., Steunebrink, B.R., Schmidhuber, J.: LSTM: a search space odyssey. IEEE Trans. Neural Networks Learn. Syst. 28, 2222–2232 (2016)
4. Hochreiter, S., Schmidhuber, J.: Long short-term memory. Neural Comput. 9, 1735–1780 (1997)
5. Karpathy, A., Johnson, J., Fei-Fei, L.: Visualizing and understanding recurrent networks. arXiv Preprint arXiv:1506.02078 (2015)
6. Pascanu, R., Mikolov, T., Bengio, Y.: On the difficulty of training recurrent neural networks. In: International Conference on Machine Learning, pp. 1310–1318 (2013)
7. Williams, R.J., Zipser, D.: Gradient-based learning algorithms for recurrent. In: Backpropagation Theory, Architectures and Applications, p. 433 (1995)
8. Srivastava, N., Hinton, G., Krizhevsky, A., Sutskever, I., Salakhutdinov, R.: Dropout: a simple way to prevent neural networks from overfitting. J. Mach. Learn. Res. 15, 1929–1958 (2014)
9. Zhao, Z., Chen, W., Wu, X., Chen, P.C.Y., Liu, J.: LSTM network: a deep learning approach for short-term traffic forecast. IET Intell. Transp. Syst. 11, 68–75 (2017)
10. Kang, D., Lv, Y., Chen, Y.: Short-term traffic flow prediction with LSTM recurrent neural network. In: 2017 IEEE 20th International Conference on Intelligent Transportation Systems (ITSC), pp. 1–6 (2017)

11. Zhuo, Q., Li, Q., Yan, H., Qi, Y.: Long short-term memory neural network for network traffic prediction. In: 2017 12th International Conference on Intelligent Systems and Knowledge Engineering (ISKE), pp. 1–6 (2017)
12. Zhang, Q., Wang, H., Dong, J., Zhong, G., Sun, X.: Prediction of sea surface temperature using long short-term memory. IEEE Geosci. Remote Sens. Lett. **14**, 1745–1749 (2017)
13. Wang, J., Deng, W., Zhao, J.: Short-term freeway traffic flow prediction based on improved Bayesian combined model. J. Southeast Univ. (Nat. Sci Ed. 1) **42**, 162–167 (2012)
14. Haykin, S.: Neural Networks and Learning Machines. Prentice Hall, Upper Saddle River (2009)
15. Orjuela-Cañón, A.D., Hernández, J., Rivero, C.R.: Very short term forecasting in global solar irradiance using linear and nonlinear models. In: 2017 IEEE Workshop on Power Electronics and Power Quality Applications (PEPQA), pp. 1–5 (2017)
16. Almonacid, F., Pérez-Higueras, P.J., Fernández, E.F., Hontoria, L.: A methodology based on dynamic artificial neural network for short-term forecasting of the power output of a PV generator. Energy Convers. Manage. **85**, 389–398 (2014)
17. Men, Z., Yee, E., Lien, F.-S., Wen, D., Chen, Y.: Short-term wind speed and power forecasting using an ensemble of mixture density neural networks. Renew. Energy **87**, 203–211 (2016)
18. Davydenko, A., Fildes, R.: Forecast error measures: critical review and practical recommendations. In: Business Forecasting: Practical Problems and Solutions, p. 34. Wiley (2016)
19. Chai, T., Draxler, R.R.: Root mean square error (RMSE) or mean absolute error (MAE)?–Arguments against avoiding RMSE in the literature. Geosci. Model Dev. **7**, 1247–1250 (2014)
20. Rivero, C.R., et al.: Bayesian enhanced ensemble approach (BEEA) for time series forecasting. In: 2018 IEEE Biennial Congress of Argentina (ARGENCON), pp. 1–7 (2018)
21. Rivero, C.R., Pucheta, J., Baumgartner, J., Laboret, S., Sauchelli, V.: Short-series prediction with BEMA approach: application to short rainfall series. IEEE Lat. Am. Trans. **14**, 3892–3899 (2016)
22. Rivero, C.R., Pucheta, J.A., Sauchelli, V.H., Patiño, H.D.: Short time series prediction: Bayesian Enhanced modified approach with application to cumulative rainfall series. Int. J. Innov. Comput. Appl. **7**, 153–162 (2016)
23. Rivero, C.R., Patiño, D., Pucheta, J., Sauchelli, V.: A new approach for time series forecasting: bayesian enhanced by fractional brownian motion with application to rainfall series. Int. J. Adv. Comput. Sci. Appl. **7** (2016)

Entropy and PCA Analysis for Environments Associated to Q-Learning for Path Finding

Manuel Garcia-Quijada$^{(\boxtimes)}$ ⓘ, Efren Gorrostieta-Hurtado ⓘ,
Jose Emilio Vargas-Soto ⓘ, and Manuel Toledano-Ayala ⓘ

Faculty of Engineering, Autonomous University of Queretaro, 76010 Queretaro,
Querétaro, Mexico
manex01@gmail.com

Abstract. This work is based on the simulation of the reinforcement learning method for path search for mobile robotic agents in unstructured environments. The choice of the learning and reward coefficients of the Q-learning method affect the number of average actions that the algorithm requires for reach the goal from the start position. In addition, another important factor is the randomness degree and environment size over which the path must be calculated, since they affect the time of convergence in the learning. Likewise, a performance metric of the Q-learning algorithm is proposed, based on the Entropy and Principal Component Analysis of the environment representative images. The analysis by Entropy only allows to determine, in a scalar form, the environment randomness degree, but it does not provide information about the dispersion location. In contrast, the analysis by PCA allows to quantify not only the randomness, but also helps to estimate the direction of greater randomness of the environment. The advantage of this analysis by PCA and Entropy is that one could estimate the actions number or movements required for path search algorithms based on the randomness of unstructured environments.

Keywords: Entropy · PCA · Unstructured environment · Q-Learning · Path planning

1 Introduction

Routing problems in 2D or 3D physical environments is a common problem in areas like Transportation, Robotics, Communications, etc. The main problem has been addressed from the Computer Science, Artificial Intelligence, Optimization, and others. A part of the problem is transport physical quantities or information from a point A (start) to point B (goal), something common in systems whose environments can be structured, unstructured or even unknown. An unstructured environment are those environments that have a set of obstacles or restrictions and free or transitable zones without a predefined order [1], but its configuration is in that way that allow the information flow from an area to another by means of an automated physical or virtual agent.

A robotic autonomous agent is an appropriate entity for transport information or material in unstructured, complex or intricate environments. In this context, the agent

© Springer Nature Switzerland AG 2019
A. D. Orjuela-Cañón et al. (Eds.): ColCACI 2019, CCIS 1096, pp. 209–222, 2019.
https://doi.org/10.1007/978-3-030-36211-9_17

must overcome problems related about the interaction in diversified environments and its actions that cannot be preprogrammed for all possible states and existing conditions. As Félix Ingrand established: "Autonomy and diversity imply need for deliberation" [2]. The constant search for path planning problem solutions for robotic agents belong to a set of problems known as Markov Decision Processes (MDP). They allow to understand the interaction between a robotic agent and its environment. In the context of the MDP, they have fundamental elements to describe them: (1) State of the system; (2) Actions; (3) Transition probabilities; (4) Rewards; (5) Policy and (6) Performance metric [3, 4].

Reinforcement learning provides a wide variety of techniques used to solve path problems that allow the tracing or routing calculation, whether optimal or not. One of these algorithms is the learning by reinforcement Q-learning and its simplicity allow to be used for discrete environments. Created in 1989, it is known that it was proposed by Watkins [5]. Q-learning is a widespread tabular method to find solutions related to path problems of mobile robots in unstructured environments. The primary objective, not the only one, is the prevention of possible collisions of the agent with environmental obstacles (hereinafter, the term environment is equivalent to using the term maze) or even with other agents in a system of so-called multi-agents. A collision can represent slight and/or severe damage to the environment for the agent or both. The Q-learning technique can be combined with other artificial intelligence techniques, such as convolutional neural networks, artificial vision, etc., whose purpose is to improve path planning focused on the detection of objects [6]. This would allow researchers to achieve a substantial advance in the integration of the robotic agent into real environments to meet well-defined objectives of mobility, mapping, assistance and location, complying, of course, with the ethical and legislative schemes.

On the other hand, is well known that random or unstructured position of obstacles in the training environment significantly affects the performance of the learning algorithms in path planning. Path planning has been approached with local and global techniques such as Graph Theory, Fuzzy Logic, Ant Colony, Genetic Algorithms, Neural Networks and many other artificial intelligence techniques [7]. However, beyond analyzing the nature of the environment to determine the complexity in which the robot should be trained, research is aimed at extracting the main topological characteristics of the environment and building simple and compact models that allow them to be integrated into knowledge and agent training [8]. The path planning for static and discretized environments does not represent great complexity and demand of computational resources; but the same problem, addressed with dynamic environments, supposes a higher complexity due to the geometric variability and existing conditions of the environment, altogether with the resources required to implement the learning algorithms calculation.

This work focuses on analyzing how the geometric complexity of the environment affects the path learning algorithm for mobile robots. The learning method used is Q-learning for discrete states and that the performance can be correlated, by the analysis of the environment based on two methods: (a) by Entropy of images and (b) PCA (Principal Components Analysis). Considering the first results, the combination of both methods can be a basic tool for analysts in order to decide about employ and implement learning methods based on the environment analysis, focused on selective and adaptive programming schemes. In other words, the approach could help for select learning parameters about the Q-Learning method and even help to decide which learning method could be used to address the problem of path planning depending on the environment complexity [4, 5].

2 Mathematical Background

2.1 Reinforcement Learning

The algorithm of reinforcement learning is based on the Bellman formulation for MDP. This equation evaluates the present and past state-action of the mobile robotic agent. An MDP is a 4-parameter array $\{S, A, T, R\}$, where S is the set of states, A is the set of actions, T is a probabilistic transition function and R is the gratification or reward function.

$$Q_{t+1}(s_t, a_t) = Q_t(s_t, a_t) + \alpha[R_{t+1}(s_t, a_t) + \gamma\, max_{a \in A} Q_t(s_{t+1}, a) - Q_t(s_t, a_t)] \quad (1)$$

where $Q(s_t, a_t)$ is a function of evaluating states and actions at a time instant t, α is the learning rate where $0 < \alpha \leq 1$, $R(s_t, a_t)$ is an instantaneous gratification, positive or negative, when an action a_t is performed on a state s_t, γ is known as a gamma function whose typical values are in the interval [0, 1] and from this function depend the future reward values [9].

2.2 Entropy

The Entropy, now adopted by Information Theory, is based on the work that Shanon did in the communications field [10]. The image Entropy is a statistical quantitative measure commonly used to characterize randomness, disorder or noise in a visual image [11, 12]. The equation for discrete variables is:

$$H(X) = -\sum_i p(x_i) \log_2 p(x_i) \quad (2)$$

where X is a discrete variable with states $x_i \in X$, $p(x_i) = P\{X = x_i\}$ is a probabilistic function, i.e. is the image normalized histogram. In general, Entropy is related to the information compression. For example, if an image contains random patterns with few possibilities of compression, Entropy value is usually high, for opposite, an image with low Entropy can be highly compressible, since it has redundant information that can be omitted, which implies that this type of images has regular patterns defined.

2.3 PCA

Principal components analysis (PCA) is a data analysis technique, based about analyzing eigenvalues and eigenvectors of the covariance matrix. It has been used mainly for dimensionality reduction, patterns detection, classification images details extraction, edge detection and orientation, etc. [13, 14]. For an image, let

$$\mathbf{x} = \begin{bmatrix} x_1 & x_2 & \cdots & x_m \end{bmatrix}^T \tag{3}$$

a data vector, and let

$$\mathbf{X} = \begin{bmatrix} x_1^1 & x_1^2 & \cdots & x_1^n \\ x_2^1 & x_2^2 & \cdots & x_2^n \\ \vdots & \vdots & \ddots & \vdots \\ x_m^1 & x_m^2 & \cdots & x_m^n \end{bmatrix} \tag{4}$$

the samples matrix of $\mathbf{x}$ where x_i^j, $j = 1, 2, \ldots, n$ are the variable discrete samples x_i, $i = 1, 2, \ldots, m$. The i-th row of the sample matrix $\mathbf{X}$, denoted by $X_i = \begin{bmatrix} x_i^1 & x_i^2 & \cdots & x_i^n \end{bmatrix}$ is known as the sample vector x_i. The average value of X_i is calculated as

$$\mu_i = \frac{1}{n} \sum_{j=1}^{n} X_i(j) \tag{5}$$

and the sample vector X_i is centralized as

$$\bar{X}_i = X_i - \mu_i = \begin{bmatrix} \bar{x}_i^1 & \bar{x}_i^2 & \cdots & \bar{x}_i^n \end{bmatrix} \tag{6}$$

where $\bar{x}_i^j = x_i^j - \mu_i$.

Thus, the centralized matrix $\mathbf{X}$ is

$$\bar{\mathbf{X}} = \begin{bmatrix} \bar{X}_i^T & \bar{X}_i^T & \cdots & \bar{X}_m^T \end{bmatrix}^T \tag{7}$$

Last, the covariance matrix o the centralized set is calculated as

$$\Omega = \frac{1}{n} \overline{\mathbf{X} \mathbf{X}}^T \tag{8}$$

The target of PCA, is to calculate an orthonormal transformation matrix $\mathbf{P}$ that allows to decorrelate $\mathbf{X}$, i.e.

$$\bar{\mathbf{Y}} = \mathbf{P} \bar{\mathbf{X}} \tag{9}$$

in a way that the covariance matrix of $\bar{\mathbf{Y}}$ is diagonal. Since the covariance matrix Ω is symmetric, it can be rewritten as:

$$\Omega = \Phi \Lambda \Phi^T \tag{10}$$

where $\Phi = \begin{bmatrix} \phi_1 & \phi_2 & \cdots & \phi_m \end{bmatrix}$ is an orthonormal matrix of eigenvectors and $\Lambda = diag\{\lambda_1, \lambda_2, \ldots, \lambda_m\}$ is the main diagonal o the eigenvalues matrix with $\lambda_1 \geq \lambda_2 \ldots \geq \lambda_m$. The terms $\phi_1, \phi_2, \ldots, \phi_m$ and $\lambda_1, \lambda_2, \ldots, \lambda_m$ are the eigenvectors and eigenvalues respectively of Φ. Doing

$$\mathbf{P} = \mathbf{\Phi}^T \tag{11}$$

$\overline{\mathbf{X}}$ can be decorrelated, that is, $\overline{\mathbf{Y}} = \mathbf{P}\overline{\mathbf{X}}$ and $\mathbf{\Lambda} = \frac{1}{n}\overline{\mathbf{Y}}\overline{\mathbf{Y}}^T$.

In summary, the energy of a signal can be concentrated in a small data set [15]. The first component of the PCA method fits toward the environment variability is greatest, the second component is adjusted in an orthonormal way to the first, and so on if there are more components. This peculiarity is very interesting in randomness images analysis in order to establish a quantitative metric to determine the dispersion degree or the image randomness level.

3 Experimental Setup

For this work, the training process used was Q-learning, programmed in MATLAB. The matrix of experiments is shown in Table 1. The coefficients choice was arbitrary but was done in order to cover a wide range of variability, we consider low and equal value for α and γ coefficients and dissimilar coefficients also were considered.

Table 1. Test matrix for reinforcement learning method.

Coefficients		Environment	Test			
α	γ	size $n \times n$	Training iterations	Test by coefficients pair	Total test	Total learning iterations
0.3	0.3	$n = \{13, 14 \ldots, 17\}$	50	$\sum_{13}^{17} 3n(n-1)$	50	5250
0.6	0.6					
0.9	0.9					
0.3	0.9					
0.5	0.7					
0.7	0.5					
0.9	0.3					

For the experimental environment, different sizes of discretized mazes were proposed, for which the robotic agent must to find out a path between the Start and the Goal. The obstacles dispersion was done in a random way in order to obtain a better variability and avoid inducing biases by using groups of predefined mazes with easy solution.

Each maze was generated from a discrete random matrix of size $n \times n$ whose representation is shown in Fig. 1. The same figure also shows the resulting environment whose premise is that it was passable, for which the connectivity of the free squares from the beginning to the goal, and thus prevent the agent from being trapped in isolated areas that would take the algorithm to an infinite loop and inhibit to the robotic agent to reach the goal.

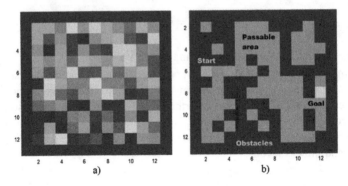

Fig. 1. (a) Random matrix example 13×13 used as base to generate a passable maze; (b) Resulting environment maze based on a random matrix.

In addition to the coefficient's variation, different sizes of mazes were proposed to analyze their impact on the algorithm performance. The Start and Goal positions were proposed on opposite sides of the environment to guarantee complex paths.

For the representative matrix of the maze, each obstacle and surrounding walls were associated with the number 0, and all the passable space was associated with a 1. In this way, a binary image associated with the maze was generated and we applied the Entropy and PCA tests. The choice of these analyzes is due, as mentioned in Sect. 2 to the fact that both techniques quantify the data randomness and for that, the images of the maze were used.

The general structure of the program is shown in Fig. 2, which is represented as a block diagram. For the evaluation of the function $Q_t(s_t, a_t)$, a tetra-dimensional array $\mathbf{Q}$ of size $n \times n \times 4$ was used, where n is the maze size per side for store each state values s_t as result of the actions a_t that the agent robotic performs for each movement.

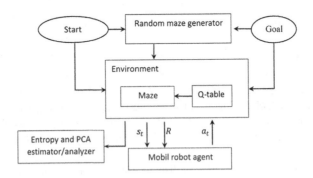

Fig. 2. Block diagram for reinforcement learning with randomness estimation based on environment PCA and Entropy analysis.

The cost of each action is stored in the matrix Q indexed by the actions a_t of each movement that the robotic agent has made as shown in (12).

$$a_t = \begin{cases} U = 1 & up \\ L = 2 & left \\ R = 3 & right \\ D = 4 & down \end{cases} \tag{12}$$

The actions are associated with a cost or rewards for the robotic agent, whose rewards or punitive actions are given by the following values: if it confronts an obstacle in position x and is given a discount or punishment of -1, if the movement is possible, the reward is 0, and if the agent achieve the goal, the reward is the maximum value 100.

For each action, the matrix **Q** values are updated so that, once the goal is achieved, the iteration result is maximized, a new iteration is started, and so on until the agent succeeds in repeating the same trajectory every time with lower cost or, in other words, with maximum reward for the actions exercised for each state.

The environment analysis with the Entropy method, each experiment is associated with a constant calculated as the total average of actions performed in the simulation to reach the goal for each iteration and its relationship with the Entropy of the maze, i.e.

$$C_e = \frac{\overline{\sum a_T}}{E} \tag{13}$$

where C_e is the Entropy constant associated with the experiment as a function of $\overline{\sum a_T}$ which is the average of the sum of the total actions a_T for all the iterations for each experiment, and E is the Entropy of the environment or corresponding maze.

About the PCA analysis, the PCA of the experimental maze was performed in addition with an ideal reference environment. An ideal environment is when there are no obstacles, that is, the whole area is free to transit, and the robot can go forward in a straight line from the start to the goal. We can infer that many actions are not required to achieve the goal. In contrast, in an unstructured environment, the problem is complicated, because the agent must explore solutions that force it to pass through states where even the reward is negative. In this way, the PCA analysis contrasts the main components of the experimental random environment, with the direction of the main component of an ideal reference environment and, subsequently, to evaluate the maximum obstacles dispersion on the ideal reference. This technique provides a quantitative metric regarding the degree of disorder of an unstructured environment; thus, a randomness coefficient can be calculated over an ideal environment. This coefficient is determined as follows: the main components of the reference or ideal images and the robot's maze are obtained, both with same size and same starting and goal position. So, let:

$$\Phi_I = PCA(I_I) \tag{14}$$

$$\Phi_L = PCA(I_L) \tag{15}$$

matrices 2×2 where $\boldsymbol{\Phi}_I = \left[v_1^I \ v_2^I \right]$ has the main vector components of an ideal binary image I_I. A similar definition is for $\boldsymbol{\Phi}_L$ that contains the main components of the binary image for the agent random maze I_L.

Figure 3 shows the typical eigenvectors orientation v_1 and v_2 with respect to the main components for two images examples of equal size 16×16. These eigenvectors represent the direction of maximum variability of their respective image. It is worth mentioning that these eigenvectors are normalized according to the importance of their respective eigenvalues, which are obtained according to the PCA methodology.

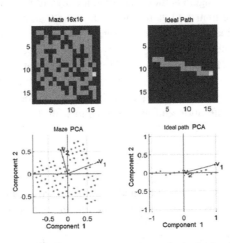

Fig. 3. Maze images and ideal path with PCA analysis, both with size 16×16.

For the maze eigenvectors, a rotation was applied that depends on the direction of a rectilinear ideal path, thus:

$$\boldsymbol{\Phi}_{LR} = T_R\left(\boldsymbol{\Phi}_L, -\theta_I\left(\phi_1^I\right)\right) \tag{16}$$

where $\boldsymbol{\Phi}_{LR}$ is the set of principal components rotated in the opposite direction to the angle $\theta_I(\phi_1^I)$ of the main component ϕ_1^I of the ideal reference image, T_R is the transformation of rotation. Once the rotation to the maze eigenvectors was made, the arithmetic sum of the perpendicular components of the maze is carried out over the main reference component, thus:

$$A_{L/I} = \phi_{L1y} + \phi_{L2y} \tag{17}$$

Precisely, such components indicate the sense of greater randomness of the environment with respect to the perpendicular sense of an ideal path.

Finally, the calculation of the maze randomness coefficient associated with the actions total average of the mobile agent did, i.e.

$$C_{PCA} = \frac{\overline{\sum a_T}}{A_{L/I}} \tag{18}$$

where C_{PCA} is the principal component coefficient associated with the experiment, $\overline{\sum a_T}$ is the average of the sum of the total actions a_t for all iterations by each experiment, and $A_{L/I}$ is the maze randomness, orthogonal to an ideal route or path.

Thus, for each experiment, with the same environment parameters about size and learning coefficients (α and γ), were averaged C_E and C_{PCA} respectively to evaluate the learning performance based on the maze randomness.

4 Results and Analysis

4.1 Q-Learning Performance

A couple of examples with different size mazes are shown in Fig. 4. Their respective traced path by the robotic agent is show also. The passable maze space is the green highlighted areas, except those that are isolated and do not obey with the connectivity 4- connected and make the zone impassable.

The obstacles and perimeter walls are shown in blue. The path is represented by the yellow sequence whose start is located on the left and the goal on the right.

Figure 5 shows the total count of actions by a couple of a typical training; it is worth mentioning that the learning coefficients $\alpha = 0.5$, $\gamma = 0.7$ and $\alpha = 0.9$, $\gamma = 0.9$ were used respectively for the examples.

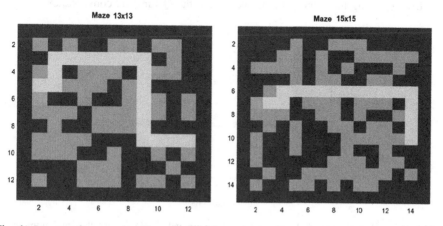

Fig. 4. Images of mazes size 13×13 and 15×15 with the path made by the robotic agent. (Color figure online)

Figure 6 show the evolution of the learning evaluation function **Q** and the number of actions taken for different stages of a training cycle, whose coefficients are $\alpha = 0.3$ and $\gamma = 0.3$. They are shown normalized (Q norm and A norm). Note that the **Q** function starts at lower negative values, this is due to the start of training, the agent is rewarded negatively if it does not achieve the goal.

As the training progresses, the gratification increases positively in proportion to the speed of the successful achievement of the objective with fewer search and exploration actions, maximizing the reward and minimizing punitive actions.

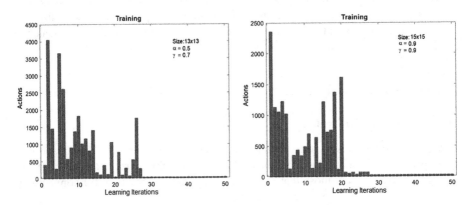

Fig. 5. Two examples of the total number of actions per training epoch for a learning cycle.

The action numbers of evolution per training period is also illustrated, thus, when the training almost ends, the number of search actions rapidly decreases, concentrating on executing only the states that provide maximum reward until the process reach stability, repeating the same path and achieving the **Q** function convergence.

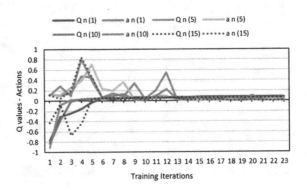

Fig. 6. Typical evolution of the normalized learning values (Q n) and the total number of actions (a n) for a training period with $\alpha = 0.3$ and $\gamma = 0.3$.

The experimentation summary for each size maze and training coefficients used is shown in Table 2. The total number of actions is the average of the three experiments per size maze for same values of coefficients. The performance described in Table 2 is shown in Fig. 7. For purposes of a better visualization, the vertical axis is shown in logarithmic scale in order to highlight the difference about maximum and minimum actions between experiments. Thus, we can observe that the total number of actions required to carry out the learning process preserves a proportionality in relation to the maze size used.

Table 2. Summary of the total actions average by experiment.

Learning coefficients							
$n \times n$	$\alpha = 0.3$ $\gamma = 0.3$	$\alpha = 0.6$ $\gamma = 0.6$	$\alpha = 0.9$ $\gamma = 0.9$	$\alpha = 0.3$ $\gamma = 0.3$	$\alpha = 0.3$ $\gamma = 0.9$	$\alpha = 0.5$ $\gamma = 0.7$	$\alpha = 0.7$ $\gamma = 0.5$	$\alpha = 0.9$ $\gamma = 0.3$
13^2	13215	17483	16599	18340	19200	11071	19907	18340
14^2	32126	15516	15516	30891	14873	21279	48642	30891
15^2	84161	17831	17686	79134	33347	78552	20006	79134
16^2	66804	43526	25848	42153	44994	18708	25558	42153
17^2	89463	200281	1004045	102769	107729	89693	71779	102769
Total actions average								

Another fundamental factor is the careful choice of learning and reward coefficients. Such values, in combination with the maze size, affect the number of actions a and, consequently, the time that the agent will use to reach the goal.

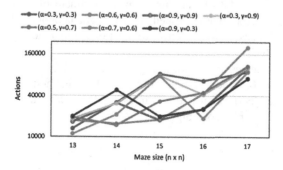

Fig. 7. Total actions average per experiment for different α and γ parameters of the Q-learning method.

Regarding the remaining combinations of coefficients α and γ, the performance of the algorithm presents a non-linear or apparently a quadratic behavior -by the geometric progression of the environment- between the different maze sizes. This could be due the large difference in coefficient values or greater proximity, cause in the algorithm some instability or slow convergence as the learning speed and the reward values are not balanced.

4.2   Randomness Environment Analysis

This section presents the correlation between the total average actions of the experiments and the randomness degree of the environment. The randomization analysis was performed with the Entropy and PCA method described in Sect. 2.2. We insist that the environment was generated randomly in order to induce as little bias as possible compared to predefined or slightly disordered environments.

The performance of the algorithm that involves the actions average of 50 epochs or iterations in which the agent is trained for each experiment is presented, the learning and rewards coefficients used were $\alpha = 0.3$, $\gamma = 0.3$ and $\alpha = 0.6$ and $\gamma = 0.6$ are shown in Fig. 8 respectively.

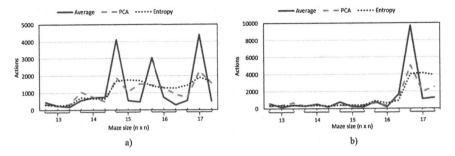

a)   b)

Fig. 8. Quotient of real and estimated actions average obtained by PCA and Entropy methods with coefficients (a) $\alpha = 0.3$ and $\gamma = 0.3$; (b) $\alpha = 0.6$ and $\gamma = 0.6$ for Q-learning.

The solid line in the graph represents the quantified average actions of the agent's learning simulation; the dotted lines represent an estimate of actions by PCA and Entropy respectively. Note that both methods have an analogous behavior, but notice that PCA method adjusts, with less error, to most of the total action's tests compared versus Entropy analysis.

The method tendencies are shown in Fig. 9, with coefficients $\alpha = 0.9$ and $\gamma = 0.9$, in addition with $\alpha = 0.3$ and $\gamma = 0.9$. Notice that both methods, Entropy and PCA, show a very similar performance but contrasting them with the measures average showed at Fig. 8, the error looks bigger.

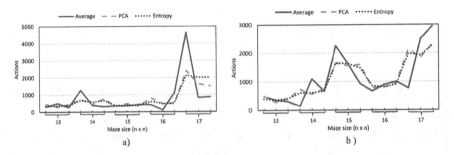

a)   b)

Fig. 9. Quotient of real and estimated actions average obtained by PCA and Entropy methods with coefficients (a) $\alpha = 0.9$ and $\gamma = 0.9$; (b) coefficients $\alpha = 0.3$ and $\gamma = 0.9$ for Q-learning.

Graphs showed in Fig. 10 describes the difference between the Entropy and PCA estimation. There are experiments in which the PCA method fits better than the Entropy method into the counting the actions number.

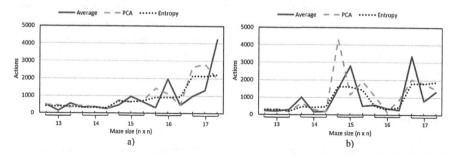

Fig. 10. Quotient of real and estimated actions average obtained by PCA and Entropy methods with coefficients (a) $\alpha = 0.5$ and $\gamma = 0.7$; (b) $\alpha = 0.7$ and $\gamma = 0.5$ for Q-learning.

The estimation performance for latest experiments is shown in Fig. 11, in these tests the learning is higher than the reward coefficient, i.e. $\alpha = 0.9$ and $\gamma = 0.3$, respectively. The correlation among two methods is remarkably different and compared to the total number actions, it suggests that the system, although converges in achieving learning, the system becomes more complicated to estimate by the Entropy and PCA methods.

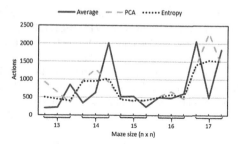

Fig. 11. Quotient of real and estimated actions average obtained by PCA and Entropy methods with coefficients $\alpha = 0.9$ and $\gamma = 0.3$.

5 Conclusions

The experimental results show that, the carefully choice of the learning and reward coefficients, are determinants in the performance of the reinforcement learning method with respect to the number of actions that the agent must perform to find the solution path. Other fundamental factors are the maze size and the degree of randomness of the environment. Experiments show that these directly affect the performance of Q-learning for mobile robotic agents. The Entropy and PCA analyzes allow to quantify the randomness of the environment. Regarding the Entropy analysis, it only allows to determine, in a scalar way, the degree of randomness, but it does not provide information in which area the greatest dispersion is concentrated. In contrast, the analysis by PCA allows to quantify not only the randomness, but also helps to estimate the direction of greater variability of the obstacles of the environment itself. In summary, considering the experiments presented, the PCA analysis method provides better results than Entropy to estimate the average of the total actions that will take the robotic agent to reach the goal. Finally, it can be anticipated that the PCA analysis could be a basic method to estimate the computational cost of learning by reinforcement of mobile robotic agents in unstructured environments.

References

1. Nurmaini, S., et al.: Intelligent navigation in unstructured environment by using memory-based reasoning in embedded mobile robot. Eur. J. Sci. Res. **2**(72), 228–244 (2012)
2. Ingrand, F., Ghallab, M.: Deliberation for autonomous robots: a survey. Artif. Intell. **247**, 10–44 (2017)
3. Sutton, R.S., Barto, A.: Reinforcement Learning: An Introduction, 2nd edn. MIT Press, MA (2012)
4. Tamilselvi, D., et al.: Q learning for mobile robot navigation in indoor environment. In: IEEE-International Conference on Recent Trends in Information Technology, pp. 324–329. MIT Anna University, Chennai (2011)
5. Xiang, Y., et al.: A PCA-based model to predict adversarial examples on Q-learning of path finding. In: Third International Conference on Data Science in Cyberspace, pp. 773–780. IEEE, USA (2018)
6. Xing, J., et al.: Application of deep reinforcement learning in mobile robot path planning. In: Chinese Automatic Congress (CAC), pp. 7112–711. IEEE (2017)
7. Patle, B.K., et al.: Real time navigation approach for mobile robot. J. Comput. **2**(12), 135–142 (2017)
8. Poncela, A., et al.: Efficient integration of metric and topological maps for directed exploration of unknown environments. Robot. Auton. Syst. **41**, 21–39 (2002)
9. Yang, S., Li, C.: Behavior control algorithm for mobile robot based on Q-Learning. In: 2017 International Conference on Computer Network, Electronic and Automation, pp. 45–47. IEEE (2017)
10. Shannon, C.E.: A mathematical theory of communication. Bell Syst. Tech. J. **2**(27), 379–423 (1948)
11. Gonzalez, R.C., et al.: Digital Image Processing Using MATLAB. Prentice Hall, New Jersey (2003)
12. Hong, D., et al.: The entropy and PCA based anomaly prediction in data streams. In: 20th International Conference on Knowledge Based and Intelligent Information and Engineering Systems, pp. 139–146. Procedia Computer Science 96, USA (2016)
13. Ng, S.C.: Principal component analysis to reduce dimension on digital image. In: 8th International Conference on Advances in Information Technology, Procedia Computer Science, vol. 1(111), pp. 113–119, Macau China (2017)
14. Gao, C.: Theory of fractional covariance matrix and its applications in PCA and 2D-PCA. Expert Syst. Appl. **1**(40), 5395–5401 (2013)
15. Zhang, L., et al.: Two-stage image denoising by principal component analysis with local pixel grouping. Pattern Recognit. **1**(43), 1531–1549 (2010)

Fail Detection in WfM/BPM Systems from Event Log Sequences Using HMM-Type Models

Johnnatan Jaramillo[1]([⊠]) and Julián D. Arias-Londoño[1,2]([⊠])

[1] Intelligent Information Systems Lab, Universidad de Antioquia,
Medellín, Colombia
{johnnatan.jaramillo,julian.ariasl}@udea.edu.co
[2] Department of Systems Engineering, Universidad de Antioquia,
Medellín, Colombia

Abstract. Currently, there is an increasing interest in predicting the behavior of active work items in Business Process Management (BPM) systems, which would make possible to monitor the behavior of such processes in a more accurate way. Given the complexity of current business processes, conventional techniques are not always effective in addressing this type of requirements; therefore, machine learning techniques are being increasingly more used for this task. This work deals with the problem of fail detection in a BPM system from event logs, based on machine learning methods. The paper explores the use of three structural learning models, Hidden Markov Models (HMM), Hidden semi-Markov models (HSMM) and Non-stationary Hidden semi-Markov models (NHSMM). The experiments are carried out using a real database of about 460,000 event logs sequences. The results show that for the given dataset, fail detection can be achieved with an accuracy of 86.70% using the HSMM model. In order to reduce the computational load of the proposed approach, the models were implemented in a distributed processing environment using Apache Spark, which guarantees solution scalability.

Keywords: Process mining · Hidden Markov Models · Hidden
semi-Markov models · Non-stationary semi-Markov models · Apache
Spark · Distributed system

1 Introduction

Business Process Management (BPM) is a methodology that seeks to control, analyze, and improve organizational processes. This methodology is supported by a type of software tools called BPM systems, and others called Workflow Management (WfM) systems, being the latter older but currently valid. The WfM/BPM systems allow making multiple definitions of the business processes, these definitions are called workflows [2], and into WfM/BPM systems, an instance of a workflow is called a "work item".

© Springer Nature Switzerland AG 2019
A. D. Orjuela-Cañón et al. (Eds.): ColCACI 2019, CCIS 1096, pp. 223–234, 2019.
https://doi.org/10.1007/978-3-030-36211-9_18

The definition of a workflow is a complex task that should be carried out by experts with a wide knowledge about the entire business process under study, since commonly business processes have implicit or hidden behaviors, which are not evident or known for most of the professionals involved in the organization. Unfortunately, very often the workflows defined for a certain business process may not adequately describe the reality, due to specific behaviors that are not included in the defined workflows. The difference between the real process and the process modeled through the WfM/BPM systems makes difficult to identify fails in the process, especially when the number of work items exceeds thousands or hundreds of thousands of items in a short period. Due to this fact, *process mining* emerges as an alternative for understanding how business processes really work from event logs registered by the WfM/BPM systems. Process mining makes it possible to identify improvements in the process, and increases the degree of automation of the business process. In fact, it may be possible to predict the behavior of the business process. This means that process mining provides a way for accurately describing the behavior of business processes, and allows redesigning and improving them continuously [1].

Several papers have shown the application of process mining methodologies to WfM/BPM systems, specifically for the refinement of workflows definitions. For example, one of the first papers where process mining is used on event logs registered by a WfM systems is [3]. In this work, a certain algorithm is used to obtain a process model of the business, which describes the business process a lot better than the workflow defined manually in the WfM system. Also, this process model deletes redundancies and allows to simplify the defined workflow. Furthermore, in [1], process mining is used to identify irregular behaviors in a real-life business process, by obtaining a process model from the event logs registered by a WfM system. According to [1], similar methodologies can be applied to systems like Customer Relationship Management (CMR), Enterprise Resource Planning (ERP), and to other systems that generate event logs.

In general, process mining has been widely used for building and refining process models generated from event logs registered by the business processes. It is also used to identify inefficient definitions of the process in workflows, and improve the business process. Nevertheless, process mining has currently other challenges, for instance, predicting the remaining time to finish a work item [13]. In [14] for example, a method for predicting the required time to finish a work item is presented. In this paper, a software tool of process mining was used to simulate event logs of some business processes of real-life. With these simulations, it was possible to answer questions related to the duration time for some tasks within the process. This kind of predictions allows having more control of the business process and improving its metrics [12]. Therefore, the next step in the process mining is to predict the future behavior of the business process, which has not been widely explored. Developing systems that allow predicting atypical behaviors has great value for the business process management [9], but is not an easy task, because business processes become increasingly complex due to their high variability degree and the presence of specific behaviors that come with the nature of the business [5].

Due to the complexity of current business processes, and given their random and stochastic behavior, process mining usually makes use of Machine Learning (ML) and probabilistic models, which are flexible and adaptable to the behavior of business processes [4]. For example, models like Hidden Markov Model (HMM) are widely used in process mining, due to their ability to model temporal sequences [4]. Many works have shown that HMMs are able to describe the dynamics of the systems event logs, and to model the changes over time of business processes [12]. However, HMMs do not take into account the time that work items spend in each state of the process. This limits their ability to predict atypical behaviors on work items that remain for a long time in a certain state of the process [4]. Consequently, it makes sense for process mining to use models that do not only take into account the occurrence time, but also the time that the process remains in a certain state. For example, Hidden semi-Markov Model (HSMM) allows detecting specific sequences from the analysis of event logs registered by the system, and taking into account their occurrence time and their duration time in a certain state [7]. HMM and HSMM suppose an homogeneous or stationary behavior in the processes, but, in the real life this is not always the case for the business processes. For this reason, Non-stationary Hidden semi-Markov Model (NHSMM) is proposed in this work, NHSMM is a modification of HSMM, and assumes that the state transition is dependent on the state duration [11,16]. These models are quite good in business processes where models that assume an homogeneous process cannot be used [16]. Nonetheless, the models mentioned before have a high computational cost that increases when new parameters are added to the model. In fact, their computational cost can increase exponentially with respect to the number of event logs sequences to analyze [8].

This paper deals with the problem of fail detection in WfM/BPM systems from a process mining perspective. The aim is to classify a set of event logs sequences generated by a WfM/BPM system in two classes. One class correspond to sequences that ended in an error state, while the other class corresponds to sequences that ended successfully. The aforementioned is the first step to develop a methodology that allows predicting in real time the final states of work items within a WfM/BPM system. The proposed approach is based on the implementation of HMM, HSMM and NHSMM on an environment of distributed processing, which guarantees the scalability of the solution.

The rest of the paper is organized as follows. The methods used for the transformation of the data are discussed in Sect. 2. Section 3 describes hidden state models of Markov. Experimental results are presented in Sect. 4. Section 5 discusses the computational complexity of algorithms and one way to improve their performance. Section 6 concludes the paper.

2   Methods

2.1   Characterization of Event Logs

The event logs used in this work describe a specific behavior in the WfM/BPM systems, and can be directly related to a work item. The behavior described by these event logs is for example; the creation of a new work element, the assignation of a work item to a specific user, the arrival of a work item to a specific queue or the invocation of an external system, etc. Each event log is represented by several features. In this paper, the features taken into account for characterizing the event logs are the following:

– *Workspace identifier:* Identifier of the workspace used by the work item.
– *Operation identifier:* The internal identifier of the operation that is executing the current instruction.
– *Work class identifier:* Internal identifier of the work class to which the work item belongs.
– *Work performer class identifier:* Internal identifier of the work performer class of the queue that contains the work item.
– *Event type:* The number of the system event that is logged.
– *Originator Identifier:* The user identifier of the user that started the workflow.
– *Subject:* The subject entered by the user when a workflow is launched.
– *Response:* Value of the response that the work item was saved with. This value could be empty.

Since the listed variables are categorical, all of them were codified using the one-hot encoding strategy. However, even though the originator identifier may change over time if new users are registered into the platform, it was considered constant during the experiment.

2.2   Vector Quantization Methods

Since the features that characterize the event logs are categorical, the most suitable HMMs to model the sequences extracted from those even logs are discrete HMMs. In order to train a discrete HMM, previous vector quantization of the observations must be carried out. In this case, since all the features are categorical, the vector quantization is not mandatory. However, the effects of using a clustering technique for grouping the observations can also be analyzed.

The aim of vector quantization is to map the observation vectors from a given data space to a finite set of values represented in a simple way. This reduces significantly the effort required to store and manipulate the observations, and could help to remove redundant information [6]. There are multiple cluster analysis methods to perform this vector quantization process, among them, k-means is one of the most popular methods. In general terms, k-means tries to find the group of centroids that minimize the intra-group dispersion. Nevertheless, in this case, the vectors to be quantized are binaries, and the most common distance measures used for clustering, such as the *euclidean distance*, are not suitable for this type of data. In consequence, using the euclidean distance measure will probably not yield good results. As an alternative, the *hamming distance* measure was used. This is a widely used distance measure to compute distances between binary vectors and genetic sequences.

The hamming distance is defined as follows. If x and y are two n-tuples of $0s$ and $1s$, then, their Hamming distance is [10]:

$$d(x, y) := |\{i | 1 \leq i \leq n, x_i \neq y_i\}| \tag{1}$$

When the new centroids are calculated in k-means method, it may happen that these new centroids do not exist within the data set on which the clustering is being done, and it could represent a difficulty when binary vectors are used. Therefore, the k-mode method could be used as an alternative, since, unlike k-means, k-mode is a clustering method where the centroids belong to the given data set.

Bearing this in mind, in this paper three methods are been taken into account within the vector quantization process of the data. The k-means method, the k-mode method, and finally, a method that does not use any clustering techniques but takes advantage of the discrete nature of the observations and assigns a unique identifier to each event.

3   Hidden State Models of Markov

3.1   Hidden Markov Model (HMM)

Hidden Markov Models are defined as a two-stage stochastic process [6]. The first stage consists of a discrete stationary stochastic process that has a finite space of states. This stochastic process is also known as Markov chain model, which describes the transition probabilities between states, where that probability depends only on the immediately previous state. This dependence is known as the Markovian property.

The second stage of the stochastic process defined in HMM corresponds to the generation of new observations over time. The probability distribution associated with this event depends only on the current state of the process. These observations allow visualizing the behavior of the process, because the states generated from these observations cannot be known, for this reason this model is called a hidden states model.

An HMM can be defined as continuous or discrete. A continuous HMM uses parametric probability density functions (typically assumed to be Gaussian or mixtures of Gaussian functions) associated with each state of the process. On the other hand, discrete HMMs use probability mass functions over a set of a previously defined set of symbols, commonly called codebook or dictionary.

A discrete HMM is defined as a tuple $\lambda = (\mathbf{A}, \mathbf{B}, \pi)$, where:

– **A** is a transition probability defined as:

$$\mathbf{A} = \{a_{ij} \equiv P\left[S_t = j | S_{t-1} = i\right]\} \tag{2}$$

where $S_t = j$ represents the state of the process at time t. The number of hidden states is M.
– **B** is the observation matrix. The probability to emit an observation v_k in the state j, is denoted by:

$$\mathbf{B} = \{b_{j(v_k)} \equiv P\left[v_k | S_t = j\right]\} \tag{3}$$

The maximum number of possible symbols is denoted by K, and the set of all possible is denote by $\mathbf{V} = \{v_1, v_2, \ldots, v_K\}$.
– The initial probabilities are represented by a vector π, which is given by:

$$\pi = \{\pi_j \equiv P\left[S_0 = j\right]\} \tag{4}$$

– A sequences of observations is denoted by $O_{1:T} \equiv (O_1, O_2, \ldots, O_T)$, when $O_t \in \mathbf{V}$, and corresponds to the observation in time t.

There are three problems associated with the use of HMMs: the learning problem, the evaluation problem, and the decoding problem. The first one corresponds to the estimation of the model parameters $(\mathbf{A}, \mathbf{B}, \pi)$ from a dataset of a particular problem. The second one corresponds to the estimation of $P(O_{1:T}|\lambda)$, or the probability that a model λ emits a particular observation sequence, and the last one is focused on the estimation of most probable state sequence given a model λ and an observation sequence. Because of the computational complexity, the solutions to these problems are based on algorithms from dynamic programming.

3.2   Hidden Semi-Markov Model (HSMM)

Hidden semi-Markov Model does not take into account the constant or geometric distributions of the duration times of each state in the process that is generally assumed in HMM [6]. In HSMM, the duration in a state is explicitly defined and is given by a random variable, which means that the probability to remain in a state is given by a distribution function. Such a distribution may be a continuous probability density function like as a Gaussian, Poisson or Gamma distribution [11]. Also, in HMM usually one observation is assumed by each state, however, in HSMM this is not assumed, and many observations can be emitted for one state, this flexibility can be very helpful to model a business process with greater precision [15]. In fact, in WfM/BPM systems is very common that each state generates several observations or event logs.

In HSMMs a new discrete random variable is defined to represent the duration that the process remains in a certain state. The set of values for this variable is denoted as follows: $\mathbf{D} = \{1, 2, \ldots, D\}$, where D is a hyperparameter of the model that represents the maximum allowed duration in a state. There are several variations of HSMM, two of the most commons are the *explicit duration HSMM* or HSMM, and the *variable transition HSMM* or NHSMM, both are explained below:

Explicit Duration HSMM. This is the most common variation of HSMM, when a state transition is assumed independent of the duration of the previous state $a_{(i)(j,d)}$, and the state transition to the same state $a_{(i)(i,d)} = 0$ are not allowed. For this variation, it is not recommended to use a large value of D [16].

An standard HSMM or explicit duration HSMM is defined as follows:

- The matrix **A** now represents the state transition probability from i to j for a time d, where $i \neq j$ [16], and is denoted by:

$$\mathbf{A} = \{a_{(i)(j,d)} \equiv P\left[S_{[t+1:t+d]} = j | S_t] = i\right]\} \tag{5}$$

- The matrix **B** is also redefined like as:

$$\mathbf{B} = \{b_{j,d(o_{t+1:t+d})} \equiv P\left[o_{t+1:t+d} | S_{[t+1:t+d]} = j\right]\} \tag{6}$$

- The vector of initial probabilities of states π is redefined as:

$$\pi = \{\pi_{i,d} \equiv P\left[S_{[t-d+1:t]} = j\right]\}; t \leq 0 \tag{7}$$

Variable Transition HSMM. This is another variation of HSMM, also know as Non-stationary Hidden semi-Markov Model (NHSMM). NHSMM models the dependence of transition probabilities on the duration of the states [11]. This means that NHSMM assumes that the transition state is dependent on the duration of the state, which makes it better to describe processes of hidden non-stationary Markov states, which are in homogeneous processes [16].

This model takes into account not only the explicit duration of a state, but also selects the transition according to the exact duration. NHSMM has demonstrated that in complex tasks of pattern recognition it presents a better performance than standard HSMM [11]. In this case, the probability of transaction among hidden states is defined as $a_{(i,h)(j,d)} = a_{(i,d)(j,1)}$. The parameters **B** and π are defined in the same way than in the HSMM, and the matrix **A** now represents the state transition probability from i to j when the process wait in i for a period of d times [16]. Therefore A is defined as:

$$\mathbf{A} = \{a_{(i,j)(d)} \equiv P\left[S_{t+1} = j | S_{[t-d+1:t]} = i\right]\} \tag{8}$$

4   Experiments and Results

4.1   Dataset and Experimental Setup

The event logs taken into account for this work were generated by a WfM system. This system supports a real-life business process related to banking. Further, the event logs are stored in a table of a relational database, which contains around sixty millions of event logs that correspond to 460,000 event logs sequences. These sequences are mapped into two groups; the first group has event logs sequences that finish successfully, and the second group has event logs sequences that finish incorrectly or with some error. In this dataset, 40% of the samples correspond to sequences that ended incorrectly, and the remaining 60% to sequences that ended correctly.

To evaluate the performance of the different models, cross-validation technique with five folds was used. The training parameters of the models also were varied, for example, the parameter M was searched between 10 and 50, and the parameter D between 3 and 6. The performance of the models was estimated using sensitivity, specificity, precision and the geometrical mean between sensitivity and specificity. The experiments were run on a cluster of Apache Spark with HDFS. This cluster was deployed into six on-premise servers. The jobs were launch with 6 executors, and for each executor were set 2 cores and 16 gigabyte of RAM.

4.2 Results

The first step for the training of the HMM-based models is to define the best method for vector quantization. For the k-means and the k-mode techniques, it is necessary to estimate which is the optimum value of k or clusters. To estimate this value, the clustering algorithm is executed several times varying the value of k up to 300, and a score that describes how well the model for this particular value of k is estimated in every execution. The score is basically the sum of squares of the distances of each point to his centroid. With this score, the best value for k can be determined. In the third case, when a clustering technique is not used, it is necessary to map each value of the original space to a new space of values, which generates a sequence of consecutive integers.

According to the experiments, the best values for k-means and k-mode are 57 and 300 respectively, and the number of values for the new space generated by the third method is 4039. These values are used as input to the HMM, HSMM and the NHSMM models, and correspond to the size of the observations dictionary of the model.

Table 1 shows the performance of HMMs models for each of the vector quantization methods discussed in Sect. 2.2. Every section includes the evaluation of the model by varying the number of hidden states (M).

According to the results shown in the Table 1, the best result is obtained when no clustering algorithm is used for the vector quantization. For the k-means and k-mode techniques, the best performance was achieved using 40 states in the HMM. However, when no clustering was used, the results were more stable and the model with 20 states achieved the best performance.

Regarding the HSMM model, the experiments include the hyperparameter (D), and were performed with a value of M equal to 10. This value was fixed because the difference between the accuracy of row *ten* and the row *eleven* of the Table 1 is small. Further, increasing the value of M, goes the computational load of the training algorithm up for all the evaluated models. A similar criteria was used to select the grid search for the hyperparameter D; small values were taken because high values of D may easily produce overfitting for the HSMM and increase the computational load. The results of this experiment are shown in Table 2.

Table 1. Results HMM

Clustering method	M	Sensitivity	Specificity	Accuracy	G-mean
k-means and k = 57	10	39.49%	77.85%	62.12%	54.16%
	20	42.34%	76.33%	62.39%	56.55%
	30	27.49%	84.69%	61.24%	46.80%
	40	**45.33%**	**74.46%**	**62.52%**	**58.10%**
	50	42.32%	76.27%	62.36%	56.52%
k-mode and k = 300	10	36.28%	79.56%	61.82%	47.81%
	20	45.28%	74.47%	62.50%	58.07%
	40	**45.31%**	**74.46%**	**62.51%**	**58.08%**
	50	45.31%	74.46%	62.51%	58.08%
Without clustering and k = 4039	10	74.10%	70.28%	71.84%	72.17%
	20	**74.35%**	**70.37%**	**72.00%**	**72.34%**
	30	74.41%	70.23%	71.95%	72.29%
	40	74.37%	70.36%	72.00%	72.33%
	50	74.39%	70.03%	71.82%	72.17%

Table 2. Results HSMM without clustering, $M = 10$ and $k = 4039$

D	Sensitivity	Specificity	Accuracy	G-mean
3	78.98%	72.97%	75.43%	75.70%
4	**99.90%**	**77.49%**	**86.70%**	**87.72%**
5	99.93%	67.84%	81.04%	82.16%
6	99.91%	75.17%	85.34%	86.53%

In this case, the best performance was obtained for $D = 4$, which is in concordance with the results presented in [16], where smaller values of D are preferred. According to the results, the HSMM provides an absolute improvement of 15% (54% in relative terms) in the G-mean in comparison to HMM. Both, the sensitivity and specificity increased in the HSMM vs the HMM model, although the improvement in the sensitivity was stronger. This result supports the hypothesis that the incorporation of the time in the modeling of business process, is an important element in order to characterize the patterns of normal and irregular events (fails) in the process.

Lastly, for the NHSMM model, there were used similar values for all the parameters than in the previous case. The results are shown in Table 3. Nevertheless, the results obtained when modeling the sequences with HSMM are still better. Also, it is important to clarify that the results obtained with the NHSMM are not decisive, since the *G-mean* value has an increasing trend as the value of D increases as well. This means that it would be necessary to perform more experiments with values of D higher to 6. However, to increase the value of

D implies a higher computational load in the training task of the models, which could make it not worthy.

For the sake of comparison, Fig. 1 shows the ROC curve of the best results for each of the evaluated models. As expected, the best ROC is by far the one provided by the HSMM model. The performance of the NHSMM degrades with respect to the HSMM model, but it is still better than the more simple HMM model.

Table 3. Results NHSMM without clustering, $M = 10$ and $k = 4039$

D	Sensitivity	Specificity	Accuracy	G-mean
3	75.21%	70.24%	72.29%	72.69%
4	75.12%	70.24%	72.25%	72.64%
5	75.25%	70.25%	72.30%	72.71%
6	**75.31%**	**70.23%**	**72.31%**	**72.72%**

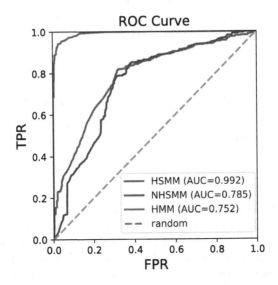

Fig. 1. Curve ROC for HMM, HSMM and NHSMM.

5 Discussion

The results show that the classification of the sequence of event logs from WfM/BPM systems can be carried out using ML methods suitable to model sequence data. An important consideration for the implementation of solutions based on this approach is the computational complexity. The algorithms used in this work have a high computational complexity, for example, in an HMM with sequences of length T and N hidden states, the complexity in terms of memory for the Baum-Welch algorithm grows linearly with T and N, this means a complexity order of $O(NT)$. However, the complexity with respect to time grows quadratically with N and linearly with T, this is a complexity order of $O(N^2T)$. Analogously, for the time-dependent models like HSMM, the complexity in terms of memory is the same as HMM, but the computational complexity for the training has an order of $O((N^2 + ND^2)T)$, where D is the maximum amount of time that remains in a state [15]. Finally, the complexity for the training in NHSMM is $O(N^2TD^2)$ [11].

For these reasons, the application of HMM, HSMM and NHSMM models to process mining tasks was avoided before. Nevertheless, currently, there is a strong and active work in the development of parallel and distributed platforms, specially oriented to data processing applications, one of such approaches is the use of HDFS systems and the Map-Reduce and Spark programming paradigms. The training of HMM-based models can take advantages from these paradigms and make possible the application of this approach within a Big Data context. The implementations of HMM, HSMM and NHSMM models used in this work were made in Apache Spark and will be available on GitHub. With this implementation, the performance of the algorithms can be scalable. This means that if the number of sequences increases, the performance of the algorithms can be maintained by adding new nodes to the cluster.

6   Conclusions

According to the results, the fail detection in WfM/BPM systems can be carried out using a process mining approach based on HMM/HSMM/NHSMM models. The performance obtained by the HSMM model is superior to the one shown by the HMM, mainly because the duration time that the process remains in one state, is an important element to model the underlying process appropriately. Also, HSMM results are superior to the one shown by the NHSMM, but, that results are not decisive, because the performance for NHSMM is better as the value of D increases.

The best performance obtained in this work was an accuracy of 86.7% in the detection of fail/non-fail even logs sequences. This is an interesting result for a first approach, but there is room for improvement. Even more considering that the model showed a bias to one of the classes.

The number of states that the HMM/HSMM/NHSMM models require to capture the dynamic of the underlying process was 10. This is a convenient result because a large number of states increases the computational cost of the models. Regarding the maximum allowed time in one state, the experiments showed that a value of $D = 4$ is a good choice for HSMM, which is in concordance with previous results that promote smaller values for this parameter. Moreover, a large value of D also has negatives consequences in the computational cost of the algorithm, as it was discussed in the previous section. However, the optimum value for these parameters depends on the dataset used.

This work is the first step to implement a system that allows predicting the behavior of the process in real time within a Big Data context. This is a complex task, due to the large volumes of information, and the specific behavior of the business processes. Nevertheless, it is one of the new challenges of process mining, which could allow having smarter business processes.

References

1. Van der Aalst, W.M.P., et al.: Business process mining: an industrial application. Inf. Syst. **32**(5), 713–732 (2007)
2. Aalst, W.M.P.: Business process management demystified: a tutorial on models, systems and standards for workflow management. In: Desel, J., Reisig, W., Rozenberg, G. (eds.) ACPN 2003. LNCS, vol. 3098, pp. 1–65. Springer, Heidelberg (2004). https://doi.org/10.1007/978-3-540-27755-2_1
3. Agrawal, R., Gunopulos, D., Leymann, F.: Mining process models from workflow logs. In: Schek, H.-J., Alonso, G., Saltor, F., Ramos, I. (eds.) EDBT 1998. LNCS, vol. 1377, pp. 467–483. Springer, Heidelberg (1998). https://doi.org/10.1007/BFb0101003
4. Da Silva, G.A., Ferreira, D.R.: Applying hidden Markov models to process mining. In: Actas da 4a Conferencia Iberica de Sistemas e Tecnologias de Informacao, CISTI 2009, pp. 207–210. Associacao Iberica de Sistemas e Tecnologias de Informacao (2009)
5. Ferreira, D., Zacarias, M., Malheiros, M., Ferreira, P.: Approaching process mining with sequence clustering: experiments and findings. In: Alonso, G., Dadam, P., Rosemann, M. (eds.) BPM 2007. LNCS, vol. 4714, pp. 360–374. Springer, Heidelberg (2007). https://doi.org/10.1007/978-3-540-75183-0_26
6. Fink, G.A.: Markov Models for Pattern Recognition, vol. 1, 2nd edn. Springer, London (2014). https://doi.org/10.1007/978-1-4471-6308-4
7. Ge, X., Smyth, P.: Deformable Markov model templates for time-series pattern matching. In: Proceeding of the Sixth ACM SIGKDD International Conference on Knowledge Discovery and Data Mining, pp. 81–90 (2000)
8. Johnson, M.: Capacity and complexity of HMM duration modeling techniques. IEEE Sig. Process. Lett. **12**(5), 407–410 (2005)
9. Kang, Y.: Probabilistic process monitoring in process-aware information systems. Ph.D. thesis, University of Pittsburgh (2014)
10. van Lint, J.H.: Introduction to Coding Theory, Graduate Texts in Mathematics, vol. 86. Springer, Heidelberg (1999). https://doi.org/10.1007/978-3-642-58575-3
11. Marhasev, E., Hadad, M., Kaminka, G.A.: Non-stationary hidden semi Markov models in activity recognition. Signal Processing -1 (Rabiner 1989) (2006)
12. Rozinat, A., Veloso, M., Van der Aalst, W.: Using hidden Markov models to evaluate the quality of discovered process models. Extended version, pp. 1–53. BPM Center Report BPM-08-10, BPMcenter.org (2008)
13. Yu, S.-Z., Kobayashi, H.: An efficient forward-backward algorithm for an explicit-duration hidden Markov model. IEEE Sig. Process. Lett. **10**(1), 11–14 (2003)
14. Van der Aalst, W.M.P., Schonenberg, M.H., Song, M.: Time prediction based on process mining. Inf. Syst. **36**(2), 450–475 (2011)
15. Yu, S.Z.: Hidden semi-Markov models. Artif. Intell. **174**(2), 215–243 (2010)
16. Yu, S.Z.: Hidden Semi-Markov Models Theory, Algorithms and Applications. Elsevier, Amsterdam (2016)

Solar Spots Classification Using Pre-processing and Deep Learning Image Techniques

Thiago O. Camargo[1]📵, Sthefanie Monica Premebida[1]📵,
Denise Pechebovicz[1]📵, Vinicios R. Soares[1]📵, Marcella Martins[1(✉)]📵,
Virginia Baroncini[1]📵, Hugo Siqueira[1]📵, and Diego Oliva[2]📵

[1] Federal University of Technology - Paraná - Ponta Grossa - (UTFPR-PG),
Ponta Grossa, Brazil
`marcella@utfpr.edu.br`
[2] Universidad de Guadalajara, CUCEI, Guadalajara, Mexico

Abstract. Machine learning techniques and image processing have been successfully applied in many research fields. Astronomy and Astrophysics are some of these areas. In this work, we apply machine learning techniques in a new approach to classify and characterize solar spots which appear on the solar photosphere which express intense magnetic fields, and these magnetic fields present significant effects on Earth. In our experiments we consider images from Helioseismic and Magnetic Imager (HMI) in IntensitygramFlat format. We apply pre-processing techniques to recognize and count the groups of sunspots for further classification. Besides, we investigate the performance of the CNN AlexNet layer input in comparison with the Radial Basis Function Network (RBF) using different levels and combining both networks approaches. The results show that when the CNN uses the RBF to identify and classify sunspots from image processing, its performance is higher than when only CNN is used.

Keywords: Image processing · Astronomy and Astrophysics · Neural network

1 Introduction

Eruptions on solar surface are correlated with solar spots and there is a probability of an event be evaluated based on the area, class and the lifetime of the spot [1]. In this sense, Coronal Mass Ejections (CME) present significant effects on Earth civilization [2]. However, the prediction of Flares and these effects are still difficult to be performed [3]. Coronal Mass Ejections is a release of huge quantity of plasma enclosed with magnetic field of the Solar Corona, Flares consist in a light flash, occurs near a solar spot and often are followed by a CME.

The sun presents areas of shear or interfacial layers forming the dynamo, which generates a main magnetic field whose movement stretches and twists the existed magnetic field lines through the solar poles, forcing the poles to writhe

A. D. Orjuela-Cañón et al. (Eds.): ColCACI 2019, CCIS 1096, pp. 235–246, 2019.
https://doi.org/10.1007/978-3-030-36211-9_19

and create bulbs, due to differential sun rotation. When this action creates bulbs, they behave as local magnetic fields in the photosphere, with their own north and south poles. These bulbs appear in the photosphere in the forms of "loops", lumps, filaments (which are not more than one protrusion view with solar bottom surface) and the sunspots.

These patches are colder regions with temperature around $4100K$, and darker than the photosphere. It is formed by a core, Umbra, which is the darkest part of the spot size of 300 to 2500 km, and greater strength magnetic field around 2000 to 2500 Mx.cm^{-2}, being more vertical. The Penumbra appears that around 50% of the spots, being a surrounding area of Umbra, about the size of 2.5 times the size of it, which has a gray scale and field strength of about 500 and 2000 Mx.cm^{-2} more horizontal [4,5]. Currently, most benchmarks to measure solar activity consider the number of sunspots present on the sun at any given time. We highlight that it is very important the noting, counting and the classification of them. However, there is a few studies on different image processing for easy sorting and counting sunspots. After the solar cycle of 11.2 years, the entire sun reverses its overall magnetic polarity: the north magnetic pole becomes the south pole, and vice versa [6]. Thus, a complete magnetic solar cycle lasts on average about 22 years, being known as Hale cycle, but the behavior varies with the variation of the activity. According to Hathaway [7], observations of sunspots and solar activity from the middle of XVII showed that the number of sunspots and the area they cover grow rapidly from a minimum (close to zero) to the maximum (3 to 4 years after reaching the minimum). However, the maximum decline to minimum is slower. This asymmetric growth and decline exhibit substantial variations from one cycle to another. This non-linear and chaotic behavior suggest that the dynamo is not only a oscillating phenomenon due to is possible to observe the solar Hale cycle [5].

Since 1981 the analysis of images provided by satellites and observatories from sun, for automated monitoring, have been done by the Solar Influences Data Analysis Center (SIDC), which has been producing monthly the International Relative Sunspot Number, Ri, calculated statistically from all contributors and available observations, using the Wolf number [8]. In order to equalize the data to find a consistent Ri, it is used the personal reduction coefficient k, which is the factor scale between the individual station and the overall network average [8].

This paper aims to extend the work presented in [COLCACI PAPER] by investigating a comparison with some networks, presenting these main characteristics and providing quality metrics for both approach not explored in [COLCACI PAPER]. The main objectives here are to identify and classify sunspots from image processing for further being explored to measure the solar activity. For this purpose, we use the numerical communication software analysis and data visualization, MatLab, besides a pretrained convolutional neural network (AlexNet) and a Radial Basis Function (RBF) network. Similar works have addressed sunspots on a image processing context, especially using computational vision, but here, in our proposal, we aim to apply machine learning techniques which can be further explored within the graphics processing approaches.

This work is organized as follow: Sect. 2 presents the background and the related investigations of images processing techniques. The Sect. 3 discusses the proposed approach to achieve the goal, while Sect. 4 shows the experiments and the computational results. Section 5 presents the conclusions from the presents results.

2   Background

Currently, sunspots are the main references to determine the level of solar activity. Besides, the captured images of the sun are the basis of several studies to develop theories and better understanding of the star. The quality, the good use and ease of observation from images is essential and, to improve these characteristics, pre-processing techniques can be addressed. This section presents a background for pre-processing and machine learning techniques usually applied on image manipulation in a general context.

2.1   Pre-processing Techniques

When manipulating images, some techniques should be applied before their complete processing. These techniques can help to make a data optimization: filling nulls, treating noise, identifying or removing outliers, and removing inconsistencies; integrating data; processing and data reduction with particular value for numeric data; normalization and aggregation; discretization of the data [9]. We list some methods to perform this processing as follows:

- Image adjust (stretching)
- RGB to gray
- Image to black and white
- Image open (growth)
- Image complement
- Region proprieties
- Image crop
- Image write.

2.2   Machine Learning

The Machine Learning techniques can be used in several automated situations because they can produce quickly and automatically models able to analyze larger and more complex data, and deliver faster and accurate results, even in a large scale [10]. Machine Learning is a part of Artificial Intelligence (AI), and present 4 major groups of approaches: supervised learning, unsupervised learning, semi-supervised learning and reinforcement learning, as seen in Fig. 1.

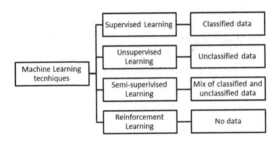

Fig. 1. Machine learning techniques.

- Supervised Learning: in these cases, the machine learns from a set of labeled data. In this case, the inputs and the respective outputs are known and the reference signal acts as a teacher, guiding the adjust of the parameters in the training phase. It is of two types, classification and regression. In the first, we have the input and tune the model to predict the output. In a regression problem, we have the output and try to find the possible inputs. Neural Network (NN) can be applied as supervised learning, and convolutional neural network (CNN) is a kind of deep neural network which presents architecture based in a multi-stage processing of an input image, generating a high-level and hierarchical features [11]. This process is fully automated, discarding external and manual classification data.
- Unsupervised Learning: in this case, there is no teacher to guide the classification procedure. The main methods of this kind is the clustering algorithms, which is a set of data mining models, that automatic grouping of data according to their similarities, like human facial expressions [12], without prior training as in the last case.
- Semi-Supervised Learning: this type of method is like a mixture of the firsts, using supervised and unsupervised procedures, being the closest thing to our way of learning [13]. Here, program learns from its own mistakes and improves its performance, that is, in addition to working to obtain the results, it the model make an analysis of future test data much better than the model previously generated.
- Reinforcement learning: these methods use observations obtained from interaction with the environment to perform actions that maximize reward or minimize risk [14]. The Markov Decision Process (MDP) [15] is an example of this typo, which is a stochastic process in which the next state depends on the current state.
The MDP present 5 values:

(1) Finite set of states (S), such as a door being open or closed;
(2) Finite set of actions (A), what possible actions can be taken;
(3) Probability model (P), the probability of a current action taking the problem to an action in the future state;
(4) Reward (R) is a value that depends on which state you are in. Rewards can be defined for states, even without actions taken;

(5) Discount factor (Y), usually between 0 and 1. This factor influences the total future reward that the Agent will receive, ie if there is a discount factor of 0.9 we know that the more advanced the Agent is, the greater your reward.

In this paper, the classification of the spots groups has been done with CNN and with Radial basis function network. Convolutional Neural Networks is one of the most know models deep learning, and also one of the most utilized. The network is composed of convolutional layers that process the inputs, normally images, because in your convolution we can filter pictures considerating their spatial structure. Most layers of a CNN are pre-trained, but the last ones are trained on a image store according the user needs. This feature turns this deep learn model very accurate.

3   Proposed Approach

This works presents an approach to classify the sun images according to the spots and some special features. We address a dataset taken from the Helioseismic and Magnetic Imager (HMI), which processes images of the Solar Dynamics Observatory (SDO).

The classification is performed according to two stages: (i) a pre-processing and (ii) a training phase, the second stage is applied to the CNN and the Radial Basis Function Network.

First, the images have been submitted to pre-processing techniques, such as stretching, threshold, object properties analysis and cropping. An image example can be shown on Fig. 2.

After the preprocessing, the training phase uses two spots groups: one with positive for O type and the another one with negative. The O type is arbitrary, defined to simplify the analysis: it is a class basically characterized by almost only penumbra. A comparison is presented in Fig. 3. The criterion used here is based on the amount of black pixels for each subfigure. All of those methods are presented in Algorithm 1.

The method utilized to reformulate AlexNet to ours purpose is transfer learning.

3.1   Preprocessing Stage

A folder with HMI images, such as the example on Fig. 2a, is created in Step 1. All these images are loaded in an array and each element is applied to Algorithm 1. In Step 3 the image is *stretched*, as shown in Fig. 2b, therefore, the contrast between the spots and the solar surface increases, and the *gray scale*, in Step 4, process a color change from RGB to a gray scale, (see Fig. 2c). This can facilitate the *thresholding* in Step 5.

The thresholding turns black the region near the group centroid (Fig. 2d), but in many cases the black object created shown itself divided in many small centroids. For this reason the *growth* of these objects is necessary, Step 6, (Fig. 2e).

Algorithm 1. A simplified pseudo-code presenting the main components of pre-processing and sorting

---

INPUT: I: HMI Intensitygram Flat images
OUTPUT: O_p: image dataset with positive to O type
$\quad\quad\quad$ O_n: image dataset with negative to O type
$\quad$ {Initialization}
$\quad$ $F \leftarrow$ *Load All HMI Images*
$\quad$ {Main loop}
$\quad$ **for** each image $\in F$ **do**
$\quad\quad$ {Treatment and Filters}
$\quad\quad$ $I_{sc} \leftarrow$ *stretching* (F_g)
$\quad\quad$ $I_{gr} \leftarrow$ *gray scale* (I_{sc})
$\quad\quad$ $I_{bw} \leftarrow$ *thresholding* (I_{gr})
$\quad\quad$ $I_{op} \leftarrow$ *oppening* (I_{bw})
$\quad\quad$ $I_{cbw} \leftarrow$ *complementing* (I_{bw})
$\quad\quad$ {Spot Detection}
$\quad\quad$ $P_{sp} \leftarrow$ *coordinates of spots groups* (I_{cbw})
$\quad\quad$ $N_{ob} \leftarrow$ *number of objects* (I_{cbw})
$\quad\quad$ {Image Cropping}
$\quad\quad$ $S_{ian} \leftarrow$ *size of the cropped images for AlexNet*
$\quad\quad$ $z \leftarrow 1$
$\quad\quad$ **for** each coordinate $\in N_{ob}$ **do**
$\quad\quad\quad$ $I_{cr}^z \leftarrow$ *Cut Image* (S_{ian}, F_g, N_{ob}^z)
$\quad\quad\quad$ $I_{testgr} \leftarrow$ *gray scale* (I_{cr}^z)
$\quad\quad\quad$ $I_{testbw} \leftarrow$ *thresholding* (I_{testgr})
$\quad\quad\quad$ {Image Testing}
$\quad\quad\quad$ **if** $I_{testbw} = BlackImage$ **then**
$\quad\quad\quad\quad$ discard I_{cr}^z
$\quad\quad\quad$ **else if** $I_{testbw} = WhiteImage$ **then**
$\quad\quad\quad\quad$ discard I_{cr}^z
$\quad\quad\quad$ **else**
$\quad\quad\quad\quad$ {Image Saving}
$\quad\quad\quad\quad$ $N_{bp} \leftarrow$ *number of black pixels* (I_{testbw})
$\quad\quad\quad\quad$ **if** $N_{bp} \in OTypeParameter$ **then**
$\quad\quad\quad\quad\quad$ $O_p \leftarrow I_{cr}^z$
$\quad\quad\quad\quad$ **else**
$\quad\quad\quad\quad\quad$ $O_n \leftarrow I_{cr}^z$
$\quad\quad\quad\quad$ **end if**
$\quad\quad\quad$ **end if**
$\quad\quad\quad$ $z \leftarrow z + 1$
$\quad\quad$ **end for**
$\quad$ **end for**

This action decreases the number of objects, which can be showed as an advantage, however, some frames with different views of the same group make the neural network learning more accurate.

For the object detection the background must be black and the object white. This condition is limited by the function *regionprops* from MatLab, (Fig. 2f). Therefore, Step 7, the *complementing* of the image is gotten Fig. 2f.

The centroid coordinates gives the parameters to crop the original image in subfigures with 227x227, Step 9, size to fit as an AlexNet input. An example of spot groups detection is presented in Fig. 2g. Thereafter, in Steps 12 to 20, a staining test is performed to ensure the validity of the figure, black and white images are rejected.

Another test is done to separate O type positive and negative in Step 20 to 27. The test is applied using the total of black pixels on the image, and a range is defined to classify the O type positive. Subfigures which do not fit in these range are classified as O type negative.

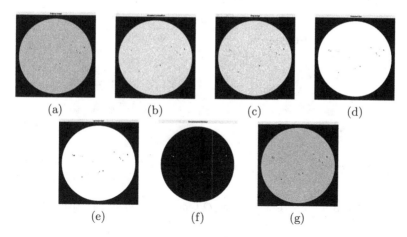

Fig. 2. Example of preprocessing stage using techniques for (a) Original Image, (b) Stretched, (c) Gray scale, (d) Threshold, (e) Grown, (f) Complemented and (g) Detected. This image is from May 15th, 2014, at 00:00 h.

3.2 Training and Testing

An image dataset has been create with the two folders of the groups of O type separated by Algorithm 1. The image dataset is randomly divided into two arrays, one to train both networks, containing 70% of the sub-figures, 15% to validation and the other containing 15% to test.

Convolutional Neural Network. The pretrained CNN AlexNet was loaded and the three lasts layers have been discarded in our proposal.

The fully connected layer contains the number of classes, weight learn rate factor and bias learn rate factor. Softmax layer, originally is responsible to gives the percent of classification of 1000 classes [11], but in this paper is reformulated to process only two classes. The last layer is the classification output layer.

The AlexNet layers parameters has been set to keep the features in the predefined layers with a small value of initial learn rate. In the fully connected layer the learning rate has been increased. The function responsible to train the CNN validates the network according to a frequency during training, and automatically stops training when no more improvement is achieved.

After the configurations the CNN is trained, then used to classify the validation/test data.

The investigation has been made computing the precision, recall and accuracy coefficients [16]. Control variables has been created to count the quantity of true positives, T_{positive}, true negatives, $T_{\text{negatives}}$, false positives, F_{positive}, and the false negatives, F_{negative}, the counting process consist in decision structures comparing the labels gave by the trained network and the labels of the test part of the image data store.

O Type

Positive   Negative

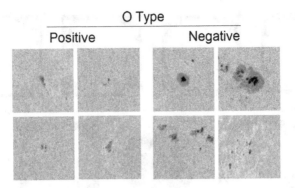

Fig. 3. Comparison between O type positive and negative.

Radial Basis Function Network. The input data for the RBF network was got from three different layers of AlexNet, data, which gives the normalization of the images, fully connected layer 6 and 8. These different inputs creates a different kind of neural network, with AlexNet fully connected layers as the RBF input the neural network can be described as a new CNN, because the SoftMax layer is no longer used, the method was replace with hyperbolic tangent method and also a different kind of SoftMax method. For the data layer as input the RBF works entirely with their method.

The Radial Basis Function network parameters was formulated to be similar to AlexNet parameters, like the network momentum, the both have 0.9, learning rate, the both have 0.0001, basically all the parameters that the two networks have in common are the same, except for the neuron quantity and the max training epochs. The neuron quantity is different according with RBF input, for the fully connected layers the neurons quantity vary between 5 and 100, for the AlexNet data layer the network have only 100 neuron, this fact is limited by computational time. The max training epochs in RBF is 500, but this value was never reached.

4   Experiments and Results

In total, 96 images in the HMI Intensitygram Flat format were analyzed, of which 920 subfigures were generated, 138 to validation, another 138 to testing and 644 to the training phase. Except for AlexNet data layer, the quantity of images had to be less than the total, this reduction was necessary because our processing machine could not handle, therefore, the total images was reduced to 400. We use Intensitygram Flat Orange 4 K images[1]. This format allows the easy manipulation for counting, identifying and classifying sunspots from image processing.

---

[1] The images can be downloaded from http://hmi.stanford.edu/.

We have investigated the neural networks performance calculating three coefficients, precision, recall and accuracy. All of these depends of some components, results of the networks prediction. True positive (TP), this component is given when there is O type positive on the subfigure and the NN detect it. False positive (FP), when there is O type negative on the subfigure and the NN classify as O type positive. True negative (TN), is given by the detection of O type negative correctly. False negative (FN), this component is given when the NN classify a subfigure containing O type positive as O type negative.

The Recall coefficient can be described as the capacity of the NN classify correctly:

$$\frac{\sum TP}{\sum TP + \sum FN} \tag{1}$$

Precision coefficient gives the proportion of correctly classification of a true positive:

$$\frac{\sum TP}{\sum TP + \sum FP} \tag{2}$$

Accuracy coefficient determine the fraction of right classifications:

$$\frac{\sum TP + \sum TN}{\sum TP + \sum FP + \sum TN + \sum FN} \tag{3}$$

The Table 1 presents all the components and the calculated coefficients for AlexNet performance.

Table 1. Performance analysis.

True positives	26
True negatives	96
False positives	9
False negatives	5
Recall	0.8710
Precision	0.7714
Accuracy	0.9130

The Table 2 shows the best and worst calculated coefficients for RBF with AlexNet layers as input.

AlexNet Confusionchart. The confusion chart is present in Fig. 4, where the rows represent the assumed classes, in this case 0 to O type negative and 1 to positive. The columns represent the target class assigned by the neural network.

The diagonal in green shows the correctly classified cases, and the diagonal in red presents the incorrectly classified. For example, 91 images were correctly classified in 0 class, representing 71.7% from the 138 testing images. On the other

Table 2. Performance comparison.

	Recall		Precision		Accuracy	
	Best	Worst	Best	Worst	Best	Worst
FC6 - SoftMax	1.000	0.4909	0.939	0.3925	0.9333	0.9333
FC6 - Hyperbolic tangent	1.0000	0.9692	0.9482	0.7393	0.9619	0.9619
FC8 - SoftMax	0.9732	0.4722	0.8925	0.4305	0.9167	0.9167
FC8 - Hyperbolic tangent	1.0000	0.9833	0.9638	0.8376	0.9381	0.9381
Data - SoftMax		0.0000		0.0000		0.7452
Data - Hyperbolic tangent		1.0000		0.6063		0.4929

hand, 8 images, or 5.8% were not classified correctly for the same 0 class. The right column in gray represents the precision highlighted in green, and the false discovery rate highlighted in red, for each class. The gray bottom row represents the recall highlighted in green and the false negative rate highlighted in red for each class. The blue cell shows the overall accuracy highlighted in green.

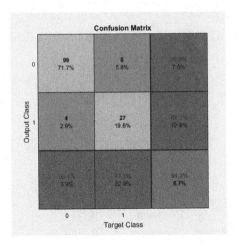

Fig. 4. Confusion chart. (Color figure online)

Network Comparison. Comparing the RBF performance according with the AlexNet layer input it's noticed that the best result achieved is with the fully connected layer 8, with hyperbolic tangent method, and the worst result is given by the fully connected layer with softmax method.

The reached results are higher than AlexNet, this can be explained by the combination of the two networks, AlexNet process the images and the Radial Basis Function Network classify the processed data. The solo RBF performance is far from solo AlexNet, Table 2 'data' row, result not pertinent, compared with Table 1, the RBF development way doesn't allows the processing of a large database, but with a pre-processed database, like the fully connected 6 and 8 layers, the RBF is able to perform a reasonable classification.

5   Conclusions

This work investigated a method to identify and classify sunspots using image processing techniques. This method consists of two steps: image pre-processing and training phase using both convolutional neural network (CNN) and the Radial Basis Function Network (RBF).

The addressed images were taken from the Helioseismic and Magnetic Imager (HMI), of the Solar Dynamics Observatory (SDO). A total of 96 images were analyzed, of which 920 subfigures were generated in the pre-processing stage, separated in 138 for testing, 138 for validation and 644 for training.

We analyzed the network performance according to the precision, recall and accuracy components. The obtained accuracy, precision and recall showed competitive results for the both considered networks. This means the proposed approach is a competitive classifier for the sunspots groups, making possible the exploration and extension for other related images. In the future we expect to investigate more techniques to identify other sun relevant features, improving the research in this spatial area.

References

1. Giovanelli, R.G.: The relations between eruptions and sunspots. Astrophys. J. **89**, 555 (1939)
2. Siscoe, G.: The space-weather enterprise: past, present, and future. J. Atmos. Sol.-Terr. Phys. **62**(14), 1223–1232 (2000)
3. Schwenn, R., Dal Lago, A., Huttunen, E., Gonzalez, W.D.: The association of coronal mass ejections with their effects near the earth. Ann. Geophys. **23**(3), 1033–1059 (2005)
4. Hoeksema, J.T., et al.: The helioseismic and magnetic imager (HMI) vector magnetic field pipeline: overview and performance. Sol. Phys. **289**(9), 3483–3530 (2014)
5. Damião, G.: Estudo da atividade solar no passado em função da radiação cósmica (2014)
6. Maluf, P.P.P.: O numero de manchas solares, indice da atividade do sol medido nos ultimos 50 anos. Rev. Bras. de Ensino de Física **25**, 157–163 (2003)
7. Hathaway, D.H.: The solar dynamo. NASA Technical report NASA-TM-111102, NAS 1.15:111102 (1994)
8. Clette, F., Berghmans, D., Vanlommel, P., Van der Linden, R.A., Koeckelenbergh, A., Wauters, L.: From the wolf number to the international sunspot index: 25 years of SIDC. Adv. Space Res. **40**(7), 919–928 (2007)
9. Han, J., Pei, J., Kamber, M.: Data mining: concepts and techniques. In: Data Mining: Concepts and Techniques, pp. 83–120. Elsevier (2000)
10. Smola, A., Vishwanathan, S.: Introduction to Machine Learning, vol. 32, p. 34. Cambridge University, Cambridge (2008)

11. Krizhevsky, A., Sutskever, I., Hinton, G.E.: ImageNet classification with deep convolutional neural networks. In: Advances in Neural Information Processing Systems, pp. 1097–1105 (2012)
12. Wang, L., Wang, K., Li, R.: Unsupervised feature selection based on spectral regression from manifold learning for facial expression recognition. IET Comput. Vis. **9**(5), 655–662 (2015)
13. Chapelle, O., Scholkopf, B., Zien, A.: Semi-supervised learning (chapelle, o. et al., eds.; 2006) [book reviews]. IEEE Trans. Neural Netw. **20**(3), 542–542 (2009)
14. Sutton, R.S., Barto, A.G., et al.: Introduction to Reinforcement Learning, vol. 135. MIT Press, Cambridge (1998)
15. Howard, R.A.: Dynamic programming and Markov processes (1960)
16. Sarwar, F., Grin, A., Periasamy, P., Portas, K., Law, J.: Detecting and counting sheep with a convolutional neural network. In: 2018 15th IEEE International Conference on Advanced Video and Signal Based Surveillance (AVSS), pp. 1–6, Nov 2018

Heuristic Method for Optimal Deployment of Electric Vehicle Charge Stations Using Linear Programming

Miguel Campaña$^{(\boxtimes)}$(iD) and Esteban Inga(iD)

Universidad Politécnica Salesiana, Rumichaca Ñan, 170146 Quito, Ecuador
{mcampana,einga}@ups.edu.ec
https://www.ups.edu.ec/girei

Abstract. The conventional automobile fleet has significantly increased the emission of toxic gases, thus reducing the quality of air. Therefore, this article proposes a heuristic planning model to promote the massive introduction of plug-in electric vehicles (PEV). Further, this article seeks to deploy electric vehicle charging stations (EVCS), such that the parking time to recharge a PEV are significantly reduced, according to the needs of the user. Besides, the trajectories (driving range) and vehicular flow (traffic) are considered as constraints to the planning problem, which are closely linked to the capacity of the road. On the other hand, clustering techniques are used taking into account real mobility restrictions as a function of minimum distances, and the relationship of the PEV with different charge supply subregions. At last, the model was developed in the Matlab and LpSolve environments. The former will enable the analysis of different trajectories and their relationship with its surroundings. On the other hand, the latter solves the optimization problem using the simplex method.

Keywords: Georeference system · Trajectory analysis · Multiple connections · Plug-in electric vehicle · Vehicular density

1 Introduction

The uncontrolled emission of greenhouse gases, strengthens the need to develop methodologies that enable the incorporation of sustainable solutions to the problem of environmental pollution [14]. The large percentage of combustion engine vehicles that circulates in the different cities around the world, undoubtedly deteriorate the quality of the air. The vehicular dynamics is of stochastic nature, and depends on multiple variables such as: (i) driving ranges, (ii) speed, (iii) trajectory, (iv) climatic conditions and (v) vehicular flow, among others. [11,18] analyze the location of charge stations considering: (i) geospatial scenarios, (ii) statistical data and (iii) maximum distances between users and EVCS. Other

Universidad Politécnica Salesiana, Quito-Ecuador.

A. D. Orjuela-Cañón et al. (Eds.): ColCACI 2019, CCIS 1096, pp. 247–258, 2019.
https://doi.org/10.1007/978-3-030-36211-9_20

works, such as [2,5] consider charge density and maximum driving ranges. In addition, [10] highlights the importance of studying the relationship between subregions of coverage considering three relevant criteria that guide the location of EVCS: (i) model, (ii) approach and (iii) trajectory. Besides, at present, only data about traffic, infrastructure and population are available as a function of conventional mobility [4,15], due to the scarce penetration of PEV. Therefore, it is relevant to carry out theoretical studies assuming meaningful criteria to try to characterize the vehicular behavior considering fundamental features of electrical mobility.

Therefore, the present model intends to contribute with a heuristic method capable of locating electrical vehicle charging stations (EVCS), such that they are placed at optimal sites thus contributing to release vehicular traffic due to potential high indices of charging coincidence, besides maximizing coverage of charge supplying for PEVs considering geo-referenced scenarios, maximum vehicular density, maximum driving ranges, distance from an user to the EVCS and its relationship with vehicular flow in the nearest subregions [8,17]. The geo-referenced scenarios enable to explore solutions, considering real trajectory variables such as: charge density and driving ranges. The charge density helps to estimate, using clustering techniques, the capacity and location of the EVCS to be deployed. Nevertheless, around 80% of the reviewed literature employs traditional clustering techniques (k-means, voronoi), skipping possible search scenarios that allow to yield the best solution. Traditional clustering techniques are sensitive to the center of mass, and in iterative processes provide random partitions. Besides, [12,13] verify the randomness of the segmentations and its close relationship with parameter k that gives the desired number of clusters, without considering certain constraints such as maximum distances, number of elements per cluster and geo-referenced availability to enable a destination node. At last, consideration of these variables are fundamental when making a decision about a topology as a close to optimum solution. Consequently, the present article seeks to integrate the aforementioned variables to investigate about close to optimum topologies. Based on what has been previously said, the model has been developed in three stages: (i) construction of the feasible mesh that satisfies the condition of maximum driving ranges, (ii) selection of geospatial coordinates to locate the EVCS and (iii) partition (segmentation) of the scenario as a function of minimum distance from the location of the PEV to the EVCS.

At last, the rest of the article is organized as follows. Section 2 analyzes the requirements to generate an infrastructures of public charging stations (IPCS) for PEVs. Section 3 presents the methodology and the problem of interest. Results are analyzed in Sect. 4, and Sect. 5 concludes the article.

2   Criteria for the Analysis of Infrastructure of Public Charge Stations

The PEVs are becoming a key feature for the development of human mobility, thus significantly reducing negative environmental impacts. The PEVs will be part of electrical networks, as elements that store mobile charge with probabilistic behavior [7,22]. In order to massively introduce the PEVs, EVCSs must be deployed and located in an ordered and planned manner, thus contributing to the sustainable development of IPCS. The sustainability is linked to the economic growth, social development and environmental protection [3,9,20]. The social dimension considers (i) harmonization of EVCS, planning the expansion of vehicular networks (trajectories) and electrical networks for supplying electric power to PEVs, (ii) traffic convergence, (iii) service capacity and (iv) impact on people's life.

2.1   Impact of EVCS in Electrical Distribution Networks

A brief analysis is carried out in this subsection, about the impact of the massive penetration PEVs on electrical distribution networks. Table 1 includes a brief characterization of the types of terminals for the charge of IPCS.

Table 1. Types of terminals for charge stations

Type	Current (A)	Time (h)	Recharge (%)	Power kW	Property	INEC standard
Slow	16	8	100	4–8	Public Private	61851
Semi - Fast	32	1.150	50–80	22	Public	61851
Fast	63	0.500	50–80	50	Public	61851
Ultra - Fast	250–400	0.170	50–80	350	Public	61851
Change - Battery	–	0.033	100	–	Public	61851

The massive integration of PEVs would cause a significant increase of the demand in electrical distribution networks, thus causing perturbations to the system. Therefore, previous studies are required to enable the integration of PEVs in a ordered and planned manner, guaranteeing high quality and supply security [16]. A convenient management criterion is the introduction of charges during off-peak hours, which are supplied at night hours; this allows to flatten the curve of demand providing an important advantage for the introduction of PEVs [1,19]. Therefore, maintaining the equilibrium between generation and consumption guarantees the correct operation of the system, and contributes to minimize the energy not supplied [21].

It can be verified in Tabla 1 that the impact on conventional electrical distribution networks is more or less complex, depending of the technology of the charge terminals. Nevertheless, public acceptance of PEVs is conditioned by the driving ranges and the development of IPCS as a function of the recharge time (parking time). Therefore, the importance of this article lies in the optimal deployment of EVCS, considering constraints of traffic density, reach distance, trajectories, driving range and closeness to electric power supply regions in geo-referenced scenarios, thus enabling to estimate the charge density in each supply subregion. In this manner, it will be possible to plan distribution electrical networks in an ordered manner, and with the location of EVCS the coverage of each subregion will be guaranteed.

2.2 Application of the Theory of Graphs for the Analysis of Vehicular Trajectories

A graph is an ordered pair of nodes constituted by vertices and edges $G(V, E)$. The vertices (V) represent PEVs and EVCS, while the edges represent the relationships between vertices. Therefore, a graph enables the analysis of topological properties, and the relationship between its vertices by means of combinatorial processes through its edges [6]. As a consequence, a graph will allow to obtain minimum routes considering a spatial perspective at the street level which, undoubtedly, will facilitate optimal planning processes. In addition, a heuristic model based on optimal trajectories will enable estimating traffic density, distances between users and EVCS, besides considering driving ranges; it also will allow to carry out an analysis between nearby EVCS.

3   Problem Formulation

This article can be considered in the basic category, due to its experimental nature employing theoretical simulation processes. It has a quantitative approach, since it seeks to determine the minimum number of EVCS that guarantees functionality of PEVs minimizing economic and social impacts. For that purpose, the model proposes an exploratory process based on assumptions. At last, since it is exploratory, the model suggests analyzing different case studies, subject to various initialization parameters that enable to identify the performance of the proposed heuristic. Table 2 shows the variables utilized in the optimization model.

There exist n EVCS (X) distributed in public access places inside an A, A_n area. The maximum driving distance (δ) is the one that allows the PEV operator to reach an EVCS with a minimum reserve of available battery. If the distance X_i to X_j is greater than (δ), it is said that it will give rise to an unsuccessful operation, thus, such trajectory is not considered. An unsuccessful operation occurs when a PEV successfully reaches at least one EVCS. This process occurs in an iterative fashion, using an exhaustive search (brute force) method considering the visit to all candidate locations of EVCSs as the stopping criterion. Once the relationship between all EVCSs as a function of their distance is verified, all redundant elements from the neighborhood are eliminated, thus giving rise to an enabling (connectivity) network ψ of length κ. Theoretical weights of traffic density α are assumed in each trajectory enabled from an EVCS X_i to a X_j.

Table 2. Variables utilized

Nomenclature	Description
X	Matrix of candidate locations for EVCS
Y	Matrix of intersections in the road network
m	Length of Y
n	Length of X
δ	Driving range
α	Vector of length traffic density (ξ)
$flag$	Binary verification variable
ψ	Combination of trajectories
ξ	Vector of pseudo optimal trajectories
$\Delta\xi$	Temporary variable
D	Vector of distances that fulfill driving range
G	Connectivity matrix
σ	Solution vector of the EVCSs close to the optimum

Once the costs (weights) as a function of traffic density have been defined, the Matlab-LpSolve interface is used to minimize the number of EVCS required to satisfy the demand of charge. It is considered that the traffic flow that enters an EVCS, must be equal to the traffic flow that departs from it. At last, once the number of EVCS has been defined, the coverage subregion of each EVCS are identified considering minimum trajectories from the position of a PEV to the site of a EVCS. Therefore, the number of subregions will depend on the length of the solution set of EVCSs to be located. As a consequence, the Algorithm 1 solves the described planning problem. In addition, the equation of Haversine is used for calculating the distance (in kilometers).

Equation 1 presents the objective function, where σ_{ij} corresponds to the relationship existing from an EVCS X_i to a X_j, such that when multiplied by a theoretical vector α of weights, the model will seek to identify the minimum number of EVCSs that guarantees satisfying the maximum traffic density. For this purpose, a fundamental concept is the uniform distribution on EVCS in the area under study. The uniform distribution will be a function of the coverage areas similar among each subregion (see Fig. 1) without the EVCS necessarily being the center of charge demand, but it is a function of the position of the corresponding candidate locations of the selected EVCS. Equation 2 guarantees the existence of candidate locations in the region under study, and indicates that in order to find relationships between EVCSs, more than one candidate location must be considered.

$$min \sum_{i,j=1}^{n} \sigma_i * \alpha \qquad (1)$$

Algorithm 1. Optimal Infrastructure of Electric Vehicle Charging Stations (OIEVCS)

1: **procedure** INPUT$(X; Y; n; m; \delta; \alpha; cont = 1.)$
2: **Step 1:** Driving Range
3:     **for** $i = EVCS\ (n)$ **do**
4:         **for** $j = intersections\ (m)$ **do**
5:             $flag = 1.$
6:             **while** $flag == 1$ **do**
7:                 $cont = cont + 1.$
8:                 $\Delta\xi = find\ path\ en\ \psi(X, Y).$
9:                 $D = haversine\ (\Delta\xi).$
10:                **if** $\psi == Nan\ ||\ D > \delta$ **then**
11:                    $flag = 0.$
12:            $\xi_{(1,i)} = [\Delta\xi; D].$
13:            $\Delta\xi = 0.$
14:            $D = 0.$
15:     $G = \xi * \alpha.$
16: **Step 2:** Optimum EVCS
17:     $\sigma = LpSolve\ (G).$
18: **Step 3:** Create Subregions
19:     Construction of Scenarios$(\sigma).$
20:     Minimum Distance of Clustering, σ_i to EVCS.
21: **procedure** OUTPUT(σ)

Subject to

$$X_i \in A_{(n)}, \forall n \geq 1 \in \Re^+ \tag{2}$$

$$\sum_{i=1}^{n}\sum_{j=1}^{n} X_{i,j} \leq \alpha_{i,j}, \forall n \in \Re^+ \neq 0 \tag{3}$$

$$d_f \leq \delta, \forall d_f, \delta \in \Re^+ \neq 0 \tag{4}$$

The traffic flow is constrained by means of Eq. 3, considering that the traffic density must not exceed the maximum capacity to serve the vehicular demand. Equation 4 indicates that the reach distance must be exclusively less or equal than the driving range δ. In addition, Eq. 4 establishes the necessary conditions to reduce the maximum reach distance that a PEV operator should drive to find a charging point. Another detail to be considered is that the PEV will be able to access a EVCS according to the subregion in which it is in, and this does not void the possibility that such electrical vehicle could charge in adjacent coverage regions. In addition, it is assumed that the maximum demand in each subregion depends on the maximum spatial capacity at the street level to accommodate a PEV.

4   Analysis and Discussion of Results

This section presents the results obtained in the simulations that were run in the Matlab and LpSolve programming environments. Table 3 presents the simulation parameters that were used to evaluate and validate the proposed methodology, considering the previously described assumptions.

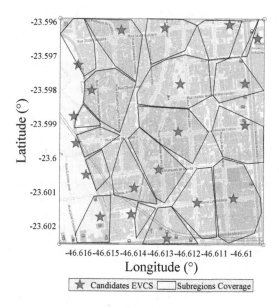

Fig. 1. Spatial perspective of candidate sites to locate EVCS *vs* initial coverage subregions (Vila Firmiano Pinto, São Paulo). Source: Authors.

Figure 1 presents the case study, which shows the chosen candidate sites to locate EVCSs. These candidate sites were selected according to possible public access areas, such as: parks, shopping centers and gas stations. The shaded subregions represent the average coverage area for supplying electrical power to the PEV, according to the chosen candidate locations. The segmentation of the scenario arises from the process of verifying the minimum distance from the position of the PEV to the closest EVCS.

Figure 2 is a box plot that shows the distribution and the central tendency of the CPU time employed by the computer, to find the solution to the deployment of EVCS subject to initial conditions. In this case, the maximum driving range is varied from smaller to greater in a vector of length $k = 10$, thus expanding the exploratory sample space. The data has been grouped in three sets defined as short distance (0.8 to 3.2), middle distance (3.2 to 5.6) and long distance (5.6 to 8.0), as can be seen in Fig. 2. The abscissa contains the data packet corresponding to each of the driving range, while the ordinates correspond to the time, in seconds, employed by the computer to explore possible solutions.

Table 3. Simulation parameters

Deployment	Number of PEVs deployed	1355
	Candidate locations	20
	Area under study	$0.6156\,[\mathrm{km}^2]$
	PEV density	$2201\,[\mathrm{VE/km}^2]$
	Geographical area	Urban
	Location of EVCS	Geospatial data
Application	Driving range	Variable [km]
	Traffic density	Variable
	Charge terminal	AC - DC

It can be seen, according to the 2nd quartile, that the CPU time increases as the driving range increases (see Fig. 2). It happens similarly with the 1st and 3rd quartiles. An additional detail that can be appreciated in the middle and long distance boxes is that most of the data exceeds the 50% of the mean value, which indicates that the distribution of data is not a constant slope function (asymmetric distribution), but an exponential function, as can be verified from the maximum values of the data set in each box of Fig. 2. Therefore, as the driving range increases so does the search sample space, which results in an increase of the computational time required to obtain a near optimal solution set.

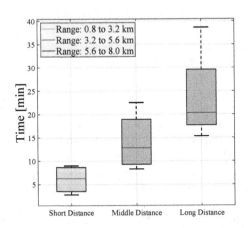

Fig. 2. Performance of the model as a function of CPU time. Source: Authors.

Figure 3 shows the number of required EVCS as a function of the variation of the driving range and the coverage area. The different spheres identified in green, violet, pink and yellow represent the near optimal solution set as a function of initial conditions and maximum driving ranges. The center and diameter of each sphere indicate the ID of the EVCS, and give a general idea of the contribution of each of them as a function of the coverage area, i.e., as the diameter increases the area covered by each EVCS is greater. Therefore, it can be appreciated that as the driving range increases, the number of EVCS (spheres) required for the deployment decreases.

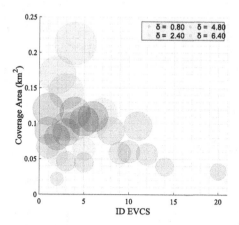

Fig. 3. Coverage percentage of each charge station as a function of the variation of the driving ranges. Source: Authors.

Another detail of interest that can be seen in Fig. 3 are the different diameters of each group of the solution vector, evidencing that the obtained clusters are not totally balanced. Nevertheless, as the number of required charge stations is smaller, the model tends to balance the clusters, effect that can be appreciated in the green spheres. This unbalance is explained by the grouping method developed in this article which groups according to the minimum distances from the location of a PEV to the nearest EVCS, once the number and locations of the EVCS have been selected using an exhaustive exploratory procedure that considers maximum driving ranges and different capacity weights randomly assigned for traveling from i to j from each georeferenced position of the EVCS. Therefore, the assigned maximum capacity of each electrical vehicle charging station will be a function of the maximum number of PEVs associated to each cluster.

Figures 4a, b, c and d present possible near optimal solutions. The color graphs express the charge density in each EVCS. It is important to note that, as the reach length increases, the number of required EVCS for the correct supply of electric power to PEVs is reduced. The red line in Fig. 4 represents the minimum route of connectivity between adjacent coverage zones. Therefore, this minimum route could be used for planning the electrical network, even the laying of fiber may be considered, thus being able to extract relevant information about the behavior of electrical mobility to enrich future research works.

Figures 4a, b, c and d show the selected model with different driving ranges, given in kilometers, with 11, 7, 5 and 4 EVCS, respectively. The model suggests this number of EVCS of a total of 20 deployed candidate locations. Therefore, the proposed model is able to minimize the number of EVCS required to constitute IPCS.

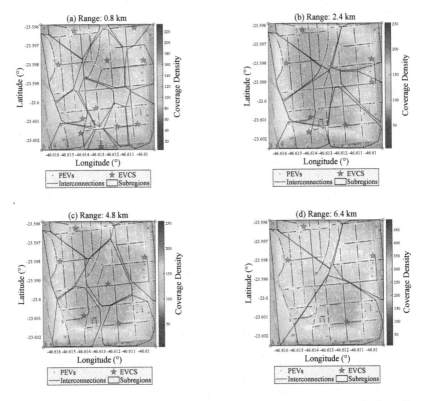

Fig. 4. Infrastructure of public charge stations for pluggable electric vehicles. Source: Authors.

5   Conclusions

The present article has demonstrated to be able to adapt to different initial conditions, considering criteria of trajectory and geospatial location with an approach oriented to the need of the user. In addition, the model considers closeness of subregions and maximum driving ranges, and by means of a segmentation process can estimate the charge density that should be served by each EVCS. Another important detail is that the model responds to theoretical geospatial perspectives that take part in vehicular networks. At last, according to constraints associated to vehicular traffic and neighborhood analysis, graph theory is used to explore the best solution set as a function of multiple trajectories, and the traffic density problem is solved applying linear programming.

Future works will seek to characterize the resulting vehicular network using simulation software (SUMO), with the purpose of estimating the number and types of recharge terminals that each EVCS should have.

Acknowledgement. This work has been conducted with the support of the GIREI (Grupo de Investigación en Redes Eléctricas Inteligentes de la Universidad Politécnica Salesiana Ecuador), under the Project Optimal Deployment of Charge Stations required for Smart Cities based on Vehicular Flow.

References

1. Akbari, M., Brenna, M., Longo, M.: Optimal locating of electric vehicle charging stations by application of genetic algorithm. Sustainability **10**(4) (2018). https://doi.org/10.3390/su10041076

2. Asamer, J., Reinthaler, M., Ruthmair, M., Straub, M., Puchinger, J.: Optimizing charging station locations for urban taxi providers. Transp. Res. Part A Policy Pract. **85**, 233–246 (2016). https://doi.org/10.1016/j.tra.2016.01.014

3. Celli, G., Pilo, F., Monni, G., Soma, G.G.: Optimal multi-objective allocation of fast charging stations. In: 2018 IEEE International Conference on Environment and Electrical Engineering and 2018 IEEE Industrial and Commercial Power Systems Europe (EEEIC/I&CPS Europe), pp. 1–6 (2018)

4. Davidov, S., Pantoš, M.: Stochastic expansion planning of the electric-drive vehicle charging infrastructure. Energy **141**, 189–201 (2017). https://doi.org/10.1016/j.energy.2017.09.065

5. Hidalgo, P.A., Ostendorp, M., Lienkamp, M.: Optimizing the charging station placement by considering the user's charging behavior. In: 2016 IEEE International Energy Conference, ENERGYCON 2016 (2016). https://doi.org/10.1109/ENERGYCON.2016.7513920

6. Inga, E., Cespedes, S., Hincapie, R., Cardenas, C.A.: Scalable route map for advanced metering infrastructure based on optimal routing of wireless heterogeneous networks. IEEE Wirel. Commun. **24**(2), 26–33 (2017). https://doi.org/10.1109/MWC.2017.1600255

7. Khanghah, B.Y., Anvari-Moghaddam, A., Guerrero, J.M., Vasquez, J.C.: Combined solar charging stations and energy storage units allocation for electric vehicles by considering uncertainties. In: 2017 IEEE International Conference on Environment and Electrical Engineering and 2017 IEEE Industrial and Commercial Power Systems Europe (EEEIC/I&CPS Europe), pp. 1–6, June 2017. https://doi.org/10.1109/EEEIC.2017.7977806

8. Lee, C., Han, J.: Benders-and-Price approach for electric vehicle charging station location problem under probabilistic travel range. Transp. Res. Part B Methodol. **106**(November), 130–152 (2017). https://doi.org/10.1016/j.trb.2017.10.011

9. Leeprechanon, N., Phonrattanasak, P., Sharma, M.K.: Optimal planning of public fast charging station on residential power distribution system. In: 2016 IEEE Transportation Electrification Conference and Expo, Asia-Pacific (ITEC Asia-Pacific), pp. 519–524, June 2016. https://doi.org/10.1109/ITEC-AP.2016.7513009

10. Ma, C., et al.: Distribution path robust optimization of electric vehicle with multiple distribution centers. PLoS One **13**(3)(2018). https://doi.org/10.1371/journal.pone.0193789

11. Pagany, R., Marquardt, A., Zink, R.: Electric charging demand location model–a user- and destination-based locating approach for electric vehicle charging stations. Sustainability **11**(8), 15 (2019). https://doi.org/10.3390/su11082301
12. Praveen, P., Rama, B.: An empirical comparison of Clustering using hierarchical methods and K-means. In: Proceeding of IEEE 2nd International Conference on Advances in Electrical, Electronics, Information, Communication and Bio-Informatics, IEEE - AEEICB 2016, pp. 445–449 (2016). https://doi.org/10.1109/AEEICB.2016.7538328
13. Shi, H., Xu, M.: A data classification method using genetic algorithm and K-means algorithm with optimizing initial cluster center. In: 2018 IEEE International Conference on Computer and Communication Engineering Technology, CCET 2018, pp. 224–228 (2018). https://doi.org/10.1109/CCET.2018.8542173
14. Shinde, P., Swarup, K.S.: A multiobjective approach for optimal allocation of charging station to electric vehicles. In: 2016 IEEE Annual India Conference (INDICON), pp. 1–6 (2016). https://doi.org/10.1109/INDICON.2016.7838934
15. Shukla, A., Verma, K., Kumar, R.: Consumer perspective based placement of electric vehicle charging stations by clustering techniques. In: 2016 National Power Systems Conference, NPSC 2016, pp. 1–6 (2017). https://doi.org/10.1109/NPSC.2016.7858946
16. Sun, H., Yang, J., Yang, C.: A robust optimization approach to multi-interval location-inventory and recharging planning for electric vehicles. Omega **86**, 59–75 (2018). https://doi.org/10.1016/j.omega.2018.06.013
17. Sundström, O., Binding, C.: Planning electric-drive vehicle charging under constrained grid conditions. In: 2010 International Conference on Power System Technology: Technological Innovations Making Power Grid Smarter, POWERCON 2010 (2010), https://doi.org/10.1109/POWERCON.2010.5666620
18. Vazifeh, M.M., Zhang, H., Santi, P., Ratti, C.: Optimizing the deployment of electric vehicle charging stations using pervasive mobility data. Transp. Res. Part A Policy Pract. **121**(January), 75–91 (2019). https://doi.org/10.1016/j.tra.2019.01.002
19. Wang, X., Yuen, C., Hassan, N.U., An, N., Wu, W.: Electric vehicle charging station placement for urban public bus systems. IEEE Trans. Intell. Transp. Syst. **18**(1), 128–139 (2017). https://doi.org/10.1109/TITS.2016.2563166
20. Yan, Y., Jiang, J., Zhang, W., Huang, M., Chen, Q., Wang, H.: Research on power demand suppression based on charging optimization and BESS configuration for fast-charging stations in Beijing. Appl. Sci. **8**(8), 1212 (2018). https://doi.org/10.3390/app8081212. http://www.mdpi.com/2076-3417/8/8/1212
21. Yao-Tang, L., Lin, G., Qi, Z., Bao-Rong, Z.: Research on the modeling of EV charging station considering V2G and its optimal configuration in photovoltaic distribution network. In: 2017 IEEE Transportation Electrification Conference and Expo, Asia-Pacific, ITEC Asia-Pacific 2017, pp. 0–5 (2017). https://doi.org/10.1109/ITEC-AP.2017.8081018
22. Zhang, Q., Xu, W., Liang, W., Peng, J., Liu, T., Wang, T.: An improved algorithm for dispatching the minimum number of electric charging vehicles for wireless sensor networks. Wirel. Netw. **25**(3), 1371–1384 (2019). https://doi.org/10.1007/s11276-018-1765-5

Fuzzy Classification of Industrial Data for Supervision of a Dewatering Machine: Implementation Details and Results

Carlos M. Sánchez M$^{(\boxtimes)}$ and Henry O. Sarmiento M

Politécnico Colombiano Jaime Isaza Cadavid, Medellín, Colombia
{carlos_sanchez54181,hosarmineto}@elpoli.edu.co

Abstract. In this document, real data collected in an industrial process are studied and analyzed, with the intention of improving the process supervision seeking for operational efficiency and saving resources, emphasizing in the information cleaning process using basic statistics and data analysis based on non-supervised clustering algorithms: Lamda, GK means and Fuzzy C-means. A general data cleaning procedure for use in industrial environments is suggested. The procedure proposed is followed in a case for a centrifuge machine for mud treatment, three versions of fuzzy classifiers were tested where fuzzy, c-means was finally selected and a result is obtained that permits detecting an inefficient operating state, in some cases the machine was running at a normal current and spending energy and other resources for a long period and the mud was not treated properly, the exit mud was practically the same as the mud at the entrance. The trained classifier has been implemented directly in the PLC used to control the machine, and the results of online classification have been verified showing that states correspond with the process behavior.

Keywords: Data cleaning · Industrial data · Fuzzy clustering

1 Introduction

The data is the boom in the level of service, in agriculture and specifically in the health sector. Large multinational companies have improved by collecting and analyzing data, with potential benefits such as cost reduction, improving the quality of clinical decisions, reducing diagnostic times, etc. [1]. According to Forbes, by 2018, 59% of the companies had adopted large data analyzes: telecommunications (95%), insurance (83%), and advertising (77%) lead the adoption of data analysis. Financial services (71%), health (64%) and technology (58%) are the next group and the manufacturing, government and education industries are the least likely users, although most of them anticipate the use of big data in the near future [2]. In Colombia, there is a growing expectation among service providers to offer solutions oriented to integration and data management for decision making. Traditionally, companies collect large volumes of information that, in general, are used very little or not used at all; it is reported that less than 0.5% of all collected data have been used or analyzed [3]. For service providers the analysis of historical data is very important, as it can help to know the behavior of

© Springer Nature Switzerland AG 2019
A. D. Orjuela-Cañón et al. (Eds.): ColCACI 2019, CCIS 1096, pp. 259–271, 2019.
https://doi.org/10.1007/978-3-030-36211-9_21

customers to improve service quality, customer satisfaction and increase profits [3]. At the manufacturing level, the management of data and the information that could be collected requires a greater effort in cleaning and analyzing the information; these data treated properly can provide valid and reliable results for decision making. The main challenge in data analysis in manufacturing companies is the lack of collaboration among departments, systems and data sources that are varied. Nowadays, new developments are required to speed up the use and application of data-based learning techniques that achieve greater use of the information available to companies or industries in the optimization of various associated resources [4]. In this paper a specific case of industrial data analysis is studied, with real data collected in a period of three months from a centrifugal machine in a wastewater treatment plant. The process of data cleansing and statistical analysis are performed, then these data are used to set up a monitoring system based on fuzzy classifiers. The classes obtained with the classifier are associated with operational states of the machine, among which efficient and inefficient process operations are identified, which in a corresponding manner require actions implemented in that sense. The proposal highlights what can be considered a generalized procedure for the collection, cleaning and analysis of data from industrial environments as a basis for future work related to the analysis of industrial data.

The paper is organized as follows: After the introduction, Sect. 2 describes the centrifugation of sludge in a wastewater treatment plant as an object of study. Section 3 proposes a general procedure for the preprocessing and data cleaning and its application to the data collected from the slurry centrifugal machine. Later in Sect. 4 and for the purpose of monitoring the classifier-based process, the fuzzy classification algorithms are described. Learning algorithm for multivariate data analysis: Lamda, Gustafson Kessel GK-means and Fuzzy-C-means the latter being the one that was finally used for its comparative advantages. Then, in Sect. 5, the classification results obtained are presented where the classes that represent inefficient operational states are identified. In Sect. 6 details of implementation are described, and finally the conclusions are presented.

2   Process Description

The process that we analyze belongs to wastewater treatment plant. The study will focus on the optimization of the sludge treatment process. This process begins with the collection of the sludge resulting from the water treatment process. This sludge is pumped to the thickener machines (centrifuges) in order to completely remove the water by adding polymers to the sludge and finally bring the waste to the final disposal. The manual data collection is done to verify the quality sludge at different points of the process and the automatic data collection is done through the control system where are registered variables such as mud flow, polymer flow, level of biodigesters, and the state of pumps. Additionally, for each of the centrifugal machines, the system records temperatures, engine speeds, loads, currents, torques and vibrations. There are two thickening machines and three dehydrator sludge machines, these centrifugal machines have a cylinder called bowl that turns in one direction, while there is an internal screw that rotates in the opposite direction to achieve this, these machines have two engines called: main drive and back drive motor. The data of the centrifugal machines were recorded every 5 s for three months. There is no an operator checking for the process all time, so if there is a problem no one can act until come to sludge building and check machine conditions.

3 Information Cleaning Process, Application to the Study Case and Description of the Data Collected

Generally, data cleaning consists of four steps: missing data imputation, outlier detection, noise removal, and time alignment and delay estimation [5]. The steps followed to gather and clean data, based on our experience in this case are:

Step 1: Data collection and centralization; to achieve this it is recommended to install a centralized server with Ethernet network connections to the various equipment in the plant and have open protocols such as Ole for Process Control (OPC) or Modbus TCP. The above allows to centralize the information in a common database, with the option to upload information in the cloud, since many data analysis service providers work in this way.

Step 2: Elimination of null data, out of range or repeated variables and adjustment of decimal number. With the tool selected by the database administrator, it is possible to eliminate null data and validate the operational ranges of the variables, in order to discard the out-of-range data that may be the product of instrumentation faults. In general, these problems should be corrected at this point if possible. This task includes completing the missing or incomplete values with the appropriate values, identifying the outliers and eliminating them, eliminating duplicates. The poor preparation of the data leads to incorrect and unreliable data mining results, and the knowledge discovered will be of low quality [6].

Step 3: Perform a basic statistical analysis, using commercially available tools or with free software such as Python that has implemented libraries for statistical analysis. Maximum, minimum and average calculations allow values to be identified far from the average and these values must be replaced or eliminated, if possible, since they significantly affect the subsequent analysis.

Step 4: Statistical analysis of correlation; this analysis allows identifying pairs of variables with a high correlation, which means that both have the same information, so one of them can be eliminated.

Step 5: Analysis of the data by sections, this analysis looks for sections of information where the data together present a minimal or no variation, in this case this section should be deleted, leaving for the later analysis only the data sections that present significant variations. These variations are related to the data source and the decision to delete or not the section should be studied with an expert in the process.

Step 6: Normalize the data, to achieve uniformity of the different variables, it is necessary to normalize the data to a range between (0, 1).

For this study case, original variables are in three encrypted files that comply, FDA (Food and Drug Administration) regulations, each file with 1.887.000 samples and a five second period between samples.

By means of the software tools of machine supervision, a preliminary analysis of the data that are collected is carried out.

Table 1 describes the variables, ranges and units after the cleaning process. The data are originally in encrypted format and it is necessary to use a control system manufacturer proper tool to export data to comma separated variable format. In this step it is important to remove headers, because they have a different format compared with the rest of information and it generates an error to read the information. Once the data are converted to the comma separated values, it is necessary to make two additional data conversions to adjust formats required for clustering analysis tools, in this case Matlab and Python accepts comma separated values, also accepts TXT format, but Lamda clustering tool requires .DAT format. Data are converted to TXT and DAT using Notepad of windows, once the conversion process to different formats is ready, it is necessary to adjust decimal numbers to be sure all the samples are in the same conditions, this procedure was done in Microsoft Excel, additionally with Python software a variable statistical analysis is done, obtaining some graphics like: Histograms, distribution chart, box diagrams, correlation matrix, dispersion chart, these graphs allow to give a global idea of the distribution of the data. In a basic analysis, it is determined if the data have a normal distribution, if not which implies that the standard deviations and correlation analysis has not sense in that case [7]. For this exercise statistical graphics were used to select the data set more proper for later analysis, so that those data that mainly focused on information collected with the machines turned off were discarded. Correlation graphic that was generated with Python software help to see a very close relationship between the torque and load, so torque variable was discarded, Fig. 1 show the correlation matrix obtained.

Table 1. File 1 data.

Item	Variable	Range	Units
1	Front Temperature	0–500	°F
2	Back Temperature	0–500	°F
3	Current	0–500	Amp
4	Torque	0–150	%
5	Vibration	0–3	"/s
6	Differential Speed	0–20	RPM
7	Sludge Flow	0–2.3	Ft3/s
9	Polymer Flow	0–0.18	Ft3/s
10	Load	0–150	%
11	Main Drive Speed	0–3000	RPM

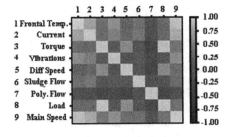

Fig. 1. Correlation matrix

Then an analysis of average, maximum and minimum values of each one of the variables was done. For statistical analysis box diagrams are very helpful, reviewing diagrams it is possible to conclude if there are variables with values out of normal range in that case it is necessary decide if replace out of range values or discard variables completely, in this example back temperature and polymer flow were discarded because many values were out of a normal operating range. You can see the box diagrams made in Python in Fig. 2. In Fig. 2 also you can see that values of current are mainly near to 200 amperes, this was a key factor to select this data set for analysis because there were five data sets of different centrifuges machines available, in the other data sets the machines were off most of the time.

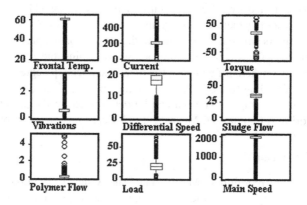

Fig. 2. Box diagrams.

Finally, data are analyzed by sections looking for data than together present less than 2% variation, so that section was deleted because if the data do not change, then they do not provide additional information. Using a Matlab algorithm all sections that do not provide information were deleted, as a result was obtained a data base with 95000 samples and the following variables: Frontal temperature, current, vibrations, sludge flow, load, main speed and differential speed. Then these data need to be normalized that is a procedure suggested for a process where the variables are in different ranges which can cause those of greater magnitude to diminish importance to others of smaller magnitude [8]. One of the ways to bring the data in a reduced range is through the "Min-Max" standardization, which consists of transforming the data to a range between (0, 1). The above is carried out by applying (1).

$$X_{(j,i)} = \frac{X_{(j,i)} - Minimum(i)}{Maximun(i) - Mininun(i)} \tag{1}$$

In this equation, X (j, i) is the attribute of the data matrix in column j and row i; Maximum (i) is the maximum value of the attribute of row (i), and Minimum (i) is the minimum value of the attribute of row (i). The Eq. (1) applied to the data matrix allows to obtain the normalized data matrix that is used for later analysis of classification.

4 Algorithms of Classification and Selection of the Algorithm for the Study Case

In this case and based on literature review, we use a fault diagnosis method that is based on historic process knowledge [9], fuzzy classifiers that have been successfully integrated in monitoring and supervision schemes of processes [10]. Among the multiple classification techniques, fuzzy techniques stand out, which present significant advantages in the classification of data revealing the transition zones between classes, which cannot be detected by crisp algorithms such as K-means [11].

By using a clustering method, the group of n data vectors $X = [x1, x2, \ldots, xn]$ each with a descriptors where n corresponds to the number of samples, is separated into m clusters (classes). The fuzzy clustering allows obtaining the membership degree matrix $U = [\mu jf]mxn$, where μjf represent the fuzzy membership degree of a sample f to the j-th cluster. According to the highest fuzzy membership degree for each sample f, the cluster where the sample is located can be determined. In the present work were used fuzzy algorithms Lamda, GK-Means and FC-Means that are described as follows.

4.1 Fuzzy Clustering

LAMDA –Learning Algorithm for Multivariate Data Analysis– is a fuzzy methodology of conceptual clustering and classification mixing the concepts of both fuzzy clustering and neural networks, and it is not an iterative algorithm. It is based on finding the global membership degree of a sample to an existing class, considering all the contributions of each of its descriptors. A numeric component of x is the normalized value of a descriptor; on the contrary, if the component is a symbolic descriptor, its value is called a "modality" [12].

The contribution of each descriptor is called the marginal adequacy degree (MAD). When the descriptor is a numeric type, the MAD is calculated by selecting one of the different possible functions [13]; among these the "fuzzy" extension of the binomial function and the Gaussian function are the most commonly used. When the descriptor is a qualitative one, the observed frequency of its attribute modality is used to evaluate the MAD. Marginal adequacies are combined using fuzzy logic connectives [14] as aggregation operators in order to obtain the global adequacy degree (GAD) of an individual to a class [12]. Fuzzy logic connectives are fuzzy versions of the binary logic operators, particularly, intersection (t-norm) and union (t-conorm). The aggregation function is a linear interpolation between t-norm (γ) and t-conorm (β) where the parameter, $0 \le \alpha \le 1$, is called exigency [15].

$$GAD\left(x'|C\right) = \alpha \cdot \gamma\left(MAD\left(x'_1|C\right), \ldots, MAD\left(x'_a|C\right)\right) + (1 - \alpha)$$
$$\cdot \left(MAD\left(x'_1|C\right), \ldots, MAD\left(x'_a|C\right)\right) \quad (2)$$

One example of Fuzzy Logic operators is: $\{\gamma(a, b) = a, b; \beta(a, b) = a + b{-}a, b\}$.

An element is assigned to the class which exhibits the maximum GAD. To avoid the assignment of a not very representative element to a class, that is an element with a small membership, a minimum global adequacy threshold is employed, called the noninformative class (NIC) [16]. Passive recognition, self-learning (the number of clusters does not have to be determined in advance) or supervised learning are possible in LAMDA. LAMDA allows processing quantitative, qualitative and interval information [17].

FC-means [18] and GK-means [19] algorithms based on a distance metric are the most known. These algorithms use an optimization criterion Jb (see (3)) that makes data clustering possible according to the similarity among individuals. The fuzziness exponent b > 1 generates clusters more, or less, fuzzy (b regulates the 'fuzziness' of the partition).

$$J_b(\mathrm{U,v}) = \sum_{f=1}^{n} \sum_{j=1}^{m} (\mu_{jf})^b (d_{jf})^2 \tag{3}$$

In these algorithms, the similarity is evaluated with the distance function $d_{jf} = (x_f - v_j)^T H_j (x_f - v_j)$ which is measured between the individuals and cluster prototypes or class centers v = {v1, v2, ..., vm}.

The FCM distance measure is Euclidean (Hj = 1). This distance produces spherical clusters in the a-dimensional space. Hj is defined according to (4) for GKM, where δj is the volumetric index of cluster j, and Fj is the fuzzy covariance matrix of cluster j. The distance, in this case, generates ellipsoidal clusters which may adapt better to the data than spherical clusters. For both algorithms the number of clusters must be given a priori.

$$H_j = [\delta_j \det(F_j)]^{1/n} (F_j)^{-1} \tag{4}$$

The FCM and GKM clustering algorithms are iterative procedures where a set of n individuals are to be grouped into m classes. The number of classes m (1 < m < n) are selected by the user. Class prototypes are randomly initialized and are modified during the iteration process. Consequently, the fuzzy partition of the data space is also modified, until matrix U stabilizes (i.e. $\| \mathrm{Ut} - \mathrm{Ut-1} \| < \varepsilon$, where ε is a termination tolerance). A characteristic of fuzzy clustering techniques is the independence with time. The resulting classifier employs in the online phase, the same similarity measure used during training, to estimate the membership degrees of the data sample at time t to the created classes.

4.2 Algorithm Selection Criteria

Since there is no a priori detailed classification even with the knowledge of the expert, it is valuable and necessary to apply non-supervised clustering algorithms, from which data associations or classes are naturally identified that represent the operating states in a coherent way. When classifying the data, it is generally searched that the results of the classification are consistent, that is to say a class is fully identified and does not reflect ambiguous states. Also, is equally important to look for minimum classes number that represents the process, this implies a process of trial and error until getting the results more adequate. Initially the Lamda algorithm is tested for which it is not necessary to define in advance the number of clusters, such classification initially throws using default parameters the separation a high number of classes that are not taken into account. Proceeding to the manipulation and adjustment of functions, connectives, and an exigency index, it is possible to obtain up to 18 machine states, but several of them are associated with the machine stopped, and therefore not relevant for the study, see Fig. 3 where the 18 numbered classes are represented on the vertical axis like horizontal lines of circles, and the process variables are also depicted in the same graphic in grayscale, the horizontal axis represents the number of samples.

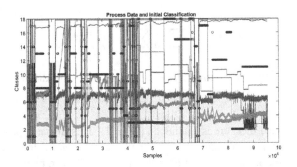

Fig. 3. Process variables and initial classification.

Then we proceed to test with fuzzy C-means algorithm using 18 classes. This exercise yields a result like that obtained with the Lamda algorithm, which is why results are tested for fewer classes by trial and error, six classes are determined. In the tests performed by FC-means after the corresponding analysis, it is concluded that the information of interest is maintained, and in front of this result the same test is performed with GK-means with 6 classes without comparative improvements.

The decision is made to select for the supervision of the sludge machine, the classification with the FC-means algorithm.

5   Results Obtained

Figure 4 shows the results of the classification for Fuzzy C-means with six classes and highlights the zone that represents the classes associated with an inefficient operation. The Fuzzy C-means classification is associated with six operational states of the machine shown in Table 2, and that table includes the alerts recommended for the operator.

When reviewing Table 2, it can be seen that there are some states that are of particular interest, as in the case of states 4, 5 and 6 where the machine is in operation for a long period, but with very low differential speed. This condition indicates that the operation is inefficient because the two screws rotate at a very close speed, and as a result the sludge is not being treated properly. In a situation like this, the operator is not warned, and the machine continues to operate inefficiently consuming energy and

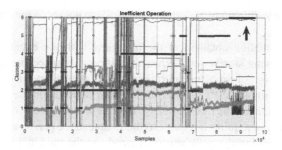

Fig. 4. FC-means classification results.

Table 2. Classes, operating states and operator alert

Class	Operating state	Operator alert
1	Stopped	OK
2	Normal operation	OK
3	Machine running	Transitional state
4	Machine operating low diff. speed	Operation alarm alert
5	Critical alarm very low diff speed	Check for sludge entry
6	Diff. speed at zero	Operation not recommended

resources because it does not have an alarm or an interlock to stop it. In the Fig. 4 it can be seen that the machine was operating at least 40 h in a not efficient way, approximately 5480 Kwh of electrical energy was lost and it is comparable to average consumption of one average family for two years.

The states 2, 3 and 1 are associated with the normal states of the machine: transition state, normal operating state and stopped machine respectively.

Finally, in Fig. 5 you can see the graph with the transitions for the six classes.

Fig. 5. Graph of states

Figure 5 was obtained from the behavior of the classes and their transitions in time. This graphic can be used as an interface to the machine operator so that in line with the process the operator can quickly see the current state with the actions that are required and visualize the possible transitions that could activate not recommendable operational states.

From the information obtained in the interview with the expert operator of the machine, the following stands out: "When the differential speed presents many changes, this is a symptom of problems; normally the differential speed should not change much" and it also suggests: "The speed differential depends on the inner ring. If the machine does not thicken the mud correctly, the ring must be changed; the ring change process is manual and requires a request to the maintenance personnel to carry out this activity. The type of ring that will be used depends on the mud that enters; this mud is analyzed manually by taking laboratory samples; if the wrong ring is used, the machine will not work correctly and the only indication will be the result of the laboratory tests".

6 Implementation Details

The implementation of the supervised system based on the fuzzy classifier (using FCM) was performed in principle in the emulator AC800F PLC brand ABB, and then be downloaded into the PLC of the machine and proceed to validation online.

Prior to the programming of the PLC, tests were carried out to verify the performance of the application both at the simulation level in a mathematical calculation program and in the PLC emulator, obtaining identical results.

The centroids U (grades of belonging representative of the classes) obtained from the classification are configured as constant values and the formula 5 is implemented to evaluate the distances based on each sampling of variables.

$$D_j = \sum_{i=1}^{N} \left(V_i - U_{j,i} \right)^2 \tag{5}$$

Dj is the distance, Vi is the variable, N = number of variables.

Then the formula 6 is implemented that allows to calculate the membership degrees GM = grade of membership, from each sample of variables to each class, M = Number of classes.

$$GM_j = \frac{1}{\sum_{k=1}^{M} D_j \backslash D_k} \tag{6}$$

Where the class is defined like j for which the maximum value of GMj is obtained. A class is obtained for each PLC task cycle in the emulator.

After downloading the application to the control system and during the first week of testing the process could record a performance in the less efficient zone corresponding to Class 6. This result shows the effective functioning of the classifier, validating the results obtained. In addition, the fact that such class 6 is not a sporadic state is also evidenced that it can be presented continuously and should be taken care of to improve the efficiency of the process.

According to the results obtained from Class 6 at diagnostic level, by which an inefficient state (not recommended operation) is recognized, it is necessary to implement the corresponding corrective actions at the supervisory level. Proposing in a next stage control action on a frequency variation of the main drive, or alert for the operator in the sense of generating stop for change of machine internal ring.

As can be seen in Fig. 6 where classes are shown on the lower part of the graphic, while the data are shown in the upper part, where the very low differential velocity (delta veloc) is effectively observed, and class 6 is clearly shown. (central circle). In the graphic 6 also (right circle), are shown one zone where the process changes to class 4.

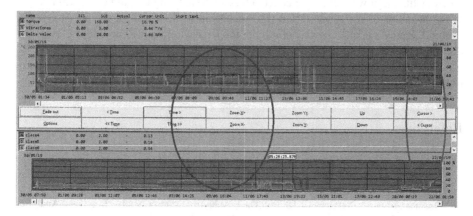

Fig. 6. Online results

The data analysis only delivers a diagnosis but the solution depends on the disposition and resources for implementation against the states that require it; That for the case study were left as work pending.

7 Conclusions

With objective to have a classifiers-based supervisor system it was necessary a preprocessing of data with some stages, until conclude with a database representative of the process. From that base it was possible to model the system by means of states (classes) that describe sludge treatment centrifuge machine and they constitute a tool for support in decisions making for process operators.

It is necessary to debug the data using different software tools and perform some tasks manually to detect range errors, repeated variables, eliminate headers or complete missing information, this procedure depends on the case, in addition to exporting the data to different formats an arduous task that can consume a lot of time if you do not have good tools for data management. Also, it is necessary to incorporate an analysis as for the selection of the variables based on the correlation evaluation between the same.

Based on procedure applied to this case study and reviewed literature, it is posed a general clear and practical rhumb in the task of data pre-processing that lead to obtain a process representative database. This process generated the need to develop a software tool to streamline tasks automatically in the preprocessing of the recorded data of the process.

Regarding the process of choosing a classifier to be integrated into the supervision system, three steps are proposed. (A) Start with the use of non-supervised classification algorithms that make it possible to search for natural associations of data in classes with full meaning regarding the operation of the process. (B) With the use of unsupervised classification algorithms, but where possible to define the number of classes a priori, it is proposed to start classifying with the same number of classes identified in the previous literal, in what could be called a task of confirming of valid classes in relation to the behavior of the process, and (C) According to the result of the previous item, continue searching for a classification with the smallest possible number of classes but keeping consistency with the functional states of the process.

The information that the operator of the machine knows about the process is very useful if it is accompanied by information collected analysis tools.

References

1. Wang, Y., Byrd, T.A., Kung, L.: Big data analytics: understanding its capabilities and potential benefits for healthcare organizations. Technological Forecasting & Social Change (2016)
2. Dresner Advisory Services 2018 Big Data Analytics Market Study. Big Data Analytics Adoption Soared in the Enterprise in 2018. Forbes (2018)
3. Cohen, M.C.: Big data and service operations. Prod. Oper. Manag. 27(9), 1709–1723 (2018)
4. Munir, M., Baumbach, S., Gu, Y., Dengel, A., Ahmed, S.: Data analytics: industrial perspective & solutions for streaming data. In: Data Mining in Time Series and Streaming Databases, Kaiserslautern, Germany, World Scientific, pp. 144–168 (2018)
5. Xu, S., Lu, B., Baldea, M., Wojsznis, W.: Data cleaning in the process industries. Rev. Chem. Eng. 31(5), 453–490 (2015)
6. Torabi, M., Hashemi, S., Saybani, R., Shamshirband, S., Mosavi, A.: A Hybrid Clustering and Classification Technique for Forecasting Short-Term Energy Consumption. Wiley Online Library (2018)
7. Davenport, T.: What to Ask Your "Numbers People". Harvard Bussines Review, pp. 2–3 (2014)
8. Lückeheide, S., Velásquez, J., Cerda, L.: Segmentación de los contribuyentes que declaran IVA aplicando Herramientas de Clustering. Revista Ingeniería de Sistemas 21, 87–110 (2007)
9. Venkatasubramanian, V., Rengaswamy, R., Kavuri, S.N., Yin, K.: A review of process fault detection and diagnosis: Part III: process history based methods. Comput. Chem. Eng. 27(3), 327–346 (2003)
10. Sarmiento, H., Isaza, C., Kempowsky-Hamon, T., Le Lann, M.V.: Situation prediction based on fuzzy clustering for industrial complex processes. Inf. Sci. 279, 785–804 (2014)
11. Heil, J., Haring, V., Marschner, B., Stumpe, B.: Advantages of fuzzy k-means over k-means clustering in the classification of diffuse reflectance soil spectra: a case study with West African soils. Geoderma 337, 11–21 (2018)
12. Aguilar-Martín, J., Lopez De Mantaras, R.: The process of classification and learning the meaning of linguistic descriptors of concepts. In: Gupta, M.M., Sanchez, E. (eds.) Approximate Reasoning in Decision Analysis, pp. 165–175. North Holland (1982)

13. Aguilar-Martin, J., Aguado, C.: A mixed qualitative-quantitative selflearning classification technique applied to diagnosis. In: QR'99 the Thirteenth International Workshop on Qualitative Reasoning, Chris Price, pp. 124–128 (1999)
14. Zadeh, L.: Fuzzy sets as a basis of theory of possibility. In: Fuzzy Sets and Systems 1, pp. 3–28. North Hollad, Berkeley (1978)
15. Piera, N., Aguilar, J.: Controlling selectivity in non-standard pattern recognition algorithms. IEEE Trans. Syst. Man Cybernetics **21**(1), 71–82 (1991)
16. Rakoto-Ravalontsalama, N., Aguilar-Martin, J.: Automatic clustering for symbolic evaluation for dynamical system supervision. In: 1992 American Control Conference, Chicago, USA (1992)
17. Hedjazi, L., Aguilar-Martin, J.: Similarity-margin based feature selection for symbolic interval data. Pattern Recogn. Lett. **32**(4), 578–585 (2010)
18. Bezdek, J.: Pattern Recognition with Fuzzy Objective Function Algorithms. Plenum Publishing Corporation, New York (1981)
19. Gustafson, D., Kessell, W.: Fuzzy clustering with a fuzzy covariance matrix. In: IEEE Conference on Decision and Control Including the 17th Symposium on Adaptive Processes, University of California, Berkeley, pp. 761–766 (1978)

Author Index

Printed in the United States
By Bookmasters